D0810166

Televangelism and
American Culture

Televangelism and American Culture

The Business of Popular Religion

Quentin J. Schultze

BAKER BOOK HOUSE
Grand Rapids, Michigan 49516

Library of Congress Cataloging-in-Publication Data

Schultze, Quentin J. (Quentin James), 1952–
Televangelism and American culture : the business of popular religion / Quentin J. Schultze.
    p. cm.
Includes bibliographical references.
ISBN 0–8010–8319–2
    1. Television in religion—United States. 2. Religious broadcasting—United States—Christianity. 3. United States—Church history—20th century. 4. United States—Popular culture.
    I. Title.
    BV656.3.S385   1991
    269'.26'0973—dc20   90–49378
                                                             CIP

To Barbara

Contents

❀ ❀ ❀ ❀ ❀ ❀ ❀ ❀

Acknowledgments

This book would not have been possible without the advice, counsel, and support of many friends and colleagues. In particular I would like to thank the following people: my colleagues in the Department of Communication Arts and Sciences at Calvin College; Yvonne Posthuma; Lois Curley; the library staff at Calvin College, especially Conrad Bult and Stephen Lambers; Betty De Vries, Dan Van't Kerkhoff, and Al Fisher of Baker Book House.

Introduction

❈ ❈ ❈ ❈ ❈ ❈ ❈ ❈ ❈ ❈

While doing graduate work at the University of Illinois I discovered an interesting fact: Some of the legendary founders of modern advertising were originally destined for careers in the ministry. That realization led me on a fascinating exploration of the relationship between modern marketing and contemporary religion. Eventually I ended up at televangelism. Watching the televangelists and reading their fund-raising letters, I found the programs and solicitations were telling examples of the union of marketing and ministry.

This book is not an exposé of popular televangelists—those colorful and entertaining preachers, singers, fund-raisers, university presidents, and political organizers. Rather, this book examines how and why televangelists are helping to transform American Christianity from a church into a business, from a historic faith into a popular religion based at least in part on superstition. An examination of these trends indicates that marketing and ministry are now close partners. Each influences the other, and not usually for good.

Televangelists are among the great entrepreneurs of our day. They are often pragmatic, self-made people who are admired for their savvy and determination. And they embody important American ideals: hard work, faith, individualism, and practicality. These qualities appeal to many viewers and attract contributors, who usually prefer to support the more successful TV ministries.

In this book I suggest that televangelism is probably the most characteristic and remunerative expression of American religion.

It is the nation's own religion, a special Protestant hybrid raised in American culture and nurtured by the mass media. Televangelism may even be the flagship of American religion, setting the style and tone of local and denominational church life.

To criticize televangelism is to criticize the broader American cultural currents that gave birth to the phenomenon and are now so heavily influenced by it. Whether we like it or not, all of us are borne along by those currents, regardless of our values and religious backgrounds or experiences. A few years ago the church I was a member of was looking for a new pastor. As I listened to congregants describe their ideal pastor, I soon realized that their concepts of worship and preaching sounded like what one sees and hears on television. They wanted charisma and flair, a pastor who would also be an entertainer in the pulpit and a star in the local community, one who would help put the church on the map by attracting newcomers every Sunday. Without realizing it, the congregation was caught in the style and spirit of contemporary televangelism. It was surrendering to the tidal forces of popular religion, hoping to beat the televangelists at the game of notoriety and success.

In this book I look closely and critically at those cultural currents—from our faith in the saving power of technology to our personality cults, from our superstitious nature to the admiration we have for well-run businesses and effective marketing. Unfortunately, most critics of televangelism have focused on the scandals and the more flamboyant behavior of a few, while ignoring the broader and more significant relationship between televangelism and contemporary American culture. Sociologist Thomas Luckmann has written, "Whereas religious ideas originally played an important part in the shaping of the American Dream, today the secular ideas of the American Dream pervade church religion."[1] Televangelism is a case in point.

Many religious groups in the United States are breathing the flowery and appealing perfume of the televangelists. Caught in the same cultural currents as the televangelists, even Roman Catholic, Presbyterian, Lutheran, and Methodist services are looking and sounding increasingly like religious television programs. A growing number of churches and denominations today are struggling with controversial new liturgies, differing views of social activism, divisive personality cults, disagreements over religiously inspired entrepreneurship, and feuds over the appropriateness of popular God-talk—all adding credence to the indications that as goes televangelism, so goes American Christendom.

I am not suggesting that the impact of national culture on religion is all bad. Only a fool would thoughtlessly criticize the religious freedom and spiritual egalitarianism that mark American Christianity. Compared with most Western nations, the United States is still strongly influenced by Christian beliefs and values. Worship and fellowship are important to millions of its citizens. Behind the scandal-riddled newspaper headlines is a diverse country of religious folk and a vast array of parish churches that contribute domestically and internationally to America's industrious and generous spirit.

However, American culture has also shaped religion in potentially troubling ways. For one thing, it has increasingly linked religion with leisure and popular entertainment; worship and entertainment are sometimes difficult to distinguish in the United States. For another, American culture has increasingly associated religious faith with popular superstition, especially the kind of "magic" found in many commercials: the wife who wins back the affection of her husband through "whiter-than-white wash" or the coed who gets a date because of her sparkling teeth. Like many advertisers, some of the televangelists promise a lot more than they can really deliver. They make it seem as if God intends everyone to be healthy and wealthy. All one needs is enough faith—and perhaps a contribution to the ministry.

Now the United States is exporting such televangelism all over the world. In Latin America, Jimmy Swaggart is far more popular than he is in North America. He is a virtual Protestant "pope" who symbolizes to Protestants and Roman Catholics alike the rising power of evangelicalism in the region. In three Central American countries alone, about three-quarters of the church-going population has watched Swaggart's television program. Under the banner of worldwide evangelism, televangelists are taking their Americanized gospels to many people and tongues. As a result, these people probably are converted more to American culture than to Christianity.

Sociologists point out that religion must adapt to the surrounding culture to survive, but it must also maintain its distinctiveness or it will be subsumed by other institutions. I suggest in this book that religion in Canada and especially in the United States has been steadily influenced by the values, attitudes, and beliefs that animate contemporary business life. To compete for members, some churches have chosen to adopt the strategies and techniques of modern marketing, including advertising and promotion. Most have survived without relying on these tactics, but an increasing number of rapidly growing churches have learned how to market themselves effectively. More than that, they have borrowed these techniques from the religious broadcasters.

A California organization, Church Growth Development International, helps local churches find new members. It is run by a Quaker who made his niche in the world as an insurance telemarketing consultant. The company's successful technique is so forthright as to beguile the average church leader. It first phones and then writes local residents, inviting them with slick, attractive brochures to friendly, upbeat services. As the head of the company admits, its success proves that a small percentage of the population can be persuaded to do or to believe just about anything.[2]

The rise of such church-growth consultants says that local churches are looking for ways to hang on to existing members and attract new ones. In short, they hope to find the most promising methods of building new congregations as well as expanding membership rosters. Recognizing that few people today identify strongly with any particular religious tradition, church consultants are creating new "traditions" out of the dust of suburban housing subdivisions and the savvy of market researchers. This is one of the reasons why the fastest-growing local churches and television ministries are often independent of established denominations.

In many moderate-sized communities and nearly every large city in the United States is at least one "megachurch" founded on the principles of modern marketing. The remarkable growth of these churches is based on the simple but revolutionary concept that even religious "products" must be matched to identifiable markets and then promoted vigorously and relentlessly.

At Willow Creek Community Church in suburban Chicago, weekend services attract nearly 12,000 people, primarily young professionals and singles. Services are held in a contemporary-style auditorium whose architecture reflects the entertainment-oriented spectacles that mark the direction of current church life. The lines between drama and worship, cathedral and theater, are not always clear. Worshipers hear not only the pastor's message, but also jazz, rock music, popular Christian tunes, and well-produced drama that might knock the socks off most community players but rattle the artistic sensibilities of classical dramatists. People are moved by these services, perhaps in the same ways that they are attracted to various forms of secular entertainment. As the church's pastor says, "This is the generation that grew up on television. . . . You have to present religion to them in a creative and visual way."[3]

That is a lesson also learned by Calvary Church of Grand Rapids, Michigan. The pastor launched "Saturday Night at Calvary" to attract the young professional crowd. Weekly from 6:00 to 7:00 P.M., "Saturday Night" reformulates worship for the television generation. A band and soloists provide contemporary music. Other volunteers use drama to deliver a message. Instead of a sermon, the pastor, clad in blue jeans and a sweatshirt and perched casually on a stool, talks informally about a topic of import to young adults. Afterward he answers questions submitted on pieces of paper. These services are designed to attract people who are either disillusioned with their existing churches or who have no church home. However, many born-again believers attend simply because they find the service more meaningful and relevant than traditional ones. As one of the producers of the service put it, compared with Sunday worship the Saturday night version is "cynical and sophisticated."[4]

Consider the fact that this is a service at an unabashedly *fundamentalist* church. These are the "fundies" and "evangelicals" portrayed by the news media as intolerant and unsophisticated. Today some of the most theologically conservative churches are among the leaders in religious marketing and promotion. In this sense they are the real liberals. Old-style mainline churches, such as Methodists and Lutherans, are far more skeptical of the new worship styles and marketing techniques. Not surprisingly, such traditional churches are not growing. Overall, the church in the United States is becoming more "American" and less traditional—more like televangelism.

It should not surprise us, then, that the styles and strategies of the megachurches, along with those of many traditional Protestant and some Roman Catholic churches, reflect the programming of the televangelists. As Marshall McLuhan and, more recently, Neil Postman have argued, the *medium* of communication shapes the *content* of the messages.[5] And the dominant communications medium in a society influences the contours and content of the entire culture. In America, where television is by far the major entertainment medium, religious faith and practice increasingly look and sound like show business. The rise of market-driven megachurches is merely part of the broader trend to incorporate image and entertainment into faith and worship.

In earlier generations the leaders in religious entertainment were itinerant evangelists and circuit riders who mastered oral communication. They preached about religion and often sold books or tracts to help pay for their travels. Now the leaders are televangelists, traveling the airways and similarly selling religious materials and artifacts. The earlier itinerant preachers greatly influenced religion throughout the country, but today's broadcast itinerants are shaping popular religious faith and practice around the world.

Day in and day out, many Americans get their sense of the spirit and purpose of religion from television. With the proliferation of religious programs on Christian stations, independent commercial stations, and cable and satellite television networks, millions of Americans are regularly exposed to broadcast religion. Even nonbelievers find themselves occasionally tuning in to some of the more entertaining televangelists, if for no other reason than to see something new or to chuckle at what seems to be the inanity of it all. Moreover, Christian bookstores prominently display the latest tapes and books of well-known televangelists. Many religious bestsellers are authored by religious broadcasters.

It appears that televangelists are among the most influential trend-setters in American Christianity. By and large, local churches imitate the popular religion that people see on television—not the other way around. Few televangelists have survived on the tube by airing local worship services. Most of them have adapted parish worship to the visual demands of commercial television.

Televangelists continually create new versions of religiosity that meet the test of the marketplace: higher ratings, more listener responses, and increased contributions. Some denominations subsidize programs to free their TV preachers from the burden of delivering messages that will "sell" in the competitive marketplace. Subsidized preachers are more likely to say what they think people need to hear, instead of what people want to hear.

Once televangelism becomes dependent on viewer response and support, the audience becomes a market and the gospel is transformed into a product. And the message is subject to change. Years ago Pat Robertson discovered through market research that viewers liked to see and hear about God's healing power, so he organized his "700 Club" around that theme. As a result, the ratings greatly improved and contributions soared.[6]

Unlike corporate executives and business managers, televangelists are not simply trying to maximize profits. Technically they represent nonprofit organizations. Generally they are on a holy mission to convert people to Jesus Christ and to expand the influence of Christianity in society. However, they usually gauge their impact quantitatively by the number of stations that carry their programs, the audience ratings, and the amount of mail, especially contributions. As a result, some of the major televangelists think and act like pragmatic businesspeople even though their mission is religious. Most televangelists are not trying to line their own pockets with cash, in spite of the impression created by the nation's news media. Instead, the TV preachers hope to accrue the enormous physical resources and financial strength needed to accomplish their religious goals. As their organizations grow, they believe, so does their power to redeem the world.

There are probably few charlatans on religious television. If hucksterism were the only problem with televangelism, simple legislation or even public outrage might take care of the situation. The problems are inherent in the system of commercial television. The message of Christ is easily lost in the barrage of images and words designed to attract viewers and cultivate regular contributors. It is difficult to communicate authentic religious faith through a medium dominated by relatively trivial drama and silly commercials. Televangelists often learn to compete with secular programs by imitating the formats of nonreligious shows. And they figure out what types of fund-raising techniques will work by examining the methods used by nonreligious marketers. The result is that their messages may look and sound more like commercials and entertainment than like spiritual truths.

Not surprisingly, some of the most successful and calculating televangelists are from the relatively freewheeling and spontaneous religious groups associated with revivalism. For example, more than half of the highest-rated weekly televangelists are charismatics or Pentecostals, whose worship usually includes more fervent expressions of feelings than do traditional Protestant or Roman Catholic services. Charismatic and Pentecostal groups

often incorporate speaking in tongues and faith healing, sometimes even on television. On the one hand their styles of religious
expression and worship simply make for entertaining television—certainly more stimulating than a lot of the secular fare on
Sunday morning, such as championship bowling programs and
prosaic public-affairs discussions.

On the other hand, charismatic and Pentecostal leaders have
learned how to organize and present their faith successfully in a
mass medium that reaches the wider society. Like an engaging
Hollywood film that smoothly moves viewers along with the story,
the most popular Pentecostal preachers carry viewers effortlessly
from music to sermon to the final appeal for funds. Yet there is a
method to it all, and often that method is the same as the one
used by the nonreligious entertainment industry and the advertising establishment.

So this book is about far more than the televangelists. It looks
at the cultural currents that carry the televangelists and American religious life down the same river of values, beliefs, and
practices.

Since, unfortunately, the news media typically lump all religious broadcasters into the same pot of cultural unsophistication
and fundamentalistic frenzy, chapter 1 will examine who the televangelists really are, distinguishing between televangelism and
religious broadcasting in general. A major focus of this book is to
differentiate between popular, audience-supported religious
broadcasting and the far less popular and necessarily subsidized
programming of particular denominations and church federa-
tions. But that is only the first among numerous important differences between the "electronic church" and the often overlooked
broadcast efforts of thousands of local churches and national
denominations.

Chapter 2 begins looking at the cultural seeds of televangelism
that are shared by its viewers and nearly the entire society. The
American faith in technology, for example, plays on a much larger
stage than Sunday-morning TV. We are a remarkably sanguine
people, and much of our optimism is directed toward the assumed
fruits of scientific research and technological invention. Many
viewers support the televangelists with the same sense of hopeful
expectation that motivates people to fund the nation's museums of
science and technology and contribute generously to its space pro-

gram. Americans tend to measure the passing of their lives partly by the technological changes that have occurred.

Our faith in technology is matched at times only by the fear that our enemies—whether international foes or secular humanists—will invent new technologies before we do. Such fear fueled our adventure into space in the 1960s, just as it drives much televangelism today. The reactionary impulse to seize control of new communications media is strongest among those who think of themselves as evangelicals and fundamentalists, but our entire society fears any outside threat to its media superiority. Technology gives the American public a particular kind of hope that transcends religion, sometimes even syncretizing religious faith and technological optimism.

Chapters 3 and 4 examine televangelism in the context of two related sides of the American experience: persona and drama. Our quest for personalized yet mythical heroes on the tube partly explains the formation of religious personality cults. At the same time, our love of simple, emotional, and moralistic stories is worked out every Sunday in dozens of religious television performances. The most popular televangelists use both persona and drama—wittingly or unwittingly—to build their audiences and galvanize viewer support. This has been true in the entertainment industry in the United States generally, and some religious broadcasters have now discovered how to use these techniques on the tube to attract and hold audiences.

However, persona and drama both require some native abilities on the part of television preachers. Like the early-American itinerant preachers, today's TV evangelists must have the right stuff to begin with or they travel a rocky and often disastrous road. In fact, it is the native dramatic ability of some televangelists, raised in the expressive Southern folk culture and nurtured on revivalism, that makes them so successful on television. The traditional, broadly educated, pensive preacher is no match on television for the revivalist performer. As in other areas of the American economy, the South is gradually taking over the business of popular televised religion.

Chapter 5 may be the most controversial part of this book. At that point I argue that the success of many televangelists reflects Americans' superstitious nature. In spite of all the churches and Bibles in this land, there is an incredible amount of biblical illiteracy, which in turn delivers naive but needy and well-intentioned adults to the hands and coffers of some televangelists. Lacking knowledge of the Scriptures and disconnected from their own religious traditions, growing numbers of Americans are absorbing with little thought the shallow "pop" faith disseminated by some TV preachers.

In particular I examine the "health and wealth" gospel proclaimed by a growing number of top-rated televangelists, including Kenneth Copeland, Oral Roberts, and Jim Bakker. Although such preachers use various kinds of religious language, their theologies are often only remotely connected to the historic Judeo-Christian tradition. At the extreme, some televangelists are modern sorcerers who claim to teach people how to manipulate God. However, that kind of superstition should not surprise us; it is but one version of the self-help mythology that plays appealingly to American audiences. If anyone can "make it" in business, why not in religion? After all, even the shy, insecure, and diminutive Jim Bakker had expensive homes and a lavish lifestyle before the scandal of 1987.

The next three chapters focus on the impact of televangelism on American religious experience and church life. Chapter 6 examines how televangelism is changing the concept of religious faith in general and the Christian gospel (Good News) in particular. The principles of marketing and promotion are greening the gospel—shaping a new, market-driven message that people prefer over the historic gospel that the church has been mandated to proclaim. Chapter 7 takes up the remarkable inconsistency between the intended and unintended consequences of televangelism. Televangelists claim to be converting the world to Jesus Christ, while research shows that they are preaching largely to the existing flock of believers. In fact, televangelism might be de-Christianizing the nation: first, by creating a new, secular gospel; and second, by convincing Christians that the task of bringing in new converts (evangelism) should be left to media professionals. Many middle- and working-class Christians in America ease their consciences by giving tithes and offerings to the televangelists while retreating to their own condos, relaxing in the privacy of their home saunas, or vacationing in their RVs.

Chapter 8 points out how religion today is increasingly "consumed" as if it were a television program: passively, unreflectively, emotionally, and comfortably from the home pew—the easy chair.

In short, televangelism turns a congregation into a mere audience and the gospel into entertainment.

The final chapter of this book offers some critical but positive suggestions for redeeming the electronic church. As the reader may clearly detect, I am not happy about the current state of televangelism. But, unlike some critics, I believe there is no simple solution, such as increased government regulation or more careful scrutiny of televangelists by the tax authorities. These kinds of responses are short-lived breezes in the wind of public concern. The church must continuously clean up its own act.

The lack of accountability within the church is a major reason for the current state of affairs. Increasingly and in the name of peace and harmony, the church refuses to keep its own house clean. Too many Christians, including pastors and denominational prelates, look the other way when confronted with televangelists' misuse of religious authority. Real accountability is impossible in the face of religious Pollyannishness. It's time for the church, television stations, and journalists to work together to clean up televangelism—and keep it clean.

I am neither an agnostic nor an atheistic critic of televangelism. I speak from within the historic Christian church—a Protestant who grew up within Roman Catholicism and who admits openly and thankfully the profoundly important role of the Jewish people in the history of God's redemption. If there are any vestiges of that historic, biblical faith left in the potpourri of American Christianity, I hope I can speak for them. But if that claim is too haughty or imperious for some readers, I ask that they consider my comments as observations by a student of American culture and a communications scholar, and not as attacks on the admittedly fallible and often ill-directed church of Jesus Christ.

Beyond the Stereotypes

❀ ❀ ❀ ❀ ❀ ❀ ❀ ❀ ❀ ❀ ❀ ❀ ❀ ❀ ❀ ❀ ❀ ❀ ❀ ❀

In today's complex world we all live by stereotypes. We couldn't function without them, since none of us has the time or energy to study the world in depth and first hand. So we rely on the news media, especially television, to provide us with relatively accurate but overly simplistic pictures and descriptions of what's happening. News reporters help us by distilling events into stereotyped renditions of the real triumphs and tragedies of life. One "all-news" radio station in Chicago proclaims to its listeners, "You give us twenty-two minutes, and we'll give you the world." After sifting through commercials, weather, and sports, listeners actually get about seven minutes of news headlines!

Religious news is especially oversimplified. For one thing, few reporters are as educated about religion as they are about economics, geography, or politics. Journalism students are encouraged to take courses in history and political science, and sometimes even the sciences, but rarely in religion or theology. Furthermore, journalists don't hold the religion beat in high esteem. Few daily newspapers, and almost none of the broadcast stations, have a full-time religion reporter. The *Los Angeles Times* and the *Chicago Tribune* are notable exceptions, but they, too, saddle religious writers with the impossible task of following many different faiths and practices. Only reporters for denominational publications are able to track closely the activities of particular religious groups. As we shall see later, however, denominational periodicals often have uncritical blinders that suggest all denominational news is *good* news.

The truth is, the media often feed the public shallow and misleading stereotypes about religion. Television viewers are served the worst stereotypes, since the normal news story is no longer than two or three minutes. It sometimes takes a visit by the pope, a "holy war" among televangelists, or a ministerial scandal to convince television news editors that religion *is* news. Newspaper readers are likely to be a bit better informed because quite a few dailies offer at least a weekly religion page. Unfortunately, most of those sections are little more than bulletin boards listing local church events along with a few wire-service stories. Whereas TV's religion coverage generally focuses on sensation, newspapers highlight the prosaic details of local church life. In both cases, religious items hardly reflect the real significance of faith and practice in American life. As the "Middletown" studies of American culture showed, the United States is a very religious nation.[1] One would never know it from the nightly news.

Televangelism in the News

The public image of religious broadcasting has been shaped significantly by the news media. Rarely is anything good or worthwhile reported about religious radio and TV broadcasts. Of course there are occasional stories about a few respected broadcasters, such as Bishop Fulton J. Sheen in the 1950s and Billy Graham in the 1970s and 1980s. Generally speaking, however, reporters ignore religious broadcasting unless they smell a steamy scandal, outrageous hypocrisy, or juicy conflict. News coverage of broadcast religion is usually limited to reports about sporadic scandals and is peppered with a few interviews and trend stories about the enormous growth and rising power of the electronic church.

Actually, broadcasting is an important part of normal religious life in the United States. At least fifteen million Americans watch religious TV shows every month.[2] Probably several million additional citizens tune in religious radio programs. For every Jerry Falwell who captures headlines about political influence there are dozens of virtually unknown broadcast evangelists who survive on the financial grace of their relatively small constituencies rather than on the glory of network publicity.

Since the late 1970s, religious broadcasting has received considerably more news coverage than in previous years. The success of conservative politicians in 1980 sent reporters hunting for reasonable explanations. Unable to account for the sudden shift in political life that launched Ronald Reagan into the White House, and alarmed about the self-proclaimed power of religious special-interest groups, especially the Moral Majority and the Religious Roundtable, reporters looked at the possible role of some of the more outspoken TV evangelists in moving the nation to the political right. At about the same time, a few reporters examined the place of Jimmy Carter's born-again faith in his presidency. It seemed to some journalists that conservative politics and fundamentalist religion were merging in potentially powerful ways. Even the *Wall Street Journal* and the *New York Times* wondered if right-wing politics and fundamentalist religion were being wed in the new Republican Party of the late 1970s and early 1980s. If so, reporters reasoned, it was time to take religious broadcasting more seriously as real news.

The fact was that only some televangelists, as they were soon called, were deemed newsworthy. Those who championed political causes on nationally syndicated television became news, while most of the others were ignored. Suddenly people such as James Robison, Pat Robertson, and Jerry Falwell attracted reporters and became official, newsworthy sources. As a result, dozens of newspapers and many magazines published articles on the "new" politically active televangelists, even though there had been similar religious broadcasters since the early days of radio. Father Coughlin and Billy James Hargis were distant memories, even though (in the 1930s and 1950s, respectively) they used broadcasting to try to swing the nation toward the right.

By the mid-1980s the news media had created a host of religious stereotypes as part of their effort to explain what they saw as the growing affinity between conservative politics and born-again religion. In only a few years they made particular phrases household words without ever giving them precise meanings. The new vocabulary included terms such as "born again," "evangelical," "fundamentalist," "charismatic," "televangelist," "electronic church," and "TV religion." Most of these words were used negatively to describe what reporters believed was happening: Reactionary religionists were trying to seize control of the democratic political process. In the eyes of many reporters, there was something sinister about politicized religion, and their stories reflected that fear.

By 1986, with Ronald Reagan successfully reelected to a second term as president, and with a few more liberals in the House and Senate, the perceived threat of conservative televangelists largely abated in the news media. There were still a few stories about evangelical religion, but the mood among journalists had changed remarkably, considering that broadcasters such as Falwell and Robertson were still preaching political themes and that Robertson was hinting at a presidential run. Apparently the news purveyors were finally able to convince themselves that religious extremists were not likely to take over American politics and that the nation's conservative mood was not merely the result of religious broadcasting.

Then with the televangelist scandals of 1986 and 1987, the news airwaves again thundered with the hooves of galloping journalists chasing some juicy stories. Tulsa evangelist and university president Oral Roberts made headlines with his claim that God would "call him home" if he did not raise $8 million within a few months for medical-student scholarships at Oral Roberts University. During the same period Jim and Tammy Bakker left the helm of their Heritage USA theme park and PTL TV network near Charlotte, North Carolina, amid public allegations by a former church secretary that Jim had seduced her six years earlier. The *Charlotte Observer,* for years Bakker's local thorn in the flesh, had found out that the PTL ministry had silenced her with a cash bribe. Various journalists soon discovered that the Bakkers had received multimillion-dollar compensation for their work at PTL, that the ministry was in potentially severe tax trouble, and that there may have been other sexual misconduct by Jim Bakker and other ranking PTL staff. At one point Bakker alleged that televangelist Jimmy Swaggart was trying to bring down the PTL empire, but those charges were never proven. Jerry Falwell stepped in to help bail out Bakker's ministry from its financial problems, only to be criticized by some of his own supporters while being lauded by the religious press for cleaning televangelism's tarnished public image.

Reports about the Falwell-Bakker-Swaggart-Roberts travails continued for nearly a year before Swaggart, the highest-rated weekly TV preacher, succumbed to publicity about his own sins. When Swaggart eventually admitted during a tearful service on his Sunday program that he had sinned, dozens of reporters queried proprietors of cheap motels on the highway between

Baton Rouge and New Orleans for evidence that would link the broadcaster to prostitution. Like the earlier stories about right-wing fundamentalism, the scandal reports were tinged with the journalists' skepticism and distrust. In early 1987, when Swaggart's supposed sins were revealed in nightly doses on the evening news, it was as if reporters had finally had their day in court with the televangelists. The Elmer Gantry stereotype was seemingly validated once and for all. Even many evangelicals openly expressed their growing disillusionment with prime-time preachers.

During a single decade, from 1978 to 1988, powerful negative religious stereotypes were reaffirmed once again. News reports implied that the fundamentalists had been caught with their hands in cookie jars (money, sex, and politics), and it was time for a serious spanking. Acting like parents, journalists took discipline in their own hands, announcing their conclusions to the public. The message was that religious fanatics are selfishly ambitious, manipulative, and hypocritical people preoccupied with sex, fame, and wealth.

In fact, the scandals of those two years, like the political sermonizing of the late 70s and early 80s, were neither new nor representative of American religious broadcasting. Scandals have always happened in that arena from its earliest days, when California revivalist Aimee Semple McPherson disappeared for weeks—allegedly with a male friend.[3] Neither scandals nor politics define the bulk of televangelism any more than they do most business or educational practices in the United States. More than anything else, such sensationalistic religious reporting reaffirmed some popular stereotypes about religion and the clergy. Even Elmer Gantry genuinely repented of his evil ways, but we never seem to hear or remember that side of the story.

In recent years only Billy Graham has consistently challenged the typical characterizations offered by ill-informed, overworked, undereducated, and religiously disinterested journalists. Amid the scandals of the late 1980s, Graham stood like an honest and humble giant among seemingly hypocritical and arrogant broadcasters such as Bakker, Roberts, and Swaggart. If some religious broadcasters represented the stereotypical Gantry, Graham's apparent moral rectitude symbolized the nation's long-standing appreciation of authentic piety and unpretentious religious devotion. The land of religious freedom used the crucifix of news to chase away the demons of religious fanaticism while preserving the angels of simple faith. All was not lost on the religious front in the nation's news media as positive stories about Graham supposedly provided the news balance that objective journalists highly prize.

The Who, What, and Why of Televangelism

Contemporary news provides little insight into the real world of televangelism. Although the printed media offer more religion news than do TV and radio, few journalists have perceptively examined religious broadcasting as to *who* the televangelists are. *What* do they believe? *Why* are they using television for religious purposes? What do they have in common? What are the effects of their broadcasts? These are the kinds of questions that beg for deeper answers than we get from the nightly news, the daily newspaper, or most of the more respectable journals of comment and opinion.

We begin our journey into the land of the televangelists with an overview of their common beliefs and practices. In spite of media stereotypes, TV preachers are not part of a unified political or religious movement. They are a rather diverse collection of pastors, preachers, and lay workers who represent different religious groups and a wide range of programming. Most of them are not "reactionary" fundamentalists, although they tend to be politically and religiously conservative. Some of them would even not prefer to call themselves "born again," in part because of the ways the media have misused this biblical term. Graham began speaking instead of new converts as being "born to heaven." Certainly not all televangelists are Pentecostals or charismatics, both of whom believe in a kind of euphoric utterance ("speaking in tongues") and a spiritual healing of the physical body.

With few exceptions, most major TV ministries in the United States are (1) audience-supported; (2) personality-led, (3) experientially validated, (4) technologically sophisticated, (5) entertainment-oriented; and (6) expansionary-minded. These six characteristics both define the electronic church and distinguish it from the broader category of "religious broadcasting." The terms *televangelism* and *electronic church* refer to religious broadcasting that reflects all or most of the above-cited characteristics. About three quarters of the twenty highest-rated weekly religious TV shows are part of this electronic church, including Copeland, Falwell, Roberts, Robertson, Schuller, and Swaggart.

Religious broadcasting is not really a church, of course, even though most televangelists are members of a denomination or pastors of their own independent congregations. Partly for tax purposes and partly to establish a base of financial support and accountability, televangelists generally start as local clergy. Two of the rising stars of religious television, D. James Kennedy and Charles Stanley, are parish pastors first and televangelists second. So is Lloyd Ogilvie of the First Presbyterian Church of Hollywood. In the past most televangelists began as itinerant revivalists. Today they usually take their local church service directly to the masses via television or radio. Or, with such more recent televangelists as Robertson and Bakker, they virtually begin their ministries on the air rather than in a local pulpit. In a strict sense, the phrase *electronic church* is an oxymoron, since a congregation meets face-to-face for worship, study, mutual edification, and fellowship.

Audience-Supported

One of the most obvious yet least understood characteristics of televangelism is its financial dependence on audiences. Televangelism is not funded like some of the local religious programs, which are aired free of charge on community-access cable TV or as sustaining broadcasts on independent and network-affiliate stations. The electronic church pays air time primarily for Sunday or early weekday mornings, and in the largest metropolitan areas the broadcast fee can be thousands of dollars. Air time on cable-TV networks such as Robertson's CBN (The Family Channel) or Bakker's old PTL network would normally cost more than time on local stations in the largest cities but less than time on the major broadcast networks (ABC, CBS, NBC).

Within forty-five or sixty days, one of these TV ministries can easily accrue debts of tens and even hundreds of thousands of dollars. The ten highest-rated weekly televangelists owe stations and networks over a million dollars per month, every month of the year. Costs include production fees, salaries, equipment, and overhead—all significantly more expensive on TV as compared to radio. Some national televangelists have monthly bills of over $4 million, and they usually have nowhere to turn for most of the financial support except to their own local church (if they have one), to their broadcast audience, or to a few wealthy supporters.

Audience-supported TV ministries are patterned after commercial radio and television in the United States. Whereas most nations around the globe first established public-funded broadcast systems, such as Great Britain's BBC or Canada's CBC, the United States championed private broadcasting from the 1920s to the 1960s, when public broadcasting first received substantial government assistance. The electronic church is the religious cousin of the American commercial broadcasting empire, which now extends around the globe. Both kinds of commercial broadcasting—religious and secular—depend on their audiences for financial survival. The televangelist who runs counter to the program preferences of viewers will never generate a following and adequate contributions to keep the program on the air. Only those with affluent local congregations, denominational subsidies, or a few millionaire supporters can ignore the desires of the marketplace for long. Even Schuller, who has one of the wealthiest congregations among the televangelists, is heavily dependent on viewers for financial contributions.

In the United States, then, televangelism is an outgrowth of commercial broadcasting. Both types of broadcasting are based on the modern concept of marketing, which insists that products and services should be tuned to the wants and needs of consumers. Not all religious messages will sell in the competitive TV environment; the most effective gospels both attract viewers and elicit donations to the ministry. To put it more starkly, the market shapes a televangelist's message and its presentation. What is said—and how—must compete effectively with other programs on broadcast TV, cable, and VCR. Televangelists face the competitive tyranny of the broadcast marketplace and the perceived needs of fickle viewers. By contrast, the mainline Protestant and Roman Catholic broadcasters have generally tried to avoid even the appearance of commercialism by refusing to solicit funds on the air or to shape program content to be competitive in the commercial-TV ratings race. That philosophy has virtually guaranteed that no mainline programs will ever rival the popularity of independent televangelists, just as public television attracts much smaller audiences than its commercial counterpart.

Televangelists, then, broadcast in the spirit of American marketing. By making their programs bend to the will of the audience, they have decided to beat the culture at its own game rather than play by other rules. As we shall see further in later chapters, there are important reasons why evangelicals are usually more comfortable with this arrangement than are mainline churches. In the United States, more than in other countries, evangelicalism is continually being reshaped to appeal to the surrounding culture and to attract new adherents. Evangelists adapt the old-fashioned gospel for whatever audiences are available. Generally speaking, that marketing concept is part of the economic and social legend of the United States, which was animated less by tradition than by hope in a free and prosperous future. In the world of televangelism, "life, liberty and the pursuit of happiness" become "air time, freedom from government regulation, and the pursuit of audience contributions."

At various times in the history of American broadcasting, both the broadcast industries and the federal government have expressed concern about paid religious programming. In the late 1920s the Federal Radio Commission, predecessor to today's Federal Communications Commission (FCC), refused to grant licenses to religious broadcasters, which they called "propaganda stations." During the 1930s and 1940s radio networks offered free broadcast time to mainline groups and refused commercial time to evangelicals. The broadcast industry, persuaded partly by mainline Protestant leaders, objected to the sectarian bias of evangelical broadcasts and especially to the apparent fanaticism of some fringe religious groups, particularly Judge Rutherford of the Jehovah's Witnesses. Ironically, the combination of government regulation and industry self-regulation forced evangelicals to deal realistically with the commercial marketplace. They fought for broadcast time, took risks, and learned how to produce programs that would attract audiences and elicit contributions.[4]

By the time TV came along in the 1950s, evangelicals had already mastered commercial broadcasting. Although the vast majority of radio evangelists never got beyond their local stations, dozens successfully syndicated their programs regionally and even nationally. Charles E. Fuller, whose "Old-Fashioned Revival Hour" probably had more steady listeners than any of today's televangelists, developed an enormous national following on syndicated and, later, network radio; some media estimated his audience at twenty million listeners.[5] Graham and Falwell grew up listening to Fuller, whose folksy, down-to-earth style played especially well in towns, small cities, and rural areas. Fuller learned how to appeal for funds without offending listeners, how to organize the radio ministry for national and even some international syndication, and especially how to communicate intimately with individual listeners through a mass medium. As radio stations and networks began eliminating free air time for mainline religious groups in the late 1940s and early 1950s, many new evangelical broadcasters were ready to set sail successfully in the commercial marketplace. For Rex Humbard, Oral Roberts, and other early TV pioneers, the new medium was a relatively natural transition from radio or the sawdust trail, where nightly offerings made or broke a ministry.

Personality-Led

The electronic church is also characterized by the strong personalities of its leaders. More than mainline churches, local evangelical churches, and national evangelical denominations, these broadcast ministries largely depend on the savvy, ability, and fame of individual preachers, evangelists, and revivalists. Like Hollywood or show business generally, televangelism relies extensively on public persona. Viewers tune in to see and hear their favorite ministers as much as to hear the message. Indeed, the televangelist and message are so intertwined that even many regular viewers equate the ministry with the preacher, when in fact there is usually a large organization that carries on the multifaceted work of the typical TV ministry.

Once again the influence of American culture on televangelism is unmistakable. Televangelism reflects the American preoccupation with stardom and celebrity status. Americans are not as much interested in ideas and perspectives, debates and dialogue, as they are in people and personality. In all walks of life, individuals who can attract customers and create a following are valuable commodities. Lee Iacocca sells automobiles for the Chrysler Corporation just as sportscaster Merlin Olsen pitches flowers for a national floral chain and Hollywood stars peddle every conceivable kind of product and service. Readers follow their favorite news columnists, and viewers tune in to particular TV reporters and anchors. As we shall see in a later chapter, the typical viewer of the electronic church knows little or nothing for certain about the private life of his or her favorite televangelist. In fact, the public image is often carefully controlled by publicity departments that help manufacture a particular persona for the TV preacher. As with other stars from the entertainment industry, there can be a wide gap between persona and real personality.

Americans like to turn ordinary people into heroes and celebrities. They have done so with the nation's founding fathers, whose public virtues were often considerably removed from their private vices. They repeatedly do so with sports stars. Every sports show and each issue of the daily sports pages in newspapers promotes the personas of particular superstars while tarnishing the reputation of others in clouds of suspicion about drug use, immoral behaviors, outrageously high salaries, and exaggerated product endorsements. No matter how critical the media are of some celebrities, the public thirst for them is unquenchable. Americans love contemporary heroes, and this is as true for televangelists as it is for other celebrities. Without the coloration of specific personalities, televangelism would soon collapse under the weight of the marketplace.

Persona also attracts workers to a ministry, inspires them, encourages them, and builds their confidence. Visionary and motivational leaders are able to rally the organization enthusiastically around a hope that transcends the day-to-day frustrations and problems within a ministry. Nearly every one of the major TV ministries was built partly on the remarkable ability of one man to communicate inspirationally his vision to the workers. Of course in some cases this has led to dangerous situations where followers refused to hold their own leaders accountable for their actions. This happened in PTL under the leadership of Bakker, who sometimes announced new projects on the air to surprised staff without board approval. In a broader sense, however, this kind of personality-driven leadership style has a long and important place in American political and industrial history. Often started as relatively small, family-oriented organizations, most TV ministries follow in the footsteps of their early corporate cousins. Persona helped establish the organizations that built America.

Personality-led televangelism effectively attracts audiences and generates contributions. Just as well-known and highly respected TV-news anchorpersons attract viewers more successfully than do obscure ones, exciting and successful preachers outshine dull or uninspiring ones. Viewers are especially intrigued by televangelists whose own lives seem to be evidence for the veracity of their special religious truths and the power of their privileged relationship to God. This is partly why televangelists' autobiographies read like testimonies of the historic Christian saints who accomplished much for God through obedience and faithfulness. Viewers generally are uninterested in a secondhand God or a lukewarm TV preacher who talks a lot but fails to inspire—as have most mainline Protestant preachers on free broadcasts. Americans prefer to watch televangelists whose own worldly accomplishments and apparent close relationship with the Almighty seemingly bear witness to the program's message of hope. For this reason more than any other, many clergy criticized the first radio preachers in the 1920s, fearing that no one would attend their local churches if they could hear great religious orators in the privacy of their own homes.[6]

Experientially Validated

Televangelism is also characterized by experientially validated beliefs and practices. Once again this is not idiosyncratic to the TV ministries but is part of the broader stream of American culture. Like much of evangelicalism, televangelism is guided by a popular epistemology, a way of knowing that derives truth from personal experience. In the United States knowledge and truth have long been associated with experience: To experience is to know. The wide array of popular religion, much of it originating in California, testifies to this. As part of an incredibly diverse culture, where some people will believe practically anything that is religious or at least mystical, Americans derive knowledge and truth from individual experience as much as from communal life or traditional belief. Instead of challenging this popular epistemology, televangelists pragmatically use it to their own advantage. This, too, partly accounts for their long-standing success.

The electronic church has generally stayed clear of appeals to religious tradition, biblical scholarship, academic theology, historic Christian creeds and confessions, and even the rich body of books and essays by saints and other influential and esteemed figures from the history of Western Christianity. Except for references to biblical stories, televangelism's programs are remarkably ahistorical. They speak almost entirely of the present or of some apocalyptic future and rarely address the past, except as nostalgia about an older, moral, and decent world that never really existed. Moreover, except for some popularized twentieth-century theology, the electronic church is usually anti-intellectual; there is great suspicion of liberal preachers who equivocate about moral matters or who fail to speak plainly and directly. One of the most anti-intellectual of them all, Swaggart, harshly criticized even psychologists, whom he broadly castigated as secular humanists. Most televangelists express far less concern about the centuries-old concerns of theologians and religious scholars than about the salvation of souls and the nation's spiritual condition.

In this respect televangelism is a modern manifestation of America's self-help tradition. Today's popular psychology and self-help ideas permeate the contemporary culture, as reflected in bestseller books on topics ranging from how to manage a business and how to "dress for success" to how to teach your children to read. These kinds of practical, motivational writings now have their television versions, where successful real-estate tycoons and other experts dispense their experiential truths to viewers. Most of these shows are produced by successful people and are conducted like revival services, complete with sermons and testimonies by newfound converts. Even some public television programs create the impression that anyone can be a gourmet cook or a master carpenter. These, too, are motivational guides to personal success in a society that most people know is filled with failed dreams. Few people will ever live the grand lives of their heroes in sports, business, or religion. Nevertheless, every tale of success, whether presented by televangelists or businessmen, keeps the American Dream alive.

Like their business counterparts, most of the well-known televangelists use the success of their own ministries as an appeal to the truthfulness of their religious beliefs. They interpret their own popularity as God's blessing on their ministry. In many cases the personal stories of televangelists are truly remarkable. Bakker rose from being a shy kid in a working-class area of Muskegon, Michigan, to the head of one of the largest theme parks and most successful TV ministries in the country. Swaggart overcame a rural Southern background and a broken family to become the highest-rated weekly televangelist (with an estimated annual budget in 1986 of about $140 million). Roberts suffered as a child from a debilitating disease, but he established a successful TV ministry, a major private university with law and medical schools, and even a medical center—much of which he later lost. Schuller left rural Iowa, eventually to become founding father and senior pastor of the magnificent Crystal Cathedral in suburban Los

Angeles. To get there he preached from the roof of a snack shop at a drive-in theatre to parishioners parked in cars. These and other stories are remarkable testimonies to both the American Dream and the success of individual TV ministries.

Throughout the history of Christianity, the testimonies of living and deceased saints have edified believers and attracted new converts. In the United States, however, testimonies now tend to focus on claims about God's material blessings. Successful Christians have often spoken not primarily of their salvation, but of the evidence of their worldly accomplishments. Sometimes success among pastors is reflected in the size of their congregations or the number of converts; these have long been used by Christians as evidence of the grace of God. Today's televangelists frequently point directly to such things as the stack of letters received, the number of stations carrying the program, the audience ratings, and (at least off the air) the amount of income generated every month. Among some televangelists, the size and splendor of ministry buildings are also important indicators of success. While these kinds of material blessings are indeed related to the overall accomplishments of a ministry, they also speak importantly of how the American Dream is translated into religious life.

Such experientially validated ministries are open to various types of abuse. Some televangelists read their own histories quite selectively. When Robertson ran for president in 1988, newer printings of his autobiography reportedly eliminated the section where God had told him that Christian pastors should not run for public office.[7] No one would expect TV preachers or any other public figures to air all their dirty laundry in autobiographies, but televangelism, like American culture in general, is predictably Pollyannish and sometimes even crudely optimistic. America has strongly triumphalistic sensibilities, and televangelists are no exception. Hopeful, joyful, and optimistically prophetic words sell far better than depressing or despairing ones. Even when reporting a moral crisis or social calamity, televangelists offer a solution. Successful TV ministries testify to the American Dream and enjoin viewers to follow and believe in it also.

The most disturbing aspect of the rise of experientially validated TV ministries is their undiscerning claims about their own privileged position before God. Televangelists frequently create the impression that they have a special pipeline to the Father in heaven. As we shall see later, it is sometimes implied that this pipeline gives a televangelist particular power to manipulate God on behalf of viewers and contributors. The success of their own ministries, TV preachers claim, shows that they can teach other Christians how to appeal to God for special blessings. From this kind of thinking comes the various "health and wealth" gospels that seemingly promise viewers that they, too, can be successful. As Bakker used to say, "You can make it!" This message is not the old-fashioned gospel of the Christian faith, but a form of contemporary magic bred in American mythology about the power to overcome tragedy, to seize available opportunities, and to secure fame and fortune.

Technologically Sophisticated

The electronic church is also quite technologically sophisticated, although the programs themselves may not appear that way to the untrained viewer. Among the stereotypes about televangelists is the recurring picture of backwoods folk with an old-fashioned religion and little knowledge about modern life. The implication is that TV religion is a holdout from past ages, when people were unscientific, unsophisticated, and even irrational. Frequently the media somewhat scornfully use the term *born again* to describe televangelists' naive holier-than-thou mentality. Clearly the secular media misperceive evangelicalism generally and televangelism specifically; such stereotypes are ridiculous generalizations. The truth is that televangelists are highly sophisticated in many respects, including the technical aspects of effective TV communication. Many network journalists are not nearly as savvy about the medium that carries their reports to the nation.

On local radio and television, especially in small cities, there are indeed some remarkably inept religious broadcasters whose only audience is probably a few friends from the congregation. Among the national televangelists, however, the situation is strikingly different. Some of them have been among the leaders in developing new communications technologies. Robertson, for example, was one of the early visionaries to conceive of the growing importance of cable television in the United States and around the world. His CBN, later called "The Family Channel," was one of the first and is still among the largest cable networks in this country. Bakker's PTL network made an impressive entry into the cable industry long before many of the well-known networks were started. Paul and Jan Crouch, who started the Los Angeles-based

Trinity Broadcasting Network on satellite, established an impressive system of stations across the country.

Televangelists have organized an amazing array of advanced equipment and expert engineering for on-location video recording. Swaggart's road show would amaze technical crews and producers from the major commercial networks. His equipment is state-of-the-art, and his road crew is experienced with virtually every kind of audio and lighting situation, including outdoor stadiums, indoor amphitheaters, and night shooting. Although Swaggart's revivals are not as difficult to tape as fast-moving sports competitions, their unpredictable settings and other on-location uncertainties are among the most difficult events to record effectively.

Some of the most popular televangelists pioneered technical innovations that are now standard. Schuller had a high-definition TV screen installed in the Crystal Cathedral before most major-league sports stadiums did. Humbard had his own church in Akron, Ohio, built in the 1950s specifically for high-tech TV production, long before stadiums, arenas, and auditoriums were being designed with television in mind.[8] In computer graphics, editing, and on-location shooting, televangelists often use highly sophisticated equipment and advanced production techniques.

Like their counterparts in secular broadcasting, televangelists have pushed strongly for the best possible visual appeal in their programs. The electronic church has attempted to beat the competition at its own technical game rather than focusing only on its broadcast message. Although there are a few exceptions, by and large the electronic church is as visually sophisticated as typical network fare. Given weekly and sometimes even daily air schedules, this is a remarkable feat. Televangelists have no reruns to shorten the production season, and most programs include fund-raising appeals or other spots that usually require separate taping.

Televangelists have been very sensitive about the image projected in their programs, fearing that technically unsophisticated shows will invariably contribute to the stereotype that some people have about evangelicals. Like their broadcast brethren in network news, entertainment, and commercials, TV preachers have sought to win over viewers by using the state-of-the-art techniques that American audiences expect from television. In the minds of some critics, the televangelists' technical prowess is another sign of the dangers inherent in TV religion. These critics worry that technological skill will translate into financial growth and, eventually, political and moral influence. Indeed, they prefer to have their stereotypes about evangelical hicks confirmed rather than challenged by reality.

Although on the air some high-rated evangelists appear to be homespun orators, the truth is that TV sermons, simple fund-raising appeals, and folksy conversation are often only the facade on an elaborate combination of technical know-how and communicative genius. Swaggart's repentance sermon in 1987, offered to the nation as his confession of sinfulness, was a masterful stroke of video, organized visually and aurally around the biblical theme of forgiveness. The congregation cried with Swaggart and gathered around him, holding hands and hugging as the show ended. The televangelist never admitted the nature of his sins, but even skeptical, nonbelieving viewers were moved by the apparent authenticity of his repentance. Sound bites of Swaggart's pulpit confession echoed through the nation's network and local TV-news programs throughout the day. It was fabulous television, more compelling than most made-for-TV films and more dramatic than any evening soap opera.

Entertainment-Oriented

Televangelists are also entertainers who have learned how to package successful dramatic techniques for contemporary religious audiences. In fact, most of the highest-rated TV preachers have adapted successful formats from secular programs. Like the industry generally, they creatively reformulate, combine, and synthesize the dramatic styles used by variety shows, talk shows, and other TV genres. Roberts inaugurated entertainment-oriented religious TV with his prime-time variety specials in the 1950s.[9] Since then, dozens of TV preachers have figured out how to dress the old-fashioned gospel in novel, entertaining clothing.

In the 1970s and 1980s numerous televangelists experimented with and refined their personal versions of talk shows. Imitating people such as Johnny Carson and Merv Griffin, Robertson, Bakker, and Crouch pioneered their own relatively successful renditions of the talk-pray-sing formula. Meanwhile, Schuller integrated aspects of the old-style variety show into his Sunday-morning services, which were produced specifically for the TV camera. While his local church's evening services were fairly traditional in terms of North American Calvinism, the televised version used short, upbeat homilies, guest stars from Hollywood and sports, well-performed choral ensembles and solos, airy shots of the interior of the Crystal Cathedral, serene images of the outdoor fountains, and majestic skyward pictures of the glass cathedral on a smog-free Southern California day. By the mid-1980s practically all the major televangelists had borrowed important techniques from nonreligious shows. Even Swaggart's old-fashioned revivalism on TV bore the marks of contemporary variety shows; the cameras alternated between shots of the excited audience and those of the performers, including Swaggart and singers.

The electronic church still includes preaching and singing, mainstays of Christian liturgy, but few programs are complete broadcasts of actual church services or revivals. Today's televangelism takes advantage of the medium's established formats, offering viewers programming in tune with their established preferences and tastes. Mimicking sawdust-trail revivalism and stadium-filled crusades, the new broadcast versions emphasize spontaneity and dramatic excitement. They are special events designed to attract and hold bored viewers who live relatively drab and uneventful everyday lives. Like traditional itinerant preaching and tent revivalism, televangelism is also religious entertainment. TV preachers combine and recombine amusement, drama, and worship in ever-changing ways. They have become part of the tradition of popular religious entertainment in the United States, shaping the church's concepts of worship and liturgy.

As a later chapter will illustrate, some televangelists have capitalized on the use of conflict, character, and setting to tell their religious stories. Their programs are anchored in the effective use of fundamental dramatic principles, and even non-Christian viewers may sometimes tune in because of a show's theatrical appeal. After all, some televangelism is genuinely more entertaining than many non-religious programs, which are comparatively dull and predictable. In particular, Swaggart's stage presence and emotional voice are powerful dramatic instruments. When televangelists mix revivalistic drama with variety- and talk-show formulas, the programs often appeal to viewers from many Christian traditions. Whereas televised church services always cast a denominational shadow on broadcasts, talk shows and variety programs can partly hide the underlying theological and sectarian styles of worship and liturgy. Televangelism creatively combines popular dramatic devices and traditional religious practices. The revivalist or evangelist becomes a talk-show host, a variety-show emcee and, above all, a performer.

Expansionary-Minded

Finally, televangelism in America is increasingly the hub for new religious institutions and movements. TV ministries bring Christians together over the airways and give them new visions of Christian faith and practice. Like the surrounding culture, the electronic church identifies success with size and visibility: the bigger and more well-known, the "better" the ministry. Televangelists are growth-oriented; they hope to bring more and more people into an ever-widening array of activities sponsored by the TV program.

For many other religious broadcasters, especially mainline Protestants, the producers feel that all they need to do is successfully inform viewers about religious perspectives on important church or public issues. This is not satisfactory for most of the major televangelists, whose expansionary vision continually calls for new programs, additional organizations, larger audiences, more contributions, and bigger buildings. While the intellectuals and theologians investigate, discuss, and debate, televangelists are busily building communications networks and establishing new organizations or causes. Televangelists are pragmatic, action-oriented individuals who believe that virtually any problem has a simple solution that requires only more money and organization.

In the world of the electronic church this expansionary mind is oriented toward spin-off ministries supported by the broadcast. Programs are increasingly fund-raising vehicles for other projects, from educational institutions to foreign missions, and from homes for unwed mothers to medical facilities and even quasi-political organizations. Many televangelists are not only interested in converting people to Jesus Christ, although that usually remains the central goal. From their perspective the church's responsibility in the world is far broader than evangelism. Every year they are collectively involved in a wider range of social activism, political influence, public-policy debate, and assistance to the poor and disadvantaged. Falwell and Company disbanded the Moral Majority coalition in 1989, but during the same year the televangelist promoted a new causes, his Liberty University Life-Long School of Learning, which offered nondegree programs via correspondence.

Broadcasting is the message center for these kinds of activities, linking contributors of time and money to local and national organizations. Although the issues and problems discussed on the program change regularly with the winds of public concern and the shifting preoccupations of the evangelical community, the expansionary vision inevitably leads televangelists to explore how they might help change the world by remaking it all in their own image of worldly paradise.

It makes considerable sense to think of televangelism partly as a national collection plate that brings in the revenues to finance a host of evangelical activities. TV programs put individual preachers in touch with a cross-denominational constituency sympathetic to both the message and the spin-off ministries. Increasingly, however, the spin-offs have turned into major fund-raising appeals that also generate enough contributions to keep the broadcasts going. Compared with even a decade ago, today's popular televangelists are far more extensively involved in nonbroadcast activities as a way of building stronger ties with their audience and contributors. Most viewers will limit contributions to keep a program on the air, but they will often donate substantially more to emotional causes such as feeding the hungry, preventing abortions by supporting unwed mothers, and promoting traditional family values.

The expansionary vision of televangelists is forced on them partly by the increasingly competitive fund-raising environment in which they operate. Knowing that their viewers will give more to a multidimensional ministry, they often launch new projects at the times of their greatest financial need. Constituencies are always looking for new causes to support. Moreover, because a sizable proportion of the audience of the electronic church has never contributed, every new project offers the potential to tap into the hearts and pocketbooks of previously uncommitted viewers. Unlike more traditional religious broadcasting, which was organized almost entirely around communicating a spiritual message, the new televangelism reflects the same kinds of diversification taking place throughout the national economy. This type of economic expansion lowers risk by spreading the resources of the electronic church across a broader spectrum of activities and a wider pool of supporters.

Conclusion

Contemporary televangelism is far more important and complex than media stereotypes suggest. The electronic church is neither a strange religious aberration nor a crazy collection of reactionary zealots. On the contrary, it is an important reflection of many social, cultural, and economic currents in American public and private life. Televangelism will survive scandals. It will also develop new programming and establish additional social and political causes. After all, televangelism is a particularly American phenomenon that has shown an extraordinary ability to adapt to the changing religious and secular environment.

The news media have largely missed the real story about the electronic church. By focusing on the more sensational and unusual aspects of televangelism, they have overlooked how truly American it is, from its marketing concept to its personality-led ministries, and from its experientially validated beliefs to its technological sophistication. Although there are certain aspects of the electronic church that should rightly concern all Americans, televangelism largely reflects the values, sensibilities, and attitudes of contemporary culture. As we shall see, televangelism's dangers are hardly its own; it shares them with many nonreligious activities and institutions, from government to sports and business. The real news is that televangelism is not so new after all.

Faith in Technology

✤ ✤ ✤ ✤ ✤ ✤ ✤ ✤ ✤ ✤ ✤ ✤ ✤ ✤ ✤ ✤

My family recently received from the local cable television company a promotional brochure on "pay per view." It offered us one free movie as a way of introducing us to the "new age of convenience" in home viewing of recent films. Indeed, the new technology was amazingly simple.

After selecting which one of the available films we wished to see, we simply called the cable company to confirm the specific time we would watch it. At that time we turned on the set to the designated channel to watch—and tape—the movie. What could be simpler? Even if we missed part of the movie because of a phone call or some other interruption, we could watch it again later by replaying the tape. Most amazing of all, though this movie was free, it normally would have cost less than the charge for two tickets at a theater, and about the same as two tape rentals at the local video shop. Since the film was not yet available for rental, it seemed like a great deal.

The promotional brochure specified all of the advantages of this new technology, comparing the "old days" of theater-going and video rental to the modern times of pay-per-view video. Prior to this system (a period called B.C. for "before choice"), film fans had to get into a vehicle, drive to the theater or rental shop, pay for a film, view it, and then either drive home or return the tape to the rental store. Dressed in sheepskins, these Neanderthal movie fans were portrayed as uncivilized primitives. In contrast, the brochure depicted "Modern Man, A.C." (after choice) as sophisticated and knowledgeable. The modern family simply checks the program guide, calls the cable company to order a showing, and then sits down to view the movie in the convenience of its own home.

Obviously such promotional material is satirical. Movie theaters and video shops are not leftovers of a distant Stone Age. Nevertheless, the brochure captures one of the most popular American myths: New technologies always make life better by saving time and enhancing the quality of life. The key advantages are supposedly convenience and choice, which are thought to combat inefficiency and liberate consumers from corporate or governmental control.

Unfortunately the fruits of new technologies are not always beneficial. In the case of pay-per-view movies, the ones offered to us during the free viewing period would hardly edify most people. My family could find only one that would probably not offend or bore—or both. And only one could really be considered family entertainment. The "choice" of "modern man" hardly looked so great.

Worse yet, two experiences at a video rental store several months earlier left me rather pessimistic about the video revolution. While standing in line waiting to rent a tape for a college class, I could not help noticing rather embarrassingly the affectionate embraces and kisses between two teenagers ahead of me. In nosy fashion, I glanced at the two tapes they were renting; both were chain-saw, cut-'em-up flicks. I pondered how such movies were incorporated into their obviously romantic relationship. The next evening, while returning the tape I had rented the night before, I found myself behind a fidgety thirty-year-old man with a fistfull of X-rated tapes. Once again I wondered about the utility of the new VCR technology. Was it really a reflection of advanced civilization, or one more promise gone sour when confronted by humankind's fallen nature?

In this chapter I address one of the most unexamined aspects of both American culture and televangelism—the national "faith" in technology. Americans certainly love new technologies, especially those that offer entertainment, communication, or transportation. The automobile and the television set, just to name two, have totally pervaded American social and cultural life. More recently there has been an explosion in the popularity of video games. In 1987 Americans spent about the same for Nintendo video games (about $1.7 billion) as they did for world missions.[1] Americans pump money endlessly into the latest technological fads; when one fad dies, another rapidly appears to take its place. Consider how quickly radio, television, FM radio, color TV, VCRs, and home video cameras have all burst on the scene. It seems that the American imagination gravitates naturally toward new gadgetry of all kinds.

How strong is this faith in technology? Consider the fact that solutions to real human problems are almost always conceived of in technological terms. This is true in the health area; many ill and even dying people wait hopefully for a scientific-medical cure: a new technology. Consider as well that solutions to the problem of environmental pollution are sought mainly in new technologies, rather than in conservation, recycling, reduced consumption, simpler lifestyles, and the like. The focus of this chapter is not on the inherent ills of technology, especially television, but rather on Americans' rather blind and naive hope in the benefits of technological progress. As we shall see, this is one of the keys to understanding why Americans are far more enthusiastic about high-tech religious broadcasting than are most peoples of the world. Many Americans expect the latest communications gimmickry to provide the means for treating spiritual ills, especially those that could be cured by worldwide evangelization.

Spiritual Nemesis

Before we look closely at how America's faith in technology affects its religious broadcasting, it is important to address the pessimistic counterpart of that faith. There are many well-educated, thoughtful, and articulate critics of televangelism who are absolutely convinced that television cannot communicate the gospel authentically. In their minds, the tube is antithetical to the Christian faith, an evil monster that perverts and distorts Christianity. We should listen to these detractors, even if their criticisms are somewhat misguided, for they rightly challenge the idea that technology is a magical cure-all.

Among the most engaging prophets of televisual doom was British broadcaster and writer Malcolm Muggeridge. In a provocative series of lectures on contemporary Christianity delivered in London in 1976, Muggeridge attempted to extirpate the technological faith that so many Westerners have in the benevolent power of mass communication, especially television. He called television "the greatest single influence in our society today, exerted at all social, economic and cultural levels."[2] For him, television's biggest threat is the way it injects the reality of Christ into the fantasy of television. The tube creates a make-believe world thoroughly at odds with the image of God in human existence. In fact, the fantasy is so strong and attractive that it might have been part of the fourth attempt to suborn Christ after the failure of the three previous temptations. Muggeridge depicts this imaginary fourth temptation as follows:

An enormously rich Roman tycoon by the name of Lucius Gradus the Elder hears Jesus speaking to a crowd. Seeing how Jesus can emotionally move the group, Gradus envisions making Christ into a potential star—even a superstar. He instructs his representatives in Jerusalem to "puff Jesus" and prepares to put him on a new television show. Christ's potential audience would be the entire Roman Empire, not simply the "rag, tag and bobtail lot following him around in Galilee." The program would be sponsored by Lucifer Inc., which would help "put [Christ] on the map, launch him off on a tremendous career as a worldwide evangelist, spread his teaching throughout the civilized world, and beyond. He'd be crazy to turn it down."[3] Of course Jesus refused the offer, as he had the other three temptations.

Muggeridge's tale of the fourth great temptation illustrated his view of the power of the media to "exploit the weaknesses and wretchedness of men," including their carnality, greed, vanity, credulity, and arrogance. He believed that the tube is not the only but the greatest conveyor of such sinful fantasy that has ever existed. By appealing to human fallenness, television promotes *eros* over *agapé*, celebrity status over a broken and contrite heart. As a result, viewers are left with "no sense of order whatsoever, social, political, economic or any other. . . ."[4] All the users of television—the pornographer, the advertiser, the ideologue and politician—contribute to such evil effects by exploiting people's evil nature.

In a similar vein, English professor and writer Virginia Stem Owens tries to reveal the incongruity between the technology of television and the life of authentic faith. Directly attacking some of the televangelists in her book *The Total Image*, Owens extends Muggeridge's argument about the tube's inability to communicate the real "grotesque gospel" of Jesus—God becoming man, the glory of the cross, the resurrection of the body—which cannot be shared "through the electronic extension of our senses." Because the viewer assumes that electronically transmitted messages are more real than spiritual truths, which cannot be communicated visually, television hinders the cause of Christ and the purpose of evangelism. The gospel is concerned with what the camera cannot hope to capture, claims Owens.[5]

If most televangelists have exaggerated faith in technology (as I believe they do), critics like Muggeridge and Owens have insufficient faith in God's power to use television for his own ends. Both the idea that television is inherently evil and the belief that it can never be used to communicate authentic faith in Christ are overly simplistic dismissals of an important technology that the church *should* use. Much of this book suggests that televangelists use the tube naively and even wrongly—that their faith in the technology gets in the way of their own critical appraisal of how well and how appropriately they are using it. At the same time, however, the outright rejection of the concept of using television for Christian communication is unfortunate, misguided, and unfair.

As we shall discover in later chapters, television is not a neutral medium; it invariably communicates some messages better than others. Here Muggeridge and Owens are fundamentally correct. Nevertheless, nearly all the criticisms they level against the medium are the result of how it is used, not its inherent nature. Critics of televangelism too often blast the medium rather than the messengers. Moreover, while upholding the spiritual realm enthusiastically, they adopt a Gnostic perspective that sees evil in part of the material world, an outgrowth of the very Creation.

Technological Optimism

Few Americans, let alone a handful of televangelists, share the critical views of television held by elite writers such as Muggeridge and Owens. The national imagination has always linked technological development to human progress. As a result, Americans, including televangelists, have generally been technological optimists. In the case of television, cable channels, remote controls, satellite transmitters and receivers, VCRs, large screens, and enhanced audio all become symbols of what most people believe are better and more pleasant ways of life. If the tube is sometimes perceived as a nemesis, it is more typically a marvel.

In 1951, as the television networks were first linking stations from coast to coast, viewers tuned in to a remarkable broadcast that for some symbolized a new kind of technological progress and social optimism. On the screen simultaneously were two marvels of human technology: the Brooklyn and Golden Gate bridges. Well-known journalist Edward R. Murrow was on hand to narrate the amazing event. He proudly announced that "for the first time in the history of man, we are able to look at both the Atlantic and Pacific coasts of this great country at the same time. . . . No . . . age was ever given a weapon for truth with quite the scope of this fledgling television."[6] Although television might indeed have become something of a "weapon for truth," by the mid-to-late 1950s it was increasingly clear to many observers that the tube would become far more like the nation's own jester than its truthteller.[7] Instead of hard-hitting news or informative public affairs programs or even thought-provoking drama, television delivered variety shows, situation comedies, detective stories, westerns, and soap operas. American technological optimism, once endorsed by one of the most credible national journalists, looks in hindsight like futuristic nonsense.

Belief in the benefits of technology has deep historical roots in this nation's public life, extending far back before even radio broadcasting. Romantic American poet Walt Whitman captured the technological sublime in his nineteenth-century "Passage to India":

> A worship new I sing,
> You captains, voyagers, explorers, yours,
> You engineers, you architects, machinists, yours,
> You not for trade or transportation only,
> But in God's name, and for thy sake O soul.[8]

Whitman's verse reflects the way that Americans have often defined success and progress in distinctly material and especially technological terms. Transportation and later communication technologies were particularly powerful symbols of the nation's development, perhaps because they were thought to be conduits for cultural, religious, and educational improvements. In any case, technology became in the United States a tremendously fascinating and even mystical representation of progress. Theologian Reinhold Niebuhr wrote, "The most dominant characteristic of modern culture is the mastery of technics by the culture and over the culture," especially in the United States. For this reason, he claimed, the French call America "technocratic."[9] American historian Daniel Boorstin refers to America as the "Republic of Technology."[10]

As every major innovation in communications came along, American writers and orators offered secular prophesies about the marvelous future that would soon result. The telegraph, for example, would "annihilate time and space," diffuse knowledge with the "speed of thought," and "make the whole land one being." Similarly, early radio would supposedly end personal or rural isolation, level class distinctions, standardize language, elevate cultural taste, promote world peace, and even perfect democracy. Television, when it arrived in the late 1940s, was expected to accomplish all these things plus correct eye defects.[11] The point here is not that everyone believed what now seem to be outlandish predictions. Rather, the important conclusion is that Americans have generally been an optimistic people who invested much of their hope, and certainly their imagination, in a rosy future that would supposedly be a specific result of technological advances.

Unfortunately, it is usually difficult to see the silliness of such technological optimism at the time. The popular media are always dotted with such exhortations, but rarely do most people question them. In recent years the VCR and cable television have best captured the contemporary imagination. As the pamphlet touting pay-per-view cable films suggested, there was now great consumer "choice" and far more "convenience" than in any previous period of movie or television viewing. What the pamphlet did not say was that the available options are controlled by corporate giants who want every "choice" to be a potential blockbuster and therefore a profitable film. Nor did it indicate that private viewing of movies generally results in people seeing films they would not watch in public; in other words, choice feeds their evil desires and loosens personal viewing standards.

Technological optimism almost always gives an impression of great social or cultural progress where there is actually very little. Americans see technology as the product of their hard work, but at the same time they incorrectly believe that because they invented new technologies they have complete control over them. The harnessing of steam power and electricity are extremely telling examples. Both produced much public commentary suggesting that humankind was finally in charge of its own destiny —indeed, that human effort and God's will were one and the same. Electricity, in particular, was, as one historian put it, "the poetry of science; no romance—no tale of fiction—excel in wonder its history and achievement."[12]

If, as Stanley L. Jaki describes them, the three faces of technology are idol, nemesis, and marvel, Americans generally saw technology as a marvel. But, Jaki points out, "A vacuum, either in physics or in theology, cannot exist too long. Idols quickly move in where God is no longer tolerated!"[13] The idea of technology-as-nemesis had little authority, except among some elitists like Muggeridge and a few groups that either spurned modern technologies primarily for religious reasons (e.g., the Amish) or to underscore a romantic counterculture (e.g., the hippies of the 1960s and 1970s).

Romancing the Future

Contemporary televangelism shares with the national culture a remarkable faith in technology that borders on idolatry. Sometimes the idea of TV-as-nemesis is expressed by a Jimmy Swaggart, a Pat Robertson, or a fundamentalist such as Tim LaHaye, whose book *The Hidden Censors* is a right-wing critique of the humanistic secularization of the modern mass media.[14] But, more frequently, even such critics envision enormous possibilities for improving the world with television. Paradoxically, contemporary evangelicalism often perceives mass-communications technologies as ways of returning humanity to a better past and thereby guaranteeing a utopian future. In other words, televangelists have appropriated the American myth that sees technology as the vehicle for building a perfect world—in this case a world like that before the Fall.

Technological optimism is intimately connected with the Christian worldview, especially as formulated by modern Protestantism. Even nonreligious Americans generally owe their modern concept of progress to the Judeo-Christian heritage of messianic intervention and salvation. Whereas the classical Greeks saw history as an endless series of cycles, each with the same pattern of recovery and degeneration, the emerging view of history following Christ's death and resurrection was "Christian" in that it was linear and optimistic. In what essentially reflected the biblical drama, all humankind was seen as playing a predestined part in God's plan of salvation. As historian Carl Becker put it, Christianity transferred "the golden age from the past to the future

[and] . . . substituted an optimistic for a disillusioned view of human destiny."[15] Martin Marty comments that the sixteenth-century reformers eventually "popularized the picture of history as a theatre, wherein the cosmic drama is being worked out in the smallest details of the lives of great and small men and women." In other words, "History was God's workshop, and He worked through the men and women who inhabited that sphere."[16]

When the Christian view of history hit American shores, however, it increasingly linked technological development with all kinds of social and economic progress. Compared to Europeans, says historian Howard P. Segal, the United States saw its country "as a probable, not merely a potential, utopia; and this utopia was to be brought about primarily through technological changes rather than through a combination of political, economic, social, and technological changes." As a result, adds Segal, "Americans made technological progress equivalent to progress itself."[17] Popular American writings reflected this growing faith in technology; they spoke of America as the New World idealized by Europeans.[18] Various styles of utopian communities and utopian ideas sprang up across the nation. Although not all of them were based on technology-oriented thinking, most were predicated on the assumption that humankind *could* produce a better, perhaps even a perfect, world on earth.[19] What began in Europe under the influence of Christianity was popularized, even as it was transformed by pragmatic and optimistic Americans into a largely secular faith in technology. Often using biblical metaphors, Americans described their technology as "the machine in the garden" and the United States as the "garden of the world."[20]

In the United States, then, popular sentiment frequently saw technology as a means of ushering in an idyllic world of peace and harmony. Communications technologies, in particular, took on a kind of religious significance as the vehicles for undoing the curse on humankind and creating a new and more godly society. It was as if Paradise could be restored and history could be reversed, simply by using the fruits of modern technological development. In the nineteenth century the link between a hopeless present and an optimistic future, at least for evangelicals, was communications and transportation technologies. As historian Perry Miller put it, the American missionary effort was associated with the nation's "titanic entrance into the world of steam and electricity." Although preachers might still have said that the "moral and spiritual improvements of missions were more important than canals and railways," by 1848 the American "mind had become so adjusted to the technological revolution that pious language was changed from contrast to analogy. . . . Over and over again, to the point of tedium, but never to satiety, orators identified missions with the industrial 'scene of astonishing activity.'"[21]

In the national imagination, then, an Edenic past and hoped-for future come together in the technological present. From one technology to the next, Americans invest their dreams and hopes in a new world devoid of the evils of today. Whether it's as simplistic as the rhetoric about the convenience and freedom brought by the VCR, or as deeply moving and marvelous as the first walk on the moon, televised for all to see, optimism in technological progress is a fundamental characteristic of American culture. Moreover, it is a faith often infused with religious imagery, rhetoric, and meaning.

Evangelicals and Technology

In evangelical circles the faith in technology is typically linked to missionary activity. More than in other nations, Americans usually see the problem of national and worldwide evangelization in technological terms. Evangelization is normally viewed as a "mass" problem that necessitates "mass" communication. (As we shall see later, *personal* evangelization is far and away the most effective method.) Under the spell of their nation's fascination with technology, American evangelicals typically persist in finding new ways to bring the gospel to more and more people. They are even willing to support certain technological advances financially in pursuit of that goal.

Evangelicals' hope and trust in new gadgetry has often placed them at the forefront of developing and using new communications technologies. For example, nineteenth-century Bible and tract societies were leaders in both printing techniques and the organization of national distribution networks.[22] Similarly, evangelicals were probably the most involved group in early broadcasting, establishing radio stations all over the country. Later evangelicals organized elaborate syndication of their shows to hundreds of stations. (The enormously popular preacher Charles E. Fuller was heard on over a thousand stations around the world.) If not for some network-imposed restrictions on religious programs, evangelicals would have probably been leaders in radio technology. All in all, evangelicals were far more innovative in radio than most people realize.[23]

Evangelicals were similarly involved in the development and use of visual technologies. Although the electronic church burst upon the public scene in 1979 and 1980, chiefly because of the so-called New Christian Right led by Jerry Falwell's Moral Majority and certain other televangelists, evangelicals had long made use of the television medium. Oral Roberts launched some remarkable prime-time specials in 1969.[24] Rex Humbard built the Cathedral of Tomorrow in 1958 as a combination church and recording studio.[25] Controversial Billy James Hargis pioneered direct-mail fund-raising based on responses to his radio and television broadcasts. And in the late 1950s he had one of the first machines in the country that "personally" signed every letter sent to supporters.

The evangelicals' enthusiasm for cable and satellite television is even more dramatic. Pat Robertson turned a single television station into one of the largest satellite networks in the United States. First called CBN (Christian Broadcasting Network), it eventually became "The Family Channel," competing directly with other religious and, especially, secular channels for space on cable systems across the country. Similar in many respects to the Disney Channel, Robertson's network produced its own first-run drama as well as the "700 Club" and other religious broadcasts. Jim Bakker launched the successful PTL network as a full-time, satellite-distributed channel for cable systems and individual viewers with satellite dishes. The Trinity Broadcasting Network of Paul and Jan Crouch included not only cable channels, but also traditional TV stations and low-power transmissions. In 1989 TBN included 165 stations worldwide, with another 40 under construction. Many of them were small stations with very limited viewership, but they, too, illustrated the evangelical penchant for seizing mass communications media to spread the gospel.[26]

Evangelicalism's faith in technology surfaces in all denominations, but especially in the more creative and independent parachurch groups. An organization called World Mission Teams published in 1987 a "Status Report on the Great Commission." In that report the group claims that God "has provided new techniques of soul-winning evangelism that win the world for Christ *today*— how souls can be harvested by the use of modern machine 'combines' rather than the hand-scythes that have been used for almost twenty centuries." The combines are actually films that are to be translated and shown around the world. Estimating the total annual cost of the campaign at $100,000,000, the authors point out that "our superb Christian-nourishing TV networks *each* spend that much (even twice as much) each year just on we [sic] Gringos."[27]

In other words, evangelicals' essential challenge is to find new *technological* answers to every cultural, economic, political, or even spiritual problem. The reason the world has not been won to Christ, evangelicals frequently say, is that the right technology has not yet been procured for the task. However, once a particular organization such as World Mission Teams claims to have the right technology, money becomes an overriding issue. Faith in technology is softened by the reality of financial or personnel shortages, but the ultimate belief that the technology could usher in the promised blessings rarely wanes. This has been especially true in transnational broadcasting.[28] Audiences for most of such programs are very small, not principally because of technical problems, but because so little attention is given to the messages and the cultures to which they are directed. International programs from American evangelists are often translated directly from an English script and are so thoroughly ethnocentric that other cultures can make little sense of them. It is as if the technology itself, regardless of the message, will save souls. World Mission Teams claims that the best thing about a film evangelist is that he "needs no degree, no denominational credentials, no years of waiting, and but a small amount of training." The reason is technological: "Just as a jet aircraft can magnify a million-fold each step that we take on a journey, so does film evangelism magnify the productive abilities of our mission forces . . . *a thousand fold!*"

The climate of technological optimism among American evangelicals leads televangelists to articulate their success primarily in technological terms. Sometimes they speak of the number of conversions, but more often they rhapsodize about the number of stations that broadcast their signals, the number of cable systems that carry their broadcasts, the number of countries they "reach," and so forth. They imply (and viewers are to assume) that technological growth and sophistication necessarily correlate with spiritual or religious improvements. Of course this is not even a reasonably good argument, but it does raise funds from hopeful viewers who are similarly taken in by the faith in technology.

This is true on the local level as well. Cable television stations frequently have public access channels that can be used by local religious groups. Many churches have taken advantage of the situation, producing their own tapes of church services, talk shows, and Bible teaching. Often the technical quality of the shows is so poor that the camera fails to capture the action and the audio is close to unintelligible. At the same time, the sermons or teachings imply much about the faith that nonbelievers neither know nor can figure out by watching the program. In the end it is clear that just "being on" the tube, just using the technology, however poorly, is enough to tickle some evangelicals' belief that technology can overcome spiritual, political, ethnic, cultural, or other barriers.

Non-Americans have a difficult time understanding this type of faith in technology. In their eyes, most secular American broadcasting is entertaining but shallow, visually slick but thematically and intellectually weak. Similarly, they typically perceive American televangelism as much religious nonsense produced by a nation that is technologically sophisticated but culturally impoverished. Such feelings are probably partly the result of jealousy; at least in the Western World, the United States has been technologically ahead of most countries, with the recent obvious exception of Germany and Japan. Nevertheless, international perceptions of American culture carry some truth that the church ought to seriously consider.

Evangelistic Rhetoric

American evangelicalism has produced its own rhetoric of technological salvation. Usually the rhetoric does not say that technology actually saves people from their sins or their spiritual death, but it does imply that the latest technologies are God's necessary tools for worldwide evangelization. In other words, the Lord has given humankind the media principally to fulfill the Great Commission of preaching Christ and baptizing the entire world in his name. This type of discourse contradicts the critical attacks launched against television by individuals such as Muggeridge and Owens. As we shall see, neither approach can withstand careful scrutiny. Moreover, both have their interested followers who accept any rhetoric that supports what they wish to be true and already believe.

In 1986 Jimmy Swaggart unveiled a plan to spread his old-fashioned gospel to every nation on earth. He proposed packaging his top-rated weekly preaching program for broadcast to all cultures. It made some sense, because this program was already more popular in some Latin American countries than in the United States. But the goal was incredible, and the belief that his ministry alone could accomplish it was especially outrageous. Nevertheless, he and his son, Donnie, told viewers it was "D-Day or Delay," depending on the responses of viewers. If enough people contributed adequate funds, the Swaggarts said, the program could literally deliver the gospel to all nations in the free world.

Like the late media critic Marshall McLuhan, Swaggart envisioned an impending global village, founded not merely on instantaneous communication but on a kind of electronic evangelism that would supposedly communicate the gospel through space and across cultural and political boundaries direct to the hearts of humankind. Swaggart's appeal was traditionally evangelical: He would spread the gospel. But the technological character of his appeal for funds was characteristically American: All I need is more technology. The fact was that Swaggart's brand of old-style Pentecostalism would play well in some Third World countries, but it would find humorous or even hostile receptions in most industrialized nations. Moreover, Swaggart's sermons, which for a time were directed against other Christian traditions, would likely cause more divisiveness than unity or even conversion. Nevertheless, the "D-Day or Delay" theme appealed to many supporters, and before his fall in 1988 Swaggart was raising more funds than any other American televangelist.

Simply put, a faith in technology is an important part of the contemporary evangelistic rhetoric. In the late 1940s Eugene Bertermann, of the conservative Lutheran Church–Missouri Synod, captured the rhetoric pointedly in an article about the history of God's use of the media from the apostles' "primitive" and "laborious" proclamation by "word of mouth" to "the mighty . . . miracle of radio." The advantages of radio, Bertermann wrote, were its "spread" over "tremendous territories in a single moment," its "speed" of 186,000 miles a second, and its "penetration" through "walls of steel and bars of iron. . . . " He concluded that "Christians know that in God's design the radio has been invented particularly for the use of His Church and the upbuilding of His kingdom."[29] Note how Bertermann's views of radio perceive power in the medium itself, not in the way the message is communicated or even primarily in the message itself. The miracle is the technology, and many evangelicals agree.

Televangelist Jerry Falwell and Baptist church-growth specialist and theologian Elmer Towns developed their own version of this rhetoric. Moreover, they used it successfully to help convince people to support their ministry. They argued in 1971 that television was "the most effective medium for reaching people," that it was one of the "technologies for accomplishing worldwide salvation." They recommended "saturation evangelism," which would preach the gospel "to every available person at every available time by every available means. . . . The church will stand accountable at the judgment seat of Christ for its failure to utilize every means available to us to reach every creature."[30] Once again, the rhetoric of evangelism says little about the message or even the messenger, but much about the technology.

This kind of rhetoric is repeated throughout the writings, broadcasts, and fund-raising appeals of most American TV preachers. Even though relatively few people are actually converted by televangelism (a point covered carefully in a later chapter), the belief in the power of the medium effectively elicits much support. That belief is not just evangelical; it is broadly American. Advertisers hold to it. So do people who produce public-service announcements. But so also do critics of television, who fear the medium is turning minds to mush, lowering the educational performance of students, and so on down the list of television's "evils."

Electronic Exegesis

As strange as it may seem, the development of the electronic media in the twentieth century has changed how some Christians interpret Scriptures, especially biblical prophecy. In turn, the Bible's changing interpretations have apparently altered their views of electronics. Nineteenth-century American writings on the telegraph were frequently prefaced with the following quotation from Job 38:35: "Canst thou send lightnings, that they may go, and say unto thee, Here we are?" Similarly, historian and early telegraph booster T. P. Shaffner compared it to all past forms of communication as follows: "But what is all this to subjugating the lightnings, the mythological voice of Jehovah, the fearful omnipotence of the clouds, causing them in the fine agony of chained submission to do the offices of a common messenger—to whisper to the four corners of the earth the lordly behests of lordly man!"[31] From the telegraph forward, the Bible and the media have told an interesting tale of electronic exegesis.

By associating the creation of electronic marvels with the very handiwork of the Creator, Christians invested the media with biblical significance. One version of this type of thinking simply saw in the media the ultimate triumph of Christianity over other religions. Such media as the telegraph and, later, broadcasting would usher in a universal peace and harmony—a shalom over all humankind. The kingdom of God would blossom in the garden of universal communication. As one observer said of the telegraph, "It gives the preponderance of power to the nations representing the highest elements in humanity. . . . It is the civilized and Christian nations, who, though weak comparatively in numbers, are by these means of communication made more than a match for the hordes of barbarism."[32] This was an oblique reference to the Book of Revelation, with all people of all nations—at least all Christians—in universal accord before the same God and living the same culture. Such electronic exegesis was of course also highly ethnocentric and probably more American than biblical.

The other, more complex link between the Bible and electronic media was straightforwardly apocalyptic. When Jimmy Swaggart launched his "D-Day or Delay" campaign, the "D-Day" was worldwide evangelization, while the "Delay" referred to nothing less than the Second Coming of Christ. Again and again, from the telegraph to satellite communication, evangelicals have seen in each new medium the final scene in the biblical drama before the return of Christ. The most recent champions of this apocalyptic thought have been the televangelists, who never cease to believe that the media will spread the gospel worldwide prior to the Second Coming as prophesied in the Book of Revelation.

Ben Armstrong, then executive director of the National Religious Broadcasters, developed this interpretation most clearly in a book appropriately titled *The Electric Church*. Published in 1979, on the heels of extensive news coverage of evangelicalism in the secular media, the book summarized the popular theology of the time. Calling the "awesome technology of broadcasting" one of the "major miracles of modern times," Armstrong explained how the electronic media were supposedly returning the church of Jesus Christ to its early roots, two millennia ago. By breaking down the "walls of tradition we have built up around the church," wrote Armstrong, these media have resurrected a more pure Christianity. The electric church would become "a revolutionary new form of the worshiping, witnessing church that existed twenty centuries ago. . . . Members of the church gathered in homes, shared the Scriptures, prayed together, praised God. . . . They were on fire for the Lord, and their lives had been changed by Him. As a result, they changed the world."[33]

Armstrong's romanticized vision of the reformed electric church culminated in a picture of a New World created by Christians who were energized principally by televangelists, not by local pastors or even the church as an organization. In his picture of the last days before the Second Coming of Christ, the electric church is seen as the living result of the electronic evangel. Armstrong predicted that God would soon use the "electric church to revitalize the older forms of churches, empowering them to keep up with the twentieth-century challenges of a rapidly diminishing time span before the return of Jesus Christ." Finally, Armstrong suggested that such a future is so close at hand that the angel referred to in the Book of Revelation might actually be a communications satellite used by God to fulfill the prophecy of the last days: "And I saw another angel fly in the midst of heaven, having the everlasting gospel to preach unto them that dwell in the earth, and to every nation, and kindred, and tongue, and people."[34]

In electronic exegesis the media become players in the biblical drama. Even if not mentioned in the Bible, the roles assigned to the media support the rhetoric of televangelism. The Trinity Broadcasting Network's Paul Crouch, whose monthly newsletter to supporters is a bizarre combination of biblical texts and technological optimism, is the champion of the new exegesis. He makes no bones about the spiritual power of the media: "Christian television is the most powerful means whereby God's people can thrust the SWORD of the Spirit—THE WORD OF GOD—to repossess THIS WORLD for His Kingdom!"[35] And TBN is supposedly one of the most powerful messengers, reaching "a potential audience of *more than HALF THE WORLD!*"[36] The drama is clear for TBN and other such ministries—God gives the special power of electronic media technologies to particular people who are carrying out the redemption plan as outlined in Scripture.

Once this type of electronic exegesis is broadcast by the televangelists, it is nearly impossible for evangelicals to disagree. Evangelicalism is based mainly on the necessity for personal salvation and on the need for all believers to support worldwide evangelization. Some evangelicals may not like the fund-raising tactics or the preaching styles of specific televangelists, but they will almost always agree on the public goal of these ministries: to win the world for Christ. From this perspective, if televangelists are evangelizing *anyone* they must be on the side of God, and they certainly must have a place in redemptive history.

The new electronic exegesis exposes its unorthodox beliefs, however, when it addresses the role of the media in the Second Coming of Christ. Again and again, to the point of absurdity, American televangelists have directly linked the return of Christ to the contemporary use of communication electronics. Gerard Straub, former producer of Robertson's "700 Club," recalls a time at the CBN offices when a group of workers was making secret plans to televize the Second Coming.[37] As ridiculous as that was, it realistically reflected a way of thinking about the role of the broadcast media in biblical history that is widespread among televangelists. When Swaggart launched his "D-Day or Delay" campaign, he indicated that the Second Coming of Christ depended on the gospel being preached to all nations. At the same time, however, he outlandishly suggested that *his* ministry could be the one to spread the gospel around the globe. The implication is that the very culmination of biblical history through the return of the Savior is dependent on both electronics and the efforts of particular televangelists—as if God would not choose to work through different means and other people.

For over a century, at least since the development of the telegraph, Americans have frequently attributed apocalyptic significance to new communications technology. The electrical and electronic media, probably because of their "mystical" ability to transmit messages instantaneously from one place to another, have been the major characters in these End Times' stories and images. There is something especially attractive to Americans about electronic exegesis, which openly baptizes their inherent faith in technology with religious symbols and spiritual significance. Ben Armstrong's book culminated in a picture of a New World created by Christians who were spiritually energized by the Holy Ghost. In his scenario, the Holy Ghost works through communications satellites and other electronic media, creating a "revolution as dramatic as the revolution that began when Martin Luther nailed his ninety-five theses to the cathedral door at Wittenberg."[38]

It appears that the apocalyptic scenarios depicted by Armstrong and numerous televangelists may be less biblical than American. Believing the scenarios requires one to have faith in the power of the new electronic media. Clearly Armstrong does. He writes, "Today, I believe we are in the midst of a new epoch where radio and television have shattered all previous standards of effectiveness for the communication of ideas and information to the largest number of people in the shortest possible time with the greatest clarity."[39] Such a belief, when turned loose in American evangelicalism, produces a faith that technology can do the work that God has supposedly not been able to accomplish through other means.

When Jerry Falwell first decided in the late 1960s to enter televangelism, he hoped to use the medium to revive and renew the "faith of the nation." He wrote in his autobiography, "We were standing on the threshold of an incredible opportunity to preach Christ simultaneously to every television home in the country. . . ."[40] Decades later, the program barely reached a few million people. Once again the evangelistic rhetoric was far more triumphalistic than the reality of the situation merited. But it made little difference in terms of fund-raising; American evangelicals, like their nonevangelical neighbors and friends in every area of the nation, clung to the faith in technology that animated the apocalyptic vision. There were already the VCR, satellites, and cable television, and there would always be a new medium of hope. But it is difficult not to wonder if such hope, however apocalyptic or biblically exegeted, is not really part of what Frederick Ferré once called "technolatry."[41]

Transmission vs. Communication

Probably the most distressing aspect of televangelism's faith in technology is its rather naive juxtaposition of transmission and communication. Televangelists, and their enthusiastic supporters and cheerleaders, characteristically equate the sheer broadcast of sounds and images with the actual communication of messages. Today there are undoubtedly more communications media than in any previous age, and evangelicals have been quick to use most of them. But how effective has the barrage of messages been in clearly communicating anything of significance? What is the real social, moral, or spiritual gain in the contemporary cacophony of media voices?

Because televangelism so readily confuses information with knowledge and understanding, its advocates think there is far more communication taking place than there really is. Every year there are more evangelical radio and television stations, larger evangelical satellite networks, slicker evangelical shows, and more programs. At the same time, however, there is ever greater confusion about what it means to live the Christian life in a complex world. Televangelists broadcast thousands of words—but how much spiritual truth are they able to communicate? Even historian Daniel Boorstin, one of the most optimistic observers of American culture, admits that the "electronic technology that reaches out instantaneously over the continents does very little to help us cross the centuries."[42] In other words, while the electronic media easily traverse geography, they have a difficult time traversing history. The "faith of our fathers," as one hymn puts it, may be lost in the hustle of contemporary media blitzes, both religious and secular. Religious messages are among the most difficult to communicate, precisely because they involve faith, which is necessarily cultivated over time. Electronic messengers have a tough job in trying to share the essence, depth, and implications of religious faith with distant audiences.

Emphasizing technology over communication, and information over understanding, actually makes religious communication more unlikely. No matter how sophisticated the transmitting and receiving equipment, the basic problem of communicating something of value remains. In fact, the glamor of the lights and the spell of the microphone can actually interfere with the essential task of sharing the historic gospel.

Conclusion

In 1989 a survey of *U.S. Catholic* readers found that 82 percent believed the church would use the electronic media more in twenty years than it presently did.[43] Even Roman Catholics, members of one of the least-electronic churches in the United States, clearly felt the lure of the media, further proof that the American belief in progress and technological development has stretched across the various Christian traditions. Just as it seemed inevitable in 1989 (as in every previous year) that the United States would be the leader in electronic communication, it seemed to many American Christians of nearly all traditions that the church should spiritually capitalize on this potential. Even though the media had not yet won the world for Christ, there was always the hope that they would. Again, such hope reflected a deep cultural faith in technology while it elicited contributions from patrons of televangelism.

Through the last century, as James W. Carey and John J. Quirk write, the American hope in technology has been transferred from one new medium to the next.[44] Just when it seems that the existing technology is not going to usher in a better society or evangelize the world, along comes a new one. The telegraph begat the radio, which begat television, which eventually begat cable television, satellite networks, and the omnipresent VCR. Each of these advances was something of a new beginning for people who trusted in the social progress or spiritual development that it would bring. What Samuel Morse said in the first telegraphic transmission across the Eastern Seaboard could be repeated meaningfully with every new technology: "What hath God wrought?" For the critic or pessimist, whether a Malcolm Muggeridge, Virginia Stem Owens, or Jacques Ellul, the phrase would carry negative connotations. What, in fact, has technology done to God's creation? For the optimist, on the other hand, Morse's message symbolizes the mystery of untapped power and the spirit of technological faith.

In the United States, technology and Christianity are strange partners. Each fuels the other's best and worst aspects. Hope and faith are so intermingled with electronics and media that it is not always easy to determine what is religious and what is technological. The use of scientific know-how necessarily requires the application of values about technology, as Jacques Ellul has argued so persuasively.[45] Without human values, technologies are but useless equipment waiting to be put to work or play. Quasi-religious values permeate the use of technology, especially the electronic media, in the United States. In public and private settings, Americans affirm their belief in the benefits of new technologies, and they forge ahead, often uncritically applying the gimmickry to all kinds of political, economic, and religious situations. Televangelists, too, have done this, but not without the enthusiastic support of their constituencies.

Therefore, it is fair to ask if modern televangelism is not governed by at least some faith in technology. Given the rhetoric of evangelization and the electronic exegesis, there is little doubt that technologically directed faith does exist. Moreover, it is obvious that this faith fosters among televangelists a far greater concern with technological expansion and development than it does with actual communication. Unfortunately, this has typically led televangelists to march ahead triumphantly with new technologies without seriously considering how best to use them for communication that is distinctly Christian in both style and content. Televangelists have been especially naive about how technologies shape a message, but they have also tended to overlook the negative impact of their systems of financial support on their attempts to communicate the gospel. Pat Robertson's own approach to religious broadcasting makes this clear. "The biggest mistake that pastors make," Robertson told an interviewer, "is to superimpose their 'thing' on the media. They should discover what the media are doing and then adapt to the media format."[46]

More technology does not necessarily mean "better" technology. The value of the electronic media for televangelism, for example, is not the number of radio or television stations airing evangelical broadcasts. Nor is it merely the power of the stations or the technical quality of their transmissions. Just as society's public media can be evaluated in terms of how well they entertain, persuade, inform, and so forth, televangelism must be evaluated principally in terms of how it meets particular religious purposes and needs. The accumulation of more technology and the expansion of televisual programming *per se* offer no real religious benefits to humankind. In fact such purely technological goals will almost invariably cloud the church's own vision for programs that could truly advance the cause of Christ and glorify God.

By diverting the church's attention from God to the media, America's faith in technology actually turns people into instruments of the very machines they supposedly control. Reinhold Niebuhr wrote that "we are relatively too successful in all our technical achievements, and that we are therefore in danger of becoming slaves of the instruments of production and communication which have initially served us so well."[47] Televangelism is part of this danger as it reaches out for new media without challenging itself to review critically how it has used previous ones, with what immediate effects, and with what long-term consequences for Christianity.

Ironically, as evangelicals have employed ever new and seemingly more powerful communications technologies, they have had ever greater difficulty coordinating their efforts. David Barnett has argued that plans to evangelize the world "seem barely possible of achievement" unless Christians coordinate their efforts in a way that is "completely new and unprecedented."[48] Television, one of the most powerful means of communication, has been especially divisive and competitive among evangelicals. It has not brought the church together any more than the telegraph delivered its promised universal brotherhood in its day. If anything, the new technologies extend and deepen existing fractures and fissures in the church in the United States.

Yet hope remains. Paul Crouch of TBN writes, *"THE WHOLE WIDE WORLD* is opening up to US! Christian television is ONE of God's great end-time harvesting tools to get THIS Gospel preached to ALL THE WORLD!"[49] Crouch and many others share a common American faith in the power of communications technologies to overcome the political and cultural obstacles to world evangelization. That faith, as we have seen, is grounded in the idea of Christian historical progress, grafted to American optimism about technology in general, and given specific form by twentieth-century evangelical theology. As one writer summarized the faith in the 1930s, "There is something so uncanny and far-reaching in the persuasiveness of the radio waves that to the Christian it might well become another Pentecost. . . ."[50]

More realistically, the electronic media probably create as many new problems as they solve. Televangelism's technological optimism has not yet been validated. Certainly this "failure" has been partly the result of the fact that God does not use the medium directly, but only through imperfect messengers whose own foibles and agendas often get in the way of the task of evangelization. Of course, no medium can communicate messages perfectly between fallen creatures in a sinful world. If the new technologies are a step forward for completing the Great Commission, they are not the only means or always the most appropriate ones. God claims the whole world, electronic media and all, but he surely expects humankind to have more faith in him than in the technologies used by his messengers. In the United States, where technological progress has always been a symbol of hope and progress is usually defined materially, this is hard medicine to swallow. Americans prefer to adopt scientific advances quickly, optimistically, and naively—instead of slowly, carefully, and humbly.

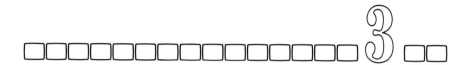

The Cults of Personality

On a cool fall morning I stood before a group of forty adults in the sanctuary of a medium-size church. I was there to lead a pre-service class on the topic of televangelism in the United States. After being introduced, I decided to begin with a quick survey of the group's TV viewing habits. "How many of you have ever watched a religious television program?" I asked. Every hand went up. "Okay," I continued, "how many of you watch one at least monthly?" All but a few arms went back up. "How many of you have heard of Jerry Falwell?" "Pat Robertson?" "Robert Schuller?" "Jimmy Swaggart?" Nearly every hand went up with every name I mentioned.

Then I tried something unexpectedly revealing. "How many of you can tell me the name of the broadcast of any of the major televangelists? A couple of hands went up, but the answers were wrong. Suddenly the sleepy adults came alive with discussion. From the front row to the drowsiest group in the back of the sanctuary, they talked excitedly and uncontrollably among themselves like high school students before the class bell rings. I had stumped them, so without any prompting they decided to prove to me that they knew the names of the major televangelism programs.

After several minutes I quieted the group and asked for their answers. This time there were many guesses, but nearly all of them were wrong. In the minds of these adults, and I presume in the minds of most Americans, televangelism is primarily the televangelists themselves. The personalities of the major TV preachers color practically everyone's knowledge of and feelings about the electronic church. I soon discovered that even in this church, where the vast majority of members regularly watched televangelists, personality was more memorable than message, doctrine, finances, or any other aspect of contemporary religious broadcasting. During a later question-and-answer period, nearly every inquiry directed to me from the group was about one or another personality: "What do you think of Schuller?" "How about Falwell?" "Is Roberts for real?"

Personalities are central to the popularity of televangelism. From Roman Catholic Bishop Fulton J. Sheen in the 1950s to the current quiver of top-rated televangelists, most picture-tube ministries have depended decisively on the telegenic appeal of a single person. There have been isolated exceptions, such as Radio Bible Class's "Day of Discovery," which without a dominant personality maintained a strong position among the ten highest-rated syndicated programs in the nation during the late 1980s and early 1990s. And of course there were numerous broadcast co-personalities on evangelical talk shows, from PTL's Jim and Tammy Bakker to Paul and Jan Crouch of the Trinity Broadcasting Network. Certainly among the weekly broadcasts, however, a single dominant personality was crucial for attracting audiences and building constituency support. During the 1970s and 1980s the weekly syndicated program ratings were led variously by Roberts, Swaggart, and Schuller. They were soon joined by Falwell, whose notoriety ballooned when he helped form the Moral Majority, and two daily religious talk-show hosts, Robertson of CBN's "700 Club" and Jim Bakker.

If personalities help televangelism gain national visibility, they are also one of its most troubling characteristics. As I will show, charismatic personalities often attract uncritical believers who submit to the authority of their leader far more than to the authority of tradition, the church, or even the Bible. And this kind of charisma is not particularly spiritual. Televangelists share some of the same charismatic qualities of other celebrities, including show business personalities.

One of the ironies in American Protestantism is how willingly some Christians join personality cults. In spite of hundreds of years of Reformation, Protestantism still yearns sometimes for its own pope-like celebrities. Especially in the United States, conservative Protestants frequently seek their own religious gurus. There appears to be a human impulse toward personality cults that transcends doctrine and faith. Such cults predate even the Roman Catholic church, extending back to the early church described in the New Testament.

Today's American culture is the soil, and television is the fertilizer, for personality cults of all kinds, from political heroes to sports celebrities and entertainment stars. Gossip magazines thrive on these personalities. So does the contemporary Christian music industry. Even evangelical book publishing is greatly affected. Like show business, evangelical mass communication of all kinds now resembles the Hollywood star system. Every Christian record company and book publisher wants to sign contracts with the most popular evangelical celebrities. Televangelism is an important seedbed for the growth of American personality cults. In the apostles' day, Paul admonished the Corinthians for being followers of various human beings rather than followers of Jesus Christ. Today he might admonish the popular televangelists, who forget that God chose the weak things of the world to shame the strong, so that no one may boast before him.[1]

Personality and Authority in America

Americans believe in individualism. They inherited the concept from the classical Greeks and used it to establish the rights and freedoms found in the Constitution and Declaration of Independence. However, this individualism was always projected into the future as a source of social and economic progress. Individuals would make the United States a great nation. Government was to serve the individual, not the other way around.

From the early days of the American colonies, immigrants linked their individualistic spirit to their hopes for the future. Settlers were looking for a land where they could chart their own destinies, where they could be themselves, and where their own personalities could shape the land. In this New World there was to be an opportunity for a new start in life. The past would not determine the future, people believed, because America had not been spoiled by some of the undesirable traditions of European society. The country was a new and noble experiment in individualism.

That hope is still alive for many people coming to the United States. Today's Asian and Latin American immigrants, like their nineteenth-century counterparts from Europe, are generally hardworking, industrious people who believe in the American Dream.

They hope to use their minds and bodies to fashion a better life for themselves. Every gain they make brings them one step closer to the dream. It is abundantly clear that the melting pot of American culture is really a chunky ethnic and racial soup held together by a common faith in progress and governed by a spirit of individualism. Each successive wave of immigration produces another ethnic group seized by that faith and spirit. While successful Americans today often sink comfortably into middle-class affluence, newcomers to the land of opportunity typically strip off their outworn traditions and plunge determinedly into the bright future.

These beliefs led to a unique culture that glorified the future and stressed the importance of individual personality. For example, early Americans were remarkably open to new religious ideas and practices. They wanted a practical religion that "worked" for individuals, as we shall see in chapter 5. In short, they wanted the kind of religious faith that mirrored their own hopes in the New World and their belief in the ability of individuals to be successful. Although "success" often meant different things to different people from a wide range of ethnic, racial, and religious backgrounds, there were increasingly two common denominators: prosperity and public notoriety.

To a large extent, success in the United States means fortune and fame. This is why gossip magazines are loaded with stories about wealthy celebrities from the entertainment industry, and why television versions of those themes are popular as well. (The *National Enquirer* is the largest-circulation paper in the country!) Gossip columnist Liz Smith says, "We don't have heroes to believe in anymore. Today, people with money are godlike. Malcolm Forbes and [Donald] Trump are absolute stars."[2] Smith might have added that such celebrities often *seek* fame with their fortunes. Money is great, but it is usually not enough for the individual who craves real success. Modern stars also want to have their names on the cornerstones of buildings, at the head of corporations, and in the titles of charitable foundations. Such notoriety completes the American image of success. According to these standards, show business (including sports) produces more successful Americans than any other enterprise. Hollywood is not just in the entertainment business. It also manufactures public personalities. So does televangelism.

Evangelical "Cultism"

This concept of success has always clashed with the Christian faith, although things have changed somewhat in the last two decades. Historically, any financially successful clergy were typically suspect to their congregations and the general public. Money was to be poured into building programs or other religious institutions, not into the pockets of pastors or other religious figures. But, by the early twentieth century, Americans were already contributing remarkable sums to particular mission enterprises or building projects led by well-known religious personalities. Like a popular nineteenth-century circuit rider, a convicting turn-of-the-century preacher with charisma could elicit contributions. A dull and uninspiring evangelist could not. For example, in 1886 the Chicago Evangelization Society raised $250,000 to convince well-known urban revivalist Dwight L. Moody to start a school for training evangelical leaders. Moody did not seek the money. Chicago evangelicals offered it to him as a statement of their desire for him to establish what later became Moody Bible Institute.[3]

It was inevitable that American views of success would influence religion. Increasingly, the successful preacher was the one who was most able not only to evangelize unsaved souls or revive waning ones, but also to create visible symbols of success. Unlike old European cathedrals or local American churches, new church buildings in the United States often reflect the concepts and personalities of individuals rather than the traditions of denominations. Religious leaders, like their business counterparts, erected larger buildings as monuments to themselves and as symbols of the power of their organizations. These structures overshadowed traditional Protestant churches and even Roman Catholic cathedrals—literally and symbolically. Among the first radio evangelists to compete architecturally was Aimee Semple McPherson, who built Angelus Foursquare Temple in Los Angeles. The structure served the needs of both worship and entertainment, including live radio broadcasts.[4] It was a religious Grand Ole Opry house. Ironically, the original Grand Ole Opry house in Nashville was formerly a church.[5]

American evangelicalism was particularly ripe for personality cults. Compared with religious groups that were anchored securely in tradition and church governance, evangelicals were independent and innovative. Evangelicals were usually not joiners as much as adaptors, revisionists, and innovators, especially with communications media. Every generation of evangelical leaders in America reshaped the gospel message for new audiences and novel media.[6] They were amazingly free and open to different ways of doing things, including evangelism. Lacking strong religious traditions, and enamored with the American version of success, evangelicals were particularly susceptible to the nascent personality cults entering broadcasting. Radio and television merely accelerated existing trends toward personality cults in American culture, including religion. No denominations were free of these problems, as the more tradition-minded Roman Catholic church discovered with political preacher Father Charles Coughlin in the 1930s, prime-time TV priest Bishop Sheen in the 1950s, and most recently Mother Angelica of the Eternal Word Network. Even mainline Protestants produced a few TV personalities, such as the Hollywood Presbyterian Church's Lloyd Ogilvie. Evangelicals, however, were among the most susceptible religious groups because of their suspicion of tradition and their strong emphasis on the preacher.

As evangelicalism developed after World War II it became the most clearly American expression of Protestant personality cults. In para-church movements of all kinds, from nondenominational Bible colleges to world mission organizations and especially domestic broadcasting, evangelicals increasingly depended upon the people-pleasing abilities and optimistic rhetoric of particular leaders. Religious publications and in-person appearances were crucial to the rise of contemporary personality cults; it seemed that every successful para-church leader had to have his own publication with a "personal" note to the constituency, and that sermon "tours" were becoming public relations vehicles. Broadcasting, however, became the most potent tool for communicating personal authority to large and distant constituencies. Mass media enabled evangelical leaders to become major celebrities with national followings.[7]

Beginning with Sheen, Roberts, and Humbard, American television offered prominent new personalities for religious viewers. It was not long, however, before evangelical leaders dominated the airways. Each one had a story to tell about his own success. Roberts overcame poor health, poverty and a stutter to make the first religiously oriented prime-time variety specials on American television.[8] Falwell succeeded in spite of his rebellious youth and an alcoholic father who died young.[9] Schuller's ministry grew from a kitschy Los Angeles drive-in church to the magnificent Crystal Cathedral in Garden Grove.[10] Robertson started his first television station with little more than spending money. Decades later he was one of the most successful cable television network executives in the nation.[11] And Bakker, a short, working-class kid who suffered from intense feelings of inferiority, eventually founded the PTL network and Heritage U.S.A. theme park, whose attendance was third only to the two Disney parks.[12]

The personal lives of these evangelical leaders, especially as portrayed in their autobiographies, form a stunning corpus of contemporary success stories.[13] These men became modern-day saints whose own lives seemingly displayed the special work of God. Like Moody and many prebroadcasting evangelical leaders, such televangelists use their past to establish their charismatic authority in the present. In their strongest forms, televangelists' autobiographies are like modern parables—testimonies to the acts of God in history. However, it is the televangelists and their public relations departments who interpret these personal scriptures for the ministry's followers. Television becomes the medium for this new "text," recalling and mirroring the actions of evangelical saints. As I will show in the next chapter, these autobiographies become ongoing dramas about the ministries.

The Magic of Televised Personality

Recently a denominationally subsidized television preacher remarked to me that "something magical happens when I speak to the camera. In my own head I know that it's just me talking. But somehow when people watch me on a recorded program it's as if they think they're communicating with me personally. I know that from some of the letters I get. The thing is, I don't feel that way about the viewers. All I see is the lens and, sometimes, the teleprompter. I have to imagine an individual sitting there in her living room watching me. Otherwise, I feel like I'm not really speaking with anyone, not even the camera crew, which is busily doing its job."

Television is a distinct medium that communicates very differently from both the printed and spoken word. It is clearly the most powerful mass medium for establishing personality cults. In fact, in the fertile American culture that breeds such cults, television is continuously establishing and maintaining society's leaders and sometimes contributing to their downfall. The tube gives authority to the voices and images of certain individuals, making them celebrities. American evangelicalism and television thrive on each other—for good and bad.

Printed messages require the reader to imagine what the voices sound like, how fast they are speaking, what kind of emotion is behind them, and what the scene looks like. It is not easy to personalize printed communication unless one already knows—or thinks one knows—the source of the messages. During my college years I received a letter from the administration that began "Dear . . . " followed by my social security number. My roommate and I laughed uproariously at the next line: "We have a personal interest in you." If the same administrator had called me on the telephone with the identical greeting, however, I would not have laughed—at least not at first. Unless it is a letter from someone we know well, printed communication is relatively distant and impersonal; we separate ourselves from the words on the paper. This is partly why printed communication is so outstanding for education. Printed words are more likely to engage the mind to think about the messages than are television and film images, which tend to elicit feelings but not thoughts. Of course these different reactions to print and moving-image media are partly learned. People can be taught to think about what they see, but neither the schools nor the churches have seriously attempted to accomplish such visual literacy.

Radio established stronger personality cults than print media by creating the impression of a personal relationship between listener and broadcaster. Because a real voice was communicated "live" (even if recorded), it normally seemed to listeners that a friend or acquaintance was speaking to them personally. Popular radio stars of past decades, such as Arthur Godfrey, depended heavily on the medium's capacity for establishing that kind of intimacy between themselves and individual listeners. So did the early disc jockeys (DJ's) on the first rock radio stations in the 1950s. Some fans listened to their favorite DJ late at night in the solemn darkness of their bedrooms, with a transistor radio under their pillow.

Radio listeners sometimes felt that well-known radio personalities, whether DJ's or actors, were no different from the real person behind the microphone. They even believed that actors such as those who played in the nightly comedy "Amos 'n Andy" were not acting. The real genius of that program, which attracted in the 1930s an estimated 40 million listeners (one-third of all Americans), was not the comic gags but the characterizations. By changing their vocal inflection, tone, dialect, and phrasing, the two actors were able to establish effective characters that made the actors invisible.[14]

Early radio evangelists such as Charles E. Fuller similarly established a feeling of personal communication with listeners. In fact, there is no way to explain Fuller's success purely on the basis of the messages he preached and the musical inspiration he offered listeners in the 1930s and 1940s. There were thousands of comparatively unpopular radio evangelists with similar messages trying to build national ministries. One listener wrote Fuller, "I am a young man . . . a commercial traveler by occupation covering a territory from coast to coast. . . . I have been held by some supernatural power to my room on Sunday evenings and drawn to listen to your broadcast. Why I do not know because church has never held any place in my life. I feel you are so sincere in your talks."[15] Fuller's popularity on the "Old Fashioned Revival Hour" undoubtedly resulted significantly from his ability to use radio effectively to establish a personal ethos with millions of listeners. Even though the humble Fuller was not trying to establish a personality cult, his intimate broadcasts made him the most popular radio evangelist of all time.[16]

Televised Intimacy

Television adds seemingly real images to radio's intimate voices, providing an even more powerful means for establishing personality cults. As Malcolm Muggeridge and others have argued, televised images invariably appear real.[17] This is especially true for television news. Common sense and everyday experience tell us that cameras do not lie. What viewers see on home television sets is what the camera is actually recording with its lens. What you see is what is actually taking place—or so the viewers assume. Even when viewers disagree with the interpretation of televised news, they trust the images they see with their own eyes. To the average viewer, television, like the home video camera, simply documents on film what really happens. News programs may be biased, viewers presume, but only because the personal biases of reporters slant the interpretation of the televised images.

In reality cameras *do* deceive. Someone has to decide what the camera will show the viewers and what it will ignore, what it will highlight and what it will push to the visual background. When the hostages were being held in the United States embassy in Iran, nightly television reports from the area around the compound created the sense that the entire nation was in revolutionary chaos and that Iranians were all gun-toting extremists. The camera rarely showed the calm that existed only a few blocks away. Just as a radio voice is created by the microphone, a television image is produced by the camera. Someone must control the camera, like the microphone. In these electronic media, sounds and images are reproduced as versions of the original ones. The sounds and images of people are not the people themselves, but viewers naturally assume that voices and photographic images are more personal and real than the printed word.

Television visually communicates one type of "real" image better than all others: the human face. Large panoramic shots communicate effectively on the enormous film screen, but not on a nineteen-inch TV tube, which compacts sunsets and mountains into poorly detailed miniatures. Neither can television effectively capture close-up images in spite of the popularity of some nature shows on public and cable television. In a film theater a close-up of an ant is so real it can startle viewers, while on television the images of that ant appear relatively indistinct and unspectacular. The human face, on the other hand, communicates well on television. Facial expressions that convey human emotion are easily gleaned from a high-quality television picture. Although the new large-screen television technologies might improve the range of images that the medium can communicate effectively, for the vast majority of people TV conveys human emotion through facial images.

Televangelism makes good use of that principle. Along with the laughing looks of comedy stars, the tragic expressions of soap opera characters, the authoritative stares of newscasters, and the sensuous glances of commercial models are the expressive faces of televangelists. Day in and day out—on cable, over the air, and through satellites—the facial images of televangelists are delivered electronically to viewers. In the privacy of viewers' homes, television recreates those images on the picture tubes. There the televangelist takes on a new persona. The TV viewer sees both more (and less) than what someone in the studio audience sees. The TV pulpit, auditorium stage, or talk-show set recedes to the visual background while the televangelist's face expands to fill the screen. Through this process the viewing of televangelism becomes an entirely different experience than attending a crusade or participating in a local revival. In face-to-face interaction the viewer decides what to see within the limits of the human eye. On TV, by comparison, the camera sets the technological limits and the camera operators and film editors determine what the viewer actually sees.

Televangelism's personality cults begin with the desires of the viewers for someone to follow and are enhanced by the intimate way that the medium communicates. Even if the televangelist does not seek to gain authority over his viewers, little that he can do visually will discourage some viewers from wanting to become followers. Television inherently creates the illusory sense that preacher and viewer are communicating personally. As Malcolm Boyd put it in the early days of the medium, a religious broadcaster can triumph as a personality "without having achieved any essential relatedness at all."[18] The negative side of this is that televangelists can create the "illusion" of personal concern for a "faceless audience" regardless of whether or not they actually have such concern.[19] The image appears to tell the truth, that the televangelist is your friend, while hiding the real truth, that there is no relationship whatsoever between the typical viewer and the televangelist.

In its strongest forms, such televisual intimacy substitutes the televangelist for God. The televangelist is presumed to be like God, communicating through space directly to millions of individual personalities. He is not only a preacher, but the source of truth and knowledge. He is not only a person, but the special person that represents God to his people. The televangelist becomes the mediator of not only the message, but the relationship with God. However, the spiritual communication that takes place in the name of the televangelist is not always in the name of Christ.

Even in situations where television does not give preachers such priestly status, it typically elevates their standing in the church. Televangelists may not have a high official status in the church, but unofficially they are looked up to as specially gifted individuals. The medium provides them a privileged place in public life among their followers. Even in denominations with their own subsidized broadcasts, a broadcaster automatically becomes one of the most authoritative voices among all clergy. He is typically invited to local churches and keynoted at denominational conventions as the major speaker. He will often be quoted or cited in denominational publications, and he might even address the clergy at denominational business meetings. A denomination's broadcaster becomes a symbol of the strength and visibility of the entire denomination. Radio and television were able to put various denominations "on the map" by giving them a personal media presence in the wider culture.[20]

TV Charismatics

It is very possible that the rise of television, including televangelism, has fueled the recent growth of personality-oriented Christianity. The spectacular growth of the charismatic movement in the 1970s and 1980s paralleled the sweep of the medium throughout American society. Even into the 1960s, some denominations were highly critical of television and film, but by the 1970s only fringe religious groups such as the Amish and some Mennonites were still trying seriously to keep television out of the homes of their members. Now, in the 1990s, it is impossible to distinguish among religious groups based solely on their television viewing habits. The tube was ubiquitous, and so was the charismatic movement. In fact, there was hardly any distinct movement left. Charismatics existed throughout the churches and across the spectrum of religious television. Cable television and satellite dishes helped deliver into millions of homes a new wave of charismatic religious leaders, including Bakker and Robertson. Television may have helped establish a new religious sensibility and a new style of popular worship heavily dependent on personality. In other words, the charismatic movement, formerly characterized by people who *believed* in things such as divine healing and especially speaking in tongues, gave way to a charismatic *style* of religious life strongly characterized by emotion and personality.

The most intriguing aspect of the contemporary charismatic movement is its broad appeal. Historically speaking, Pentecostals, although sharing some beliefs and practices of charismatics (for example, healing and speaking in tongues), were always distinct organizations and movements identified by denominations and to some extent even by social class, educational background, and region of the country. The new charismatics, on the other hand, span the scope of American Christianity. *Christianity Today* magazine, which represents mainstream American evangelicalism, commissioned a Gallup Poll in 1979 to determine how many charismatics and Pentecostals there were in the country. The magazine found that 19 percent of all American adults considered themselves to be Pentecostal or charismatic Christians—an almost unbelievable figure. Moreover, this charismatic movement stretched across the spectrum of organized American Christianity, from Roman Catholic (18% charismatic) to Baptists (20%) to Methodists (18%) and to Lutherans (20%). However, only a small fraction (17%) of those who called themselves Pentecostal-charismatic actually spoke in tongues.[21] In other words, the rapidly growing charismatic movement of the 1970s and 1980s was distinguished more by its style of religious expression than by its beliefs or doctrines, more by *how* it worshiped than whom or why it worshiped.

There are numerous explanations for the historic popularity of the charismatic expression of Christian faith. Perhaps it is indeed the work of God in the church—a spiritual awakening characterized by emotional expressions of the faith. Charismatic worship has always included such practices: raised hands during worship, popular and spontaneous singing, long and impassioned prayers, more congregational participation in liturgy. Another, not necessarily contradictory, explanation is that many mainline Protestant and Roman Catholic churches simply have not changed liturgically and organizationally to meet the spiritual needs of people in a modern culture. Accordingly, worship can become a rather boring, static, and meaningless activity—a series of actions that mean little to the average member and simply keep church buildings maintained and services going. From this perspective, the charismatic movement has been a grass-roots attempt to revive worship and enliven the experience of faith. And it has led to the conversion of many people.

While there is merit in both explanations, depending on one's views of how God works in the world, neither explains precisely why the charismatic movement has taken its present form. I suggest another possibility—that the new charismatic movement has been at least partly the natural culmination of religious expression in a culture increasingly dominated by the medium of television. In all its dimensions the charismatic movement seeks to turn loose the personality of the believer and the personality of God in the act of worship. In other words, this expression of faith has never been based primarily on traditional practices, scriptural interpretation, preaching, or the sacraments. It was always centered on *personal* experience, with the song leader or pastor establishing the direction of the experience. These leaders were like video directors, orchestrating the live performances of the church audience. (In the next chapter I will discuss at length the dramatic aspects of televangelism linking them to popular liturgy in the churches today.)

Regardless of how authentic charismatic worship is, and Christians disagree on that matter, it normally transfers religious authority away from organizations and toward particular leaders. *Charisma* magazine is one of the most celebrity-oriented evangelical magazines in the country, frequently profiling well-known evangelical broadcasters. Although charismatics are encouraged to experience and express their faith for themselves, they are to do so under the directions and patterns established by their leaders. In this sense, then, the charismatics in televangelism are the cutting edge of popular American Christianity. They have figured out how to establish their authority through a visually oriented mass medium with hundreds of thousands and even millions of viewers. Their talents as preachers are also their gifts as worship leaders and television "personalities." Like turn-of-the-century urban revivalists, they judge success in terms of how well they can move an audience to emotion, not necessarily in terms of the accuracy of their messages.

The nature of television as a personality-driven, facially expressive medium helps explain why charismatics have increasingly dominated the top-ten weekly syndicated religious-program audiences during the past twenty years. Roberts led the weekly ratings for years. Then Swaggart and Schuller vied for the lead, with Swaggart dropping considerably after the scandals of 1986 and 1987. Among the most popular new televangelists is Copeland, a Pentecostal who once worked for Roberts. Although televangelists such as Schuller, Falwell, and D. James Kennedy would not call themselves charismatics, they adapted their television programs to elements of personality-oriented communication. They made themselves symbols of Christian authority on a wide range of social, political, and religious issues. And they strived for the kind of emotional responses from their viewers that would result in larger audiences and more involvement in their ministries by those audiences.

As a product of a televisual culture, the new charismatic Christianity is not primarily a denominational movement, an ecclesiastical structure or even a set of particular doctrinal beliefs. It is a popular style of religious expression that transcends historical differences among Christians. As Pierre Babin said, even when the pope goes on TV, "he is more symbol than word." On the tube the pontiff is able "to be everywhere and has an aura of prestige, an affective, sensory influence which puts him in a totally different position to his predecessors."[22] Indeed, it appears that in the televisual 1970s and 1980s Pope John Paul II became the "charismatic" leader of the largest religious organization in the world. Few people realized, however, that the Vatican had its own public-relations department, which was enormously successful at orchestrating international television coverage of the pope's many trips.[23] This was to be the first pope with televisual charisma.

Sun-Belt Televangelism

While the pope travels the world on behalf of the Roman Catholic church, American televangelism is an increasingly Southern phenomenon. Popular televangelism requires a specialized talent for communicating (some would say the gift of the Holy Spirit), and in today's cultural climate the North is no match for the South. In the religious ratings war, where personal charisma is the most powerful weapon, the North is clearly an underdog.

Throughout American history the North's churches have reflected largely the sociocultural milieu of white, middle-class, professional, and managerial life. Northern churches and North-centered denominations were organized increasingly like businesses and corporations, while their pastors became more and more like professional managers. Sermon styles mirrored the academic lectures that seminarians heard from their mentors. Most important of all, preaching in the North was often merely a semi-scholarly exposition of a text, delivered unemotionally by a refined minister who seemed more interested in impressing his pastoral colleagues than in moving a congregation to spiritual decision or action. In short, Northern churches, especially the mainline Protestant ones, became a hybrid of business and academic organizations generally ruled by rationality and bureaucratic decision making. Every aspect of church life was affected by these developments, and many churches and some denominations are still struggling to overcome them before they lose all remaining members. In the TV age, such churches will simply not grow, and many will not survive. They are struggling not just against congregational apathy or disinterest, but against the very grain of the televisual culture.

Southern churches continue to be more directly influenced by the region's oral culture, which puts more emphasis on storytelling, vernacular, and especially on the power of the speaker to engage an audience. Even in mainline Protestant churches in the South there is considerably more off-the-cuff delivery of sermons than reading of prepared texts. The preacher has greater verbal and visual clout, and sermons are more like spontaneous events or immediate revelations of God's Word than carefully deliberated and researched treatises on theological subjects. This more spontaneous style of pastoral communication has been the bread-and-butter of Pentecostal churches for years, but only in the last decade have many theologians begun to take it seriously as a potentially valid and powerful mode of preaching. What the theologians are now calling "narrative preaching" is an intellectualized and scholasticized attempt to reclaim what some Christian groups never lost—a more dramatic and charismatic presentation of the gospel. After all, the Jews, too, were essentially an oral culture when Christ arrived amidst the flourishing of Greek culture. In effect, the Northern churches in America followed the Greeks while the South followed the Hebrew styles of communication—at least until television delivered the Southern style directly to the Northern living rooms.

Most of the popular televangelists of recent years have been from the South: Falwell, Robertson, Swaggart, James Robison, Charles Stanley, Roberts, Copeland. The others have generally adapted the Southern tradition. Bakker was from a small Pentecostal church in a working-class community in Michigan. Schuller established a simple, alliterative, conversational style of preaching that maintains its white, Northern refinement while freeing him to be rather personal and emotional. Charles Stanley of Atlanta, a Southern Baptist, probably has most effectively kept essential elements of both Northern and Southern rhetorical traditions so as to appeal to both. He is practical but propositional, emotional but level-headed, persuasive but inoffensive, animated but controlled, doctrinal but biblical, discursive but narrational. Stanley's meteoric rise in televangelism during the late 1980s was certainly due as much to his ability to put these styles together as it was to the actual content of his sermons. He was one of the few televangelists who appealed to viewers nearly across the spectrum of American society. Through all these characteristics he was able to convey a remarkable humility and sincerity. Those were key traits, especially in the late 1980s as televangelism coped with the public skepticism caused by the Swaggart and Bakker scandals.

The Southern, Pentecostal communication style is the most compatible with television. Swaggart, who represented that style better than anyone else on the tube, was clearly the most powerful weekly television preacher. Compared with the academic, managerial, or professional styles of Northern preachers, Swaggart's televisual style was leagues ahead of the Yankee competition. Given a choice, few viewers would watch the faces or actions of staid, sophisticated, scholarly preachers. Audiences much prefer to see a good storyteller use his face and voice to make the Scriptures seemingly come alive. It is no accident that Swaggart had the highest weekly audience ratings among religious broadcasters. Not only were his performances often electrifying, but for most people he conveyed genuine belief in his own messages. Even viewers who disagreed with those messages tended not to question his personal integrity and especially his ability to communicate those messages with power and conviction—at least until the scandals. In fact, Swaggart's televised confession in 1988 was one of the most emotionally moving religious broadcasts of all time. With an agonized look on his face, and tears streaming down his cheeks, Swaggart conveyed genuine repentance. His repentance seemed real, even to many skeptics of televangelism.[24]

From Charisma to Cult

In spite of what some critics think, there is nothing inherently evil about televised charisma and personality-oriented communication. Like the local church, where gifted preachers attract large congregations, televangelists with personal magnetism will generally build greater audiences than TV preachers who cannot communicate effectively. Communication is always dependent on the ethos of the speaker. That ethos, in turn, is established partly by a speaker's public personality. The most popular news commentators and talk-show hosts, like the highest-rated televangelists, convey their messages through a distinct personality. Theologically speaking, human beings communicate as God does—via their own attributes as individuals. Although some televangelists try to imitate other ones, each is distinct as a person both on and off the camera.

The unavoidable fact is that talented televangelists can attract viewers who become more committed to them than to God. A gifted communicator can easily establish pseudo-relationships with his audience, many of whom begin to believe that they know their favorite televangelist intimately. (The major TV preachers recognize this, but they rarely speak publicly about it.) Some of the most fanatic admirers become so emotionally involved that they fantasize about their religious leaders, who to them represent a direct line to heaven. A similar situation is reflected in the sporadic media reports of crazed devotees who harass movie stars to gain their affection. However, the percentage of abnormally attentive fans is probably larger in televangelism than in show business, because the spiritual dimension of TV ministries often tends to attract unhappy individuals who are alienated from their own friends and relatives. These troubled souls are not looking primarily for traditional religious messages; they sometimes desperately need to relate to someone who has found God and will help them find him, too. Probably for this reason, prayer is one of the most popular topics addressed by televangelists.

Most viewers are not nearly so personally attached to a preacher they meet only on a TV screen. Nevertheless, his charisma, if not his message, can have a spellbinding effect if they feel they have lost hope and have become estranged from others. The most popular televangelists are sometimes deluged by letters from lonely, stressed, hopeless, and fearful individuals. As we shall see in chapter 6, the siren call of impending disaster, as in some apocalyptic TV preaching, tends to attract such people. Especially when crisis is the message, a preacher's TV charisma— his eloquence, persuasiveness or personal aura—can set him strikingly apart from other voices of authority in society. The television medium seemingly transforms common, sinful preachers—people who are like everyone else—into super-ordinary figures.[25] Many viewers place their hope and find their comfort in the apparently authoritative voices and face-to-face images of individuals they have never met and who are sometimes thousands of miles away. Like Walter Cronkite, who for years was the most trusted man in America, a televangelist can become a personal source of wisdom and truth.

The most gifted TV preachers, those with the greatest visual charisma, inevitably end up with their own personality cults. Jim and Tammy Bakker had some of the most committed followers among all televangelists in the 1980s. Some viewers were so loyal to the Bakkers that even after Jim went to federal prison in 1989 they continued to send donations and to disbelieve the media reports about his financial and sexual misconduct. If viewers believe that their favorite televangelist is a personal friend, they will usually put more trust in what he says than in what their local pastor preaches or even what their denomination or church professes. It is these kinds of viewers who form a televangelist's personality cult—and their faith in his integrity and wisdom is usually unshakable, even by evidence to the contrary.

Within the typical television ministry there will also be workers that staunchly believe in their leader. Indeed, televangelists tend to attract employees who find a lot more meaning in working for someone they believe in than in working for the distant and seemingly uncaring management of a large secular business. Workers in these ministries are rarely in it for the money. Although salaries are generally low, televangelism's employees are inspired by the televangelist to work hard on behalf of the ministry and to turn their spiritual labor into a meaningful endeavor. Since their work is defined as a mission, there is little room for internal critics or naysayers. Workers must have faith, and that means faith in the televangelist as well as in God.

In local churches the one-on-one relationship existing between pastors and their congregants largely precludes personality cults. Typically, only in the megachurches or "ministry centers," where size creates significant anonymity, is the climate conducive to the development of such blind allegiance to a preacher and his causes. Not surprisingly, a television ministry may begin within a megachurch. Falwell, Swaggart, Schuller, and several other televangelists are also pastors of their own large churches, where they have greater authority than the rest of the staff. Aside from televangelism, religious personality cults are most prevalent in large impersonal churches where few members know the main pastor well and where deacons and elders obediently submit to the authority of their human leader.

Even when televangelism's personality cults do not lead to distortions of the gospel message, they can corrupt a preacher and lead viewers away from God. Good-intentioned televangelists, like well-meaning politicians, are sometimes corrupted by the people around them. If followers project greatness onto their leaders, soon the leaders believe what their supporters say about them. This is most obvious in the practice of physical healing. When followers hope for healing and express a firm belief in the healer's *personal* power to cure them, even skeptical preachers eventually come to believe in their own ability to conquer diseases and restore wholeness. Most Christians would see physical healing as God's way of raising up a great leader who can turn doubts to greater faith. However, in the case of televangelists, it is often difficult to distinguish between authentic faith and media-induced ego. As Joseph Bayly put it, a "successful" Christian who becomes a celebrity "may begin to believe the publicity that's written about him/her, may come to have a bloated opinion of his importance as a result of being interviewed, having his picture on magazine covers, being adulated by a fan club that hangs on his every word and accepts his every action."[26]

In the mid-1980s Swaggart's televised sermons suggested that he had become a victim of his own fame. In those years he preached vigorously against other expressions of the Christian faith, from Roman Catholicism to Calvinism and mainline Protestantism in general. It appeared for a time, as Swaggart increasingly used his broadcasts to respond to critics, that the battle he preached about was no longer between Christ and Satan, but between Swaggart and the rest of Christianity. Later, when Swaggart was disciplined by the Assemblies of God denomination for his sexual misconduct, the televangelist asserted his independence. Swaggart apparently believed that his ministry was more important than the ministry of his own denomination—that he was above ecclesiastical law and had more authority than the denomination. Typically, spiritual arrogance is the ultimate outcome of the psychological pressures imposed on the leader of a personality cult. When the self is placed above even the church, Christ's representative body on earth, bitter feuds and schisms within congregations and across denominations frequently develop. If any Christian organization emphasizes human personality over the personality of Christ, ambition and ego lead to hatred within the church and even destruction of the individuals involved.

Religious Monarchies

Personality cults are so significant in the dynamics of televangelism that the future of a particular ministry depends heavily on the ethos of one person—the celebrity preacher himself. The result is a potential crisis of authority when this central personality retires, dies, or suffers bad publicity. Unlike most local churches and nearly all denominations, television ministries hang on the ability of one individual to attract audiences and elicit contributions. Although many people create the programs, the on-air personality is unquestionably the most important figure, the driving force that energizes the public ministry.

Like the saints in some Christian traditions, televangelists are treated as special individuals whom God has used in extraordinary ways. They become the kings of the religious world, dispensing their edicts and marshaling the troops for holy wars against secular powers or competing religious groups. Their infectious charisma rallies the followers for skirmishes of all kinds, from fights over bad publicity to struggles for more finances. Swaggart and Bakker, for example, openly fought verbal battles against publications that wrote critical articles about them. Among other things, each of these two televangelists sent letters to supporters, alerting them to the alleged false charges against him and calling supporters to complain to the offending media and send contributions to the ministry. In such situations the kings of televangelism use direct-mail messengers to dispense their decrees to their followers.

Televangelists and their households usually try to rule over distant flocks like religious royalty. In fact, the succession of leadership, a significant problem for most all of the major televangelists, often becomes a family affair. Schuller, Roberts, Falwell, and Robertson all have sons who stand in the wings, possibly waiting to assume the throne through the family name. However, in the United States, monarchical transitions are highly suspect, since the nation was formed partly in reaction against monarchies, which provided no guarantee of popular support for a titular leader. Although monarchies offer orderly and obvious transitions of power and authority, they challenge the sovereignty of the people to decide their own political fate. Not surprisingly, many Americans are especially skeptical of religious kingdoms upheld by television.

In addition, few sons of televangelists have the people-pleasing qualities of their kingly fathers.[27] It appears that these strong fathers, committed over the years far more to building the ministry than to raising a family, almost invariably produce children with less charisma than their own. Rather than struggling to find their own place in life, too many of these sons have been awkwardly thrust into the ministry. Some of them are uncomfortable with their second-class status next to their highly successful and well-respected fathers, and they may suffer insecurities about being able to live up to the standards established for them. When Robertson vacated the television ministry to run for president, he left son Tim in charge. A gifted administrator, Tim managed the CBN organization well, but he was simply not a charismatic "700 Club" host like his father. Donations to the ministry dropped (perhaps partly because some supporters contributed instead to Pat's political campaign), and Pat eventually had to return to the network after his unsuccessful presidential bid in order to bail it out financially. Not long after his return, contributions were up and the future once again looked bright, both for the network and for Robertson's Regent University, which was heavily dependent on network subsidies.

As best as I can tell, there is not a single case of a successful transition of leadership from father to son in a major television ministry.[28] Organizational and managerial momentum might keep such ministries going after the founding leader dies, but more likely personality-oriented programs will slowly wither and eventually fade away. Reruns are sufficient only for a time, except on radio, where very small constituencies can support broadcasts for years. J. Vernon McGee and Lester Roloff are examples of radio preachers whose ministries survived as taped shows after their deaths. Television viewers, however, want to know that the charisma exists in a living personality, as a real human presence, not merely as a pre-recorded icon of a deceased saint.[29]

In American culture, parvenus and plutocrats replaced European notions of family monarchies. Wealth and fame established new leadership in politics, business, and other areas of life. Instead of a direct transfer of authority through lineage, there has always been the waxing and waning of new leadership carved out of both inherent charisma and popular will. Televangelists will learn this lesson, too, as the second generation of television ministries emerges in the 1990s. Roberts will be the first to face this problem, followed by Schuller, Falwell, and others. Robertson, Roberts, and Falwell started their universities partly as institutions that would perpetuate their ministries after their deaths, and presumably after their broadcast ministries ended.[30]

Not all is lost for declining televangelist monarchies, however. Some radio and television ministries established by particular personalities have later found that they can survive by de-emphasizing personal charisma and establishing a much broader concept of ministry. The best example is Radio Bible Class, which entered television three years after the death in 1965 of the radio ministry's highly visible and well-liked founder, Martin DeHaan.[31] Called "Day of Discovery," the television production focused more on message than personality. It also emphasized a very clear, direct, and simple presentation of those messages rather than an ostentatious or highly dramatic program. Most important of all, it tied the television program to a major publishing ministry, which solidified the organization's spiritual role in the lives of its supporters. In other words, "Day of Discovery" was not entirely dependent on either one-man leadership or the television program itself. By diversifying the ministry and broadening its use of personality, the program and the entire organization thrived, even in the midst of scandals involving other well-known TV ministries.

The inability of televangelists to create their own successful religious monarchies suggests how tenuous is their long-term authority in spite of apparent short-term popularity. Unlike the saints of some Christian traditions, whose personal charisma extended over centuries in the hearts and minds of hopeful believers, television-created saints suffer the same vicissitudes of popular acclaim as film actors and news anchors. Publicity departments help televangelists establish contemporary hagiographies, which are little more than ghost-written autobiographies, but even those appeal only to the currently faithful. Used-book stores and other resale shops are the dumping ground for such once-popular stories of the rise of successful televangelists.

Ironically, the original cult of saints was developed in the Middle Ages and became a major part of Counter-Reformation piety. The Council of Trent responded to Protestant challenges "by justifying the devotion to saints."[32] Hundreds of years later, Protestant clergy on television have sometimes attempted to establish their own sainthood, despite Catholic criticisms.[33] Biblically speaking, sainthood was never envisioned as a power play between competing brands of Christianity or among clergy. In American culture, however, that is what it partly became, and no degree of attempted monarchical intervention is going to change things.

Holy Charisma

In historical perspective, televangelism's divisive cults seem only to be the latest version of personality-based holy wars. After all, Christianity has been riddled with personality cults, from the early church at Corinth to contemporary Protestantism. Even Roman Catholicism, which stresses tradition and church law as well as doctrine and sacrament, has had such problems—and not just from critics who fled to the Protestant ranks, like a Martin Luther or a John Calvin. If human personality is not evil, and if the gifts of the Holy Spirit are given to individuals, it would be naive to even attempt to extirpate all charisma from the church. As long as there are people on earth, there will be personality cults in both show business and the church.

The legitimate role of charisma in religion is primarily a matter of personal and collective motivation, since individuals use it for different ends and with selfless as well as selfish intentions. Personality cults largely reflect the abuse of charisma in human relationships. They occur when, because of both communicator ego and audience desire, faith gives way to ambition and hope turns into desperation. Soon the genuine desire to help one's fellow humans and to accomplish something worthwhile is transformed into a drive to manipulate others as a show of power. Writes Charles Colson, "We seem to think we need a big parachurch organization or a well-known celebrity in order to accomplish anything for the kingdom of God. As a result, the church has elevated popular pastors, ministry leaders, and televangelists to the dubious pedestal of fame—only to watch many topple in the winds of power, influence, and adulation."[34] Televangelism's personality cults massage the individual ego in the deceptive name of ministry. Along the way they can lead to highly autocratic styles of leadership that place nearly all authority in the hands of one person. For these reasons it makes sense that most televangelism scandals have involved pastors from Pentecostal churches, which focus on charismatic leaders significantly more than other traditions. In the future, however, scandals will involve a far broader group—televangelists whose personal charisma is more the product of television than of spiritual gifts or particular religious traditions.

Moreover, personality cults baptize invisible selfishness with the appearance of public magnanimity. The vast majority of televangelists probably believe in their hearts that they are humbly and altruistically ministering to their broadcast congregations. Whether or not they are doing so is not for them alone to determine, for personal motivation can be clouded and deeply hidden. As I will suggest in the final chapter, the church desperately needs to keep its own personality cults under control. As a public figure who represents not just himself or his ministry but the universal church of Christ, every televangelist must have his motivations evaluated by more than his own followers, who are often too emotionally attached to a favorite preacher to offer any honest or objective criticism.

The task for the church, then, is to distinguish between holy and unholy charisma. While that sounds odd, considering the fact that charismatic gifts (as religiously defined) are supposed to be "holy," it is more obvious in today's television culture than in any previous generation that not all charisma is good for leaders and their followers. Just as television can create new show-business stars overnight, it can establish "religious authorities" in only a few years or even months. Suddenly a televangelist is perceived as a spokesperson for the church or a large segment of the church, representing, for example, *all* evangelicals or fundamentalists or conservative pastors. Then he is quoted by the news media and appears on the talk shows. He may establish a political organization to further influence public life and to enhance his prestige with the media and supporting church members. In the 1980s all of this happened. As long as the airwaves are open to televangelism, these things will likely occur again.

Like show business, televangelism leads to a diminished authenticity in the ways that personalities are presented to the public. People want to believe in particular kinds of successful and seemingly influential people, but these desires do not justify creating a wide gap between a preacher's on-camera and off-camera personality. Most local congregants know what their pastor is really like from talking with him outside of church. They see the kind of car he drives, where he lives, how his children act, and all the other things that define a person's character, values, and lifestyle. For most viewers, on the other hand, televangelists only *appear* to be friends. Any sense of personal relationship is merely illusory. Simply put, there can easily develop a lack of integrity in a TV preacher who lives dual lives, public and private. The success of the ministry may require that he play a certain character on the tube, especially a character who is successful, inspired, knowledgeable, charismatic. Swaggart played such a role until the reality of his own personal life caught up with him and his viewers in the national media. In fact, Swaggart's fall seemed to indicate that he had been preaching against his own sins for a number of years.

Note the big difference between the source and nature of Mother Teresa's charisma and that of the typical televangelist. The latter must *seek* charisma if he is to establish the support of a personality cult. Mother Teresa's charisma is inherent; it is the result of her personal integrity. Her authenticity would cut through any attempt to fashion a media image for her. She *is* what she is. And what-she-is is precisely what attracts people: someone who genuinely bases her life on self-denial, service, and love. These attributes describe what she is, not what she purports to be for the television camera. Her integrity and other personal qualities, not what she accomplishes in worldly terms, make her broadly appealing, a true ambassador of Christ to the world. There is no question about whether Mother Teresa of Calcutta has *holy* charisma.

Television may not create the dangers of personality cults, but it does make them more likely, more extensive, more powerful, and highly visible. Christian charisma and Hollywood charisma can be so intertwined on the tube that it is difficult to figure out which is which. In any public arena there is both genuine and counterfeit charisma. The former truly submits human personality to God. The latter feigns sacrifice and service while promoting the self.

Conclusion

Television in the United States is the mass medium most naturally prone to personality cults. In American culture, where the tube is largely show business, and where people are more interested in the future than the past, television creates a favorable climate for religious personality cults. As Neil Postman put it, God does not play well on television.[35] Spirited televangelists do, and they offer the kind of authority that parish pastors seem to lack. They help direct a nation and its churches, both of which know little about what their forebears actually believed and practiced. Televangelism tends to reinvent Christianity in the name of each new broadcast preacher.

The emergence of televangelism's personality cults should cause seminaries, churches and denominations to take seriously the need for religious leaders who are effective communicators. Although personality cults can easily corrupt leaders and their followers, the charisma that enables them to form is not inherently evil. To the contrary, human charisma is a natural reflection of the communicative talents of a magnetic personality and people's real need for authoritative figures they can trust. Gifted leaders, whether in civil-rights movements or religious revivals, can help people transcend the limitations of individual hopelessness and powerlessness. When those leaders have integrity, they authentically express the legitimate desires of needy people, not their own selfish yearnings. Personality cults are unfortunate perversions of the inherently human quest for authority.

Finally, I hope that even amidst the evils of television's personality cults the church will see opportunities for real ministry, not just simplistic solutions to age-old problems. Cultism will continue to plague the church, as it does all areas of American life. Wherever it exists, however, are people who are searching for an authority outside of themselves. Personality cults are always evidence of the human need to have someone to follow. In Christianity that someone is none other than the Creator.

The Lure of Drama

A few years ago the publisher of a new book of mine suggested that I appear on a major daily talk show to promote the book. Since the book addressed a topic from a Christian perspective, the publisher further asked if I would be willing to appear specifically on a well-known program hosted by a leading charismatic celebrity. I gave tentative approval and waited for additional information.

Shortly thereafter I received in the mail an official questionnaire from the program's producer. Among the usual professional and personal items, the questionnaire asked for a dramatic description of my conversion—when it happened, how it happened, and how my life had changed since then. My curiosity was piqued, so I asked some friends about the show. They indicated that the program included daily guests who indeed described their dramatic conversions to Jesus Christ. In fact, the show was a loosely organized conversation about all the great things God was doing in the guests' lives, emphatically punctuated by Christian testimonies.

I was reluctant to appear on the program, but at my publisher's urging I filled out the questionnaire and returned it to the producer. Within two weeks I received a form letter indicating that I would not be a guest "at this time." The reason was not clear, but the program's format displayed the likely reason: Unlike the usual guests, including other authors, I simply lacked a spectacular conversion story. I was not mired in drugs or sex before being saved. I had not been miraculously healed. As a teacher, I certainly had not been led down Wealthy Street. Moreover, I was not a well-known celebrity either before or after "accepting Christ," as the questionnaire put it. Simply put, I had nothing dramatic to add to the program's audience appeal. All I had was a book with some provocative ideas about how to live the Christian life.

That experience taught me that popular American evangelicalism follows a dramatic trail on television. Whatever it may be like in the local church pews or in the hearts of individual believer, on-the-tube evangelicalism tends to be what advertisers call "puffed up." Television amplifies the inherent drama of the faith, making Christianity a more sensational and extraordinary phenomenon than most believers ever experience for themselves. Daily and weekly televangelism takes popular evangelicalism the way it is and then makes it even more that way—a dramatic reflection of the work of Christ in the lives of individual believers. Along the way, the tube distorts the Christian faith by hyperbole and excess. The medium creates a new version of Christianity based less on tradition, Scripture, or common experience and more on dramatic entertainment with popular appeal.

The Revivalist Legacy

Perhaps more than any other culture, America popularized and dramatized the Christian faith. Partly because the country's missionary impulse was so strong, and partly because its people were so pragmatic and industrious, American Protestantism has been highly dynamic from colonial times to the present. There were always pastors and denominational officials who criticized such a dynamic and adaptable faith. At the same time, however, there have always been free-thinking and highly entrepreneurial individuals who refused to let church tradition or organizations get in the way of accomplishing the Great Commission—taking Christ to people of all social strata and religious backgrounds.

Certainly the legacy of American revivalism is a testimony to this fact. From the first and second Great Awakenings to the revivalist energy of people such as Charles Finney, Dwight L. Moody, and Billy Sunday, American Protestantism has always had a dynamic edge that vigorously adapted the gospel message to the common folk of the day. While mainline Protestantism tended toward organizational development and the professionalization of the clergy, evangelical and later fundamentalist and especially charismatic Protestantism gravitated outward toward the popular spirit of the people. Mainline Protestantism and Roman Catholicism typically worried about the state of "the church," while evangelicalism increasingly concerned itself with the spiritual state of the individual's soul. This popular, evangelistic thrust fed the development of revivalism and eventually fueled the rapid growth of televangelism.

Contemporary Americans sometimes forget that revivalism was always a combination of entertainment and religion. Local revivals were spiritual meetings, designed to revive the faith of lost, backsliding, or sleepy souls. But they were also highly dramatic, emotional, and even exciting gatherings that delivered individuals and communities from the boredom and monotony of their everyday lives. Revivals were often like rock concerts or Fourth of July celebrations, lifting people out of the common routines of daily existence and infusing their experience with special meaning and excitement. In short, revivals were dramatic public events that repeatedly expressed the central truths of the Christian faith for popular audiences. People came not just to be taught theology or to learn about the faith's history, but to experience the reality of the faith in their own lives. As we shall see, this vicarious aspect of revivalism, which sometimes led to excess, also became the basis for televangelism's dramatic appeal. Just as there was often a major difference between the predictability of local church worship and the emotional spontaneity of the sporadic revivals, so is there today a significant difference between TV "worship" and a traditional church service.

Someone has said that three persons contributed imperceptively but decisively to the ways that the Western World thinks—Marx, Freud, and Barnum. Expecially in the United States, the impact of the latter has been greatly underplayed by historians and intellectuals, who typically focus more on people who generated ideas than on successful individuals who were pragmatic and entrepreneurial. Modern revivalism, for example, owes much to P. T. Barnum, the great circus promoter and businessman. And Barnum owes much to revivalism. He created the concept of "the greatest show on earth," a colorful orgy of visual delight that combined the bizarre and the sublime, the beautiful and the gaudy, the outrageously humorous and the enormously terrifying, as well as the truly talent-filled show and the deceptively hyped spectacle. Instead of a stage or an arch, Barnum's dramatic platform was a circus ring covered by a movable tent. And he announced the arrival of the circus with blasts from the whistle of the locomotive that brought the circus to town. It was all, as TV impresario Ed Sullivan might have said, a "really big show."[1]

Revivalism, too, was often such a big show. Urban revivalists such as Billy Sunday were legendary performers who attracted audiences partly because of their religious messages but also greatly because of their dramatic abilities. Sunday jumped energetically around a stage or pulpit, bellowing forth his "sermon" while shedding his jacket and rolling up his sleeves. Instead of being a stodgy or refined cleric, he was a dynamic, aggressive, emotional preacher who entertained audiences. Sunday's sermons, if they can be called that, were one-man performances of the contemporary realities of popular evangelicalism. He did not simply teach about the faith, as if he were a detached theological scholar or unemotional Bible teacher; he dramatically enacted the experience of that faith. Like a circus audience, roaring approvingly at the antics of clowns or cheering the bold moves of an animal trainer, Sunday's audiences were caught in the drama depicted so powerfully by this talented performer. Sunday's stories about the battle between God and Satan were as terrifying and real as any Barnum circus routine.

In *A Simplicity of Faith*, theologian William Stringfellow compared the American circus to American society. He argued provocatively that in the United States the circus is a kind of popular liturgy that reflects symbolically the "scope and diversity of Creation." In his view, the circus is one of the most explicitly American and deeply theological expressions of the Christian faith. He called the circus performance "most obviously a parable of the eschaton. It is there that human beings confront the beasts of the earth and reclaim their lost dominion over other creatures." He added that some performers, such as the death-defying acrobats, are represented in the circus liturgy as "freed from the consignment of death." Stringfellow thought that the circus performer was "the image of the eschatological person—emancipated from frailty and inhibition, exhilarant, militant, transcendent over death—neither confined nor conformed by the fear of death any more." Meanwhile, the circus clown comments on the "absurdities inherent in what ordinary people take so seriously—themselves, their profits and losses, their successes and failures, their adjustments and compromises—their conformity to the world."[2]

American revivalism and the circus share the same legacy of popular dramatic entertainment. Both are public events designed to appeal to common folk by displaying sensational and extraordinary events. Both have celebrity performers whose dramatic abilities transcend the abilities of average people. Both invite the audience to experience the drama, not principally to think about it or academically learn from it. Both are dynamic events that convey a sense of spontaneity and live performance. Both are itinerant occurrences that have no particular home or historical location but attempt to meet the people where they are at the moment. Finally, as Stringfellow suggested, the circus, like the revival drama, addresses at least symbolically the most fundamental hopes and fears of humankind.

It should be no surprise, then, that circus-styled revivalism significantly shaped the spirit and structure of American Protestantism. In its wildest forms, Protestant worship became circuslike, with staged healings, clownish preachers, and cheering congregations. However, even mainline evangelicalism has been influenced by the revivalist legacy, emphasizing the drama of conversion, testimonies of the saved, emotional expressions of faith, powerful exhortations of popular preachers, and moving music. Although evangelical worship is typically far more than entertainment, it has not remained untouched by the styles and forms of showmanship. Quite to the contrary, popular evangelicalism adapted evangelism and worship to the ways of popular drama. Aimee Semple McPherson realized this in the 1920s when she started radio station KFSG in Los Angeles. Instead of filling the airways with Bible teaching or worship services, she hired a successful vaudevillian writer to produce religious versions of contemporary popular entertainment. McPherson's programs included a competitive talent show, numerous religiously inspired radio serials, band performances, and the like.[3] The stage was set for later televangelism, which similarly adapted its programming from the legacy of revivalist entertainment. Along the way, televangelism, like popular drama, became a combination of inspiration, education, catharsis, and imitation—as well as entertainment.

Action and Emotion

Like old-style urban revivalism, televangelism in the United States adopted the techniques of popular entertainment. One type of televangelism, represented by the programming of people like Jimmy Swaggart and the early Oral Roberts, was a direct descendent of revivalism. Another type, based more directly on the television-talk-show format, combined the revivalist ethos with the folksy discussion of Johnny Carson's "Tonight Show" or, before that, radio programs such as Arthur Godfrey's daily network offering. Pat Robertson, Jim Bakker, and Paul Crouch used the latter approach, adapting it somewhat from the early variety-show format as well.[4] As Robertson explained the genesis of his "700 Club" program, "We simply took a format that had worked on commercial networks and applied it to CBN. It was a proven format that had reached millions of Americans."[5] No segment of televangelism was free from the influences of revivalism and popular entertainment, although some shows were more directly shaped by successful commercial television programming.

Television became the new stage for religiously inspired entertainment. Rather than using the circus tent or the campground's open chapel, televangelists used the home TV set. Consequently, televangelism was increasingly shaped in the image of the medium's programming, which emphasized action and emotion. On-the-tube action meant more than someone acting; it required an increasingly rapid visual pace. Emotion meant audience involvement in the story, conversation, sermon, and the like. Whenever a television offering failed to achieve both a visually stimulating pace and a vicarious audience involvement, the ratings would dip and the show would eventually disappear. Televangelism eventually came under the same constraints; its producers, directors, writers, and celebrity talent looked for ways of building action and emotion into their programming.

The medium's insatiable appetite for action and emotion has profoundly affected how it communicates religious faith. In the 1940s a group of Protestants protested to a Jewish film producer that all chaplains in war movies were Catholic. The producer's response was a telling indictment of the medium of television, not just motion pictures. Catholic priests, he indicated, were better suited to the visual media because they *did* something while ministering to a dying soldier—anointing the forehead or making the sign of the cross. The Protestant pastor, on the other hand, merely *said* something; there was little place for action, and hence less opportunity to build emotion.[6] In other words, television is not a religiously neutral medium. It soaks up and wrings out religious expressions that have certain dramatic possibilities. Meanwhile, less tangible religious expressions are simply difficult to convey through the tube.

Former network TV newsman Frank Reynolds cogently captured the medium's dramatic bias through his years of experience covering "real" stories as both a print and broadcast journalist. Television, he argued, is inherently subject to a "constant temptation to dramatize events: to turn history into a theatre, complex events into personal confirmations." He added, "Worse still is the temptation to 'stage' a situation . . . and then present it as though the cameras were naturally recording events."[7] Reynolds recognized the way TV shapes and reshapes messages, giving them new meanings and altering viewers' perceptions of reality. Religion, too, is turned into theater on television, while religious programs cleverly feed viewers messages that are designed to confirm existing beliefs. Moreover, televangelism frequently creates seemingly spontaneous, "Spirit-led" programs that are actually well planned and carefully edited to achieve the maximum effect on the audience.

Swaggart's Sorrow

Undoubtedly the master of action and emotion on televangelism has been Louisiana's Jimmy Swaggart. He is an amazingly gifted communicator whose camera crews, producers, and editors know how to craft powerful televisual messages out of seemingly old-style revivalist meetings. Swaggart conveys both interesting action and captivating emotion through his use of body language (arms, legs, upper torso, hand) and especially his highly expressive face. The preacher moves constantly and changes his facial cast repeatedly to fit the mood of the point he is making. The camera crew heightens the dramatic effect by the repeated use of tight close-ups of both Swaggart and his "live" audience members.[8] In addition, the cameras and editors establish a high degree of televisual action by frequently changing the images. Even though there is only one man on a stage, walking back and forth before the in-house audience, the cameras convey a far greater sense of action by switching every few seconds from one shot to another. In the actual stadium or auditorium there is little visually stimulating activity, since Swaggart is a small figure moving gradually across the stage. On television, however, Swaggart comes across as a highly animated, deeply emotional, enormously sincere individual. Certainly Swaggart's richly resonant voice helps establish his audience credibility, but the camera is the key to his success, since it literally creates the action and intensifies the emotion present in Swaggart's voice.

Swaggart's confession sermon in 1988 was one of the most masterful TV programs of all time, perhaps even the single most effective televisual performance of any American evangelist. Even non-Christians who had been highly critical of Swaggart specifically and televangelism generally were typically moved by the production. Accused of having sex with a prostitute, and subsequently exposed for his actions by the prostitute, Swaggart was in deep trouble with both his denomination and the media. After airing previously recorded programs for several months, Swaggart returned to the air in a production taped at his own church in Baton Rouge. Organized around the theme of forgiveness, the entire one-hour program was designed to communicate the fact that just as God forgives sinners, viewers should forgive Swaggart. In a quivering voice, Swaggart admitted his "sinfulness" without revealing any particular transgressions. By providing ample shots of his tear-drenched face, the cameras created an intense sense of both the preacher's genuine sorrow and his need for forgiveness from God and the viewers. The eye of the cameras jumped repeatedly to heartbroken congregants, who clearly suffered *with* Swaggart and held nothing against him. At the end of the show the projected images captured Swaggart hugging and crying with individual supporters.

There is little doubt that Swaggart's forgiveness program was well orchestrated by himself, the rest of the church's pastoral staff, and the television production crew. Key camera shots of Swaggart's "admission" of unspecified guilt were used extensively as TV "sound bites" on news shows across the country. Since the cameras made the worship service a public event, they carefully controlled what viewers were able to see. For example, it was impossible to see how many seats in the church were empty, apparently because of parishioners who had become disillusioned with the ministry. Also, there were no shots of disgruntled or angry congregants, some of whom tried to register their complaints vocally during the service. In addition, the cameras captured nothing of what Swaggart's own family really felt about Jimmy's sinfulness. The family became mere extras in the unfolding drama, sitting teary-eyed on the platform with the ministry's star. Not one word or image of dissension was permitted on the screen for the entire hour. The message was clear: "God and the church have forgiven Brother Jimmy. You should too."

One wonders what kind of prior discussion and planning went into the forgiveness program. What could cameras have captured in such planning sessions? What would viewers have seen if the program were taped and edited by critics of the Swaggart ministry? One thing is certain: The show was an enormously powerful drama that was planned, not spontaneous. It relied upon action and emotion to deliver a forgiven sinner to a forgiving audience. In short, it used the medium of television to distribute a carefully crafted dramatic performance to millions of individual viewers.

Swaggart is only one of the major televangelists to have mastered the techniques used extensively by religious revivalists. As will be discussed further in the next chapter, Pat Robertson organized his "700 Club" around dramatizations of God's miracle power. Although parts of each show were spontaneous, such as prayers and some of the conversation, the overall thrust and look of the program was carefully researched and produced. In fact, the various personal testimonies of guests are recorded precisely in the way cautioned against by Frank Reynolds; they are staged reenactments of conversions and especially healings, depicted as though the cameras were naturally recording events. The reason, of course, is that such staging eliminates ambiguity, uncertainty, or complexity. It turns what happened in someone's life into an opportunity for religious propaganda under the control of the program producer and the segment writer and editor. To put it differently, staged reenactments are meant to communicate one person's interpretation of an event, not the event itself. Like docudramas in general, televised depictions of healings do not duplicate the actual events. Since the producer and others have control over a reenactment, they can shape it for the purposes of maximizing action and emotion. In the end such reformulations will attract more viewers and presumably also elicit greater contributions to the ministry.

Televangelism, then, amplifies and extends the extent to which popular religion is dependent upon action and emotion for its survival. Whatever televangelism touches with its cameras and editors tends to become like mass revivalism of an earlier age and commercial television of today. On the Sunday appointed for a special offering for constructing his $18-million Crystal Cathedral in suburban Los Angeles, Robert Schuller showed dramatic sensibilities that would ultimately project his "Hour of Power" program to the top of the weekly syndicated television ratings—men wearing hard hats and pushing wheelbarrows took up the collection.[9] Later, when the cathedral was completed, Schuller originated his program there, blending revivalism, the variety show, and mainline Calvinist liturgy. It was a strange combination indeed.

The problem with televised religion is not simply that it thirsts for action and emotion. All religious expression, including worship, necessarily involves human action. And, clearly, religious faith involves emotion as well as reason. Nevertheless, the medium can easily mandate how much and what kinds of action and emotion are necessary to build a ministry that is "successful" by the standards of popularity and size. "Performing" does not necessarily mean acting or pretending, but in televangelism the line between staged fiction and dramatized reality is increasingly thin, just as it is between TV's drama and docudrama and between imaginative narrative and journalism. In the name of a bigger or more influential ministry, too many televangelists are simply imitating the styles and techniques of popular entertainment. As a result, more and more televangelism mirrors the circus-like atmosphere of network television, from its talk shows to its tabloid spectacles.

Non-Stop Sweeps

In the world of commercial television, the audience ratings race pushes program producers to sensationalize their shows. Experience tells them that sensationalism attracts viewers, no matter how critical some viewers are of such programming. Consider the case of local television news during the spring "ratings sweep" of 1990—a quarterly period when audiences are measured so stations can establish their advertising rates. New York's Channel 4 aired a special series of reports on "Sex Tapes" that featured shadowy shots of nude bodies, as well as experts debating the value of various aphrodisiacs. Los Angeles-based KCBS broadcast a four-part feature on "The Search for Sleaze," which supposedly probed the city's night life by showing mud wrestlers and X-rated birthday cakes. Obviously there is little real news value in such reports. Their purpose is to attract fickle viewers in an increasingly competitive broadcasting and cable environment. As *Newsweek* magazine puts it, "TV producers and correspondents have chucked journalism out the window in a frenzied pursuit of higher ratings and bigger bucks."[10]

Today's televangelism is beginning to chuck authentic religion in the crazy search for bigger ministries and more popular programming. The problem is not primarily the lingering negative public image of televangelism in the face of the scandals of the late 1980s, but rather the sheer competitiveness for supporters among a growing number of well-packaged programs. In the 1980s, with the growth of satellite and cable TV as well as syndicated fare, the number and accessibility of religious TV programs exploded in the United States. Televangelism became significant in the nation's public life when various TV preachers became active in politics and the secular news media started covering their activities. The fact was, however, that the market for religious television remained fairly small, since most televangelists were limited to Sunday-morning or late-night time periods for their shows. Moreover, even though there were more cable channels, the competition among those channels was very intense. As with secular fare, religious programs were chasing a relatively fragmented audience of potential viewers.

Given such competition, televangelists really had only one option if they sought to build influential and well-known ministries: They could change the content of their programs in hopes of luring viewers from other religious and perhaps a few secular offerings. Every program costs tens or even hundreds of thousands of dollars to produce and distribute to stations. Televangelists were essentially airing their broadcasts on a pay-as-you-go basis, making every one of their programs a victim of their own kind of ratings sweep. If programs would not generate adequate financial support, they would have to be taken off the air. Unlike commercial stations, which dealt with audience sweeps only every quarter, televangelism literally faced a potential financial crunch every week. Programs had to be designed to maximize viewership and thus, weekly contributions. Each show had to accentuate action and emotion, even if it meant sensationalizing the religious message. Dramatic impact became the yardstick for success for most televangelists.

When Baptist pastor Jerry Falwell took over the reins of the faltering PTL ministry after the departure of Jim and Tammy Bakker, he was plunged into one of the most difficult fund-raising jobs in televangelism. For one thing, the public image of the ministry became very low as reports about the Bakkers' financial and sexual misconduct permeated the news media. For another, Falwell's Baptist theology was not fully acceptable to many of PTL's charismatic supporters, who believed in faith healing and speaking in tongues. Finally, the Bakkers had driven PTL into such debt that bankruptcy seemed inevitable, regardless of how much on-air fund-raising was undertaken by Falwell. In response to this situation, which resembled in extreme the financial plight of most televangelists, Falwell had little choice but to appeal dramatically to viewers for donations. Almost overnight Falwell's media image changed as he tried desperately to raise cash to keep PTL alive. He pleaded, cajoled, and begged for contributions, often sounding more like the Bakkers than Falwell. Finally, in a widely telecast segment that ended up on the news networks because of its dramatic appeal, Falwell followed through on an agreement that he would go down PTL's giant water slide if enough contributions were received. It was all rather Barnumesque—a business-suited Baptist minister flying down the slide with his arms crossed like an Egyptian mummy.

Televangelism is now driven by an amazingly creative impulse to maximize the popularity and financial benefits of every program. Unlike secular TV producers, who can fall back on summer reruns while new programs are produced, televangelists must produce new shows every week and, in some cases, every weekday. This programming need results in an incredible market for new dramatic material. Few programs can rely on simple preaching or church services, as does the weekly show of Charles Stanley. Indeed, in some communities local church services are aired for free as part of their stations' commitment to regional public-service programming. Across the spectrum of most televangelism, from Roberts to Schuller and Swaggart, new TV material is essential for holding viewers and encouraging them to contribute. When Swaggart's show was preempted during the weeks immediately after his scandal broke in the national news, he aired previously recorded programs. Moreover, Falwell and a few others would occasionally rebroadcast programs that were extremely effective at generating viewer response during their first airing. Overall, however, televangelism necessitates new dramatic material that is at least as interesting and preferably more engaging than secular reruns or local public-service programs, which typically compete for Sunday-morning audiences.

In addition, as in the case of secular "sweep" periods, the dramatic qualities of a program generally have to be increased over time to hold viewers from switching to competitive shows. When NBC's "Hill Street Blues" launched in the 1980s a new kind of evening soap, called an "ensemble drama," it attracted a small but loyal audience. Over the course of the show's network run, it was increasingly sensationalized to the point where nearly every episode included some kind of bizarre, macabre, or unexpected event. By the time "Hill Street Blues" was cancelled in 1987, it was a far more outlandish peek at the private lives of a fictional police precinct than when it was inaugurated. Meanwhile, the program had attracted far more viewers and advertising revenues for NBC. In 1990, as Falwell searched on his own "Old-Time Gospel Hour" weekly broadcast for a successful technique to lift the ministry out of a slump, he hit upon a rather unconventional but highly effective device: powerful lay preachers who had emotional stories to tell. He turned the pulpit over to some professionally untrained ministers whose personal tales of salvation were compelling vignettes of Christ's redeeming work. Along the way, Falwell sold videotaped copies of the broadcasts to viewers.

In the land of non-stop sweeps, televangelists confront the same dilemma that faced circus magnate Barnum. Forced to come up regularly with new acts and seemingly more extraordinary shows, Barnum had to be designing new dramatic material all the time. Even confirmed circus-goers tired of the same old acts, although they expected to see the standard kinds of performances, from acrobats to elephant parades and chimp antics. Similarly, market-driven televangelism normally depends on novel material delivered in dramatic fashion with escalating action and emotion. In both cases, unusual or spectacular and sensational fare sells better than routine programming. In this sense, too, Swaggart's forgiveness sermon was truly compelling televangelism that attracted many curious nonbelievers along with the typical audience. Scandals are good for ratings.

A Ministry's Own Drama

Over the years it has become increasingly clear to televangelists and their marketing advisors that nothing promotes a TV ministry more effectively than the dramatic story of that ministry. To put it differently, TV ministries typically must create a "real" drama in which the televangelist, audience members and supporters are major characters. People do not give to a ministry unselectively. They contribute to those with the most interesting and engaging stories to tell about their own ups and downs in the world. Sociologist William Martin cogently captured this fact: "Both to satisfy their own aspirations and to bring in enough money to keep their operations alive, media ministers must create and sustain an impression of growth and momentum that will attract viewers, win their loyalty and enthusiasm, and motivate them to provide a dependable financial base for the ministry."[11]

Like other nonprofit organizations, and more so today, televangelism is locked into the necessity of maintaining a good image with its constituency. Since the constituency is largely evangelical, a TV preacher must establish a rather triumphalistic and religiously dramatic tale about the alleged accomplishments of the ministry. People want to support a winner, not a loser, and in evangelical terms that typically means a rhetoric of soulwinning. In one way or another, often with much tacit deception, televangelists and their marketing advisors create the appearance of a program that is converting many nonbelievers and turning the nation, and sometimes even the world, to Christ. In other words, the ministry's own story is linked creatively to the unfolding biblical drama of Creation-Fall-redemption and, in the United States especially, the Second Coming of Jesus Christ.

Before the scandal, Jimmy Swaggart was a master of triumphalistic storytelling. According to him, as depicted on television, Jimmy Swaggart Ministries was nearly single-handedly communicating the gospel to the entire free world and some of the communist world as well. Swaggart stood before a large map of the world that indicated by color which nations were receiving the gospel via his ministry and which were yet under pagan influence. As his son, Donnie, put it on the broadcast, it was "D-Day or Delay." The choice was plain: Either viewers would contribute to the cause of world evangelization, enabling the Swaggart organization to expand its ministry to new countries, or the spread of the gospel would be delayed. Moreover, the Swaggarts implied, Christ's Second Coming depended on viewer contributions, since the Savior would not return until, as predicted in the Book of Revelation, Christ was preached to all people. Swaggart's ministry had effectively yoked its own financial condition to the earthly return of Jesus Christ. During that period, Swaggart's show was the highest-rated weekly syndicated broadcast and apparently the most successful fund-raiser, generating nearly a half-million dollars weekly in contributions—well beyond that needed to keep the program on the air in all its current cities and nations.

In the spring of 1990 Pat Robertson similarly used his "700 Club" to link his ministry to international evangelization. Broadcasting live from Central America, Robertson explained to viewers how a CBN-sponsored mass-media blitz in the region was supposedly helping to usher in peace and prosperity by combating communism and fostering spiritual revival. Using quasi-documentary segments about political, economic, and religious changes occurring in Central America, the program associated CBN's own campaign with the rise of evangelicalism in the area, the decline of the Marxist Sandinista government in Nicaragua, and especially the transformation of individual lives among believers. Indeed, CBN had recently conducted the most extensive evangelistic campaign in Central America, using numerous mass media to saturate Nicaragua, El Salvador, and Guatemala with the North American-styled gospel of personal salvation. CBN spent about $1.5 million on the project, which included prime-time TV specials for three nights on all TV stations in El Salvador and Guatemala. However, the rise of evangelicalism and the decline of the Sandinista government had been occurring long before CBN's media blitz. Moreover, the "700 Club" greatly oversimplified the political and religious trends in Central America, creating an overly optimistic sense of what was happening in an area still dominated by economic strife, political instability, and injustice.

Probably the most telling example of institutional storytelling has been the TV ministry of D. James Kennedy of Fort Lauderdale, Florida. Kennedy is a gifted exegetical and expository preacher who built a large church and enthusiastic following in the 1970s and early 1980s. His early TV programs were simple broadcasts of Kennedy's Sunday-morning services, emphasizing the sermon and to some extent the music. Because of Kennedy's conservative Calvinist-Presbyterian background, the broadcast services were rather sedate and predictable compared with the Pentecostal excitement of Roberts or Swaggart or the charismatic flair and emotion of Robertson and Bakker. Still, Kennedy's TV services attracted a loyal following of viewers who valued the program's clear exegetical style and more sophisticated ethos.

In the mid-1980s Kennedy began increasingly to address public issues, including abortion, evolution, prayer in schools, and sex and violence in motion pictures. Over the course of a few years, Kennedy's TV ministry had effectively inserted itself in a broader drama of secularism vs. Christianity in American life. The program's new story was soon linked to whatever seemed to be the most emotional public issues for Christians, especially evangelicals. Kennedy's direct-mail appeals reflected the same strategy, asking viewers and supporters to respond to surveys about the nation's moral and spiritual health, and requesting funds to help Kennedy's ministry return America to its Christian roots.

Televangelism's dramatic appeal, then, is far more than what the preacher says or does on a particular broadcast. By writing their own institutional dramas, which create a role for the ministry in the very future of the nation and the world, televisual ministries are able to dramatize effectively their place in the kingdom of God and the checkbooks of viewers. More than that, they can associate contributions to the ministry with the cosmic struggle between ultimate good and evil. In this way they transform themselves from mere nonprofit fund-raisers to agencies of God. Critics of the ministry become evil characters, while supporters are trusted conspirators in the battle to save humankind from the hands of the devil. In short, the ministry's drama incorporates the contributors as essential characters in the triumphalistic story.

During live fund-raising periods on programs such as Robertson's "700 Club" and Bakker's "PTL Club," the idea of a cosmic struggle has been used repeatedly to enhance the sense of immediate financial need. As contributors call with their pledges, and as the totals are regularly displayed on camera, the ongoing action and emotion symbolically represent the movements of the church of Christ in contemporary history. The individual will of the lone viewer becomes either a path or a roadblock to the victory of Christ over sin and despair. In such a context it is difficult for many believers not to support their favorite ministry.

The Bakker Soap Opera

No ministry better illustrates the dramatic role of personal story in televisual fund-raising than Jim and Tammy Bakker's "PTL Club." Jim Bakker began broadcasting his own television program in 1974 under the name "PTL Club" ("Praise the Lord" or "People that Love"). Over the years the name of the show was changed to "The Jim and Tammy Show," reflecting the increasingly important role of these two charismatic personalities in the content of the program. The show successfully raised millions of dollars annually to finance construction of a 2,000-acre complex near Charlotte, North Carolina.

By 1986 most of the Bakkers' ministry drama had been realized: a large TV studio in a barn-shaped building, a workshop and seminar center, a two-story "Upper Room" supposedly patterned after the site of the Last Supper, an outdoor amphitheater, a youth center, a restaurant, an Olympic-size swimming pool, tennis courts, a general store and shopping mall called "Main Street," Heritage Island water park with a water slide and 45,000-square-foot wave pool, and the 504-room Heritage Grand Hotel. Funds raised on the show were also disbursed to a home for unwed mothers, a small home for handicapped children, hundreds of "People That Love" outreach centers around the country, and a variety of overseas missions projects.

During the spring of 1987 Jim resigned from the board of Heritage USA, admitting publicly that he had had sexual relations with a young church secretary years earlier while separated from his wife. Soon other televangelists made additional allegations about Bakker's personal use of ministry funds, his homosexual activities, and even his unorthodox theology. Public reports held that between 1982 and 1987 the Bakkers' combined annual income increased roughly tenfold to about $1.5 million. Expense accounts further enhanced their lavish lifestyles, which included a 55-foot houseboat, a Mercedes-Benz and a Rolls-Royce, and several homes and apartments. There was no doubt that the Bakkers had been able to raise far more money than the television ministry needed to produce its programs and broadcast them throughout the United States. After the scandal, some critics labeled the ministry a "'Dallas' with collection plates." Others said that "Mickey and Minnie had been kicked out of Disney World."[12]

Although many people, including most media representatives, were highly critical of the Bakkers, few observers took the time or effort to figure out what made the Bakkers so popular and the organization so financially solvent. The truth was that the Bakkers were enormously gifted television performers who turned the program into a real-life soap opera about their own lives and the life of the ministry itself. Just as some other televangelists successfully created appealing stories about their ministries, with viewers and contributors playing key roles, the Bakkers almost inadvertently learned over the years how to engage supporters in a spiritual battle against evil forces supposedly conspiring to destroy PTL. "The Jim and Tammy Show" was fabricated out of the actual experiences of the Bakkers and their friends who shared the dream of Heritage U.S.A. The Bakkers became the main characters in a drama about the grace of God and the actions of Satan in the lives of ordinary people. The villains were the *Charlotte Observer,* which led the media in an investigation of PTL, and the Federal Communications Commission, which examined PTL's fund-raising practices on television stations.

Every weekday Jim and Tammy appeared on their program, which was broadcast via satellite to faithful viewers across the nation. The program appealed especially to senior citizens, some of whom moved to homes at or near PTL headquarters and many others who visited the complex during holidays or extended vacations. Jim's puerile mannerisms, such as his boyish grin, emotional outbursts, and easy laughter, endeared him to these viewers. Similarly, Tammy's girlish qualities, including her doll-like appearance and frequent tears, won over many supporters. Neither celebrity seriously tried to convince the viewers that they were Nashvillian country-and-western stars or unapproachable televangelists. Instead, on the program they became vulnerable and sensitive people, almost like children, who expressed their love of and need for their viewers and contributors. In response, many supporters treated the Bakkers as their own special offspring, buying them gifts and showering donations on the ministry. Even after the scandal became public, some supporters refused to believe the media reports. In the eyes and hearts of their admirers, Jim and Tammy were prodigal children who would be welcomed back with open arms and a fatted calf.

Such familial love was only part of the story, however. During one decade of daily programs, the Bakkers had repeatedly shared

their dreams about PTL with viewers over the air and with supporters via the mails or sometimes even in person during visits to
PTL by some of the larger contributors. In those dreams the
Bakkers expressed their desire to "bring the Christian campground up to the 20th century."[13] Christians deserved to "make it,"
as Jim said repeatedly, and PTL would show that God desired
great things for his children. The PTL complex, like the program
itself, displayed an amazing level of ostentatious living. PTL represented the "good life" over against the old-fashioned evangelical
belief in self-denial. In fact it appears that the Bakkers' success
depended partly on their own flamboyant lifestyle. Their viewers
wanted to believe in the Bakkers and in PTL, which represented a
triumph over the old cultural taboos that kept many believers
from having a good time. More than anything else, PTL was a
place and a program simply to have fun. To many Christians, that
was indeed a liberating philosophy of life.

In other words, PTL's own tale of success became part of a personalized story that viewers wished to call their own. Jim and
Tammy symbolized the freedom of all Christians to have lavish,
fun-loving lifestyles. To support PTL was to embrace the triumph
of one set of cultural values over another one. As Jim told one
newspaper, "We preach prosperity. We preach abundant life.
Christ wished above all things that we prosper."[14] The PTL ministry was for a time the living proof of this philosophy, both
through the personal success stories of the Bakkers and the organizational prosperity of the entire ministry. Heritage USA became
the place where supporters could live out that philosophy without
guilt, even at the Heritage church services. For many people, especially those from conservative Pentecostal backgrounds, the
Bakkers' story was deeply attractive. For others, like televangelist
Jimmy Swaggart, PTL was spiritually and culturally apostate.

Although the Bakkers' program was troubling to some Christians, its enormous success at attracting regular viewers and committed supporters cannot be thoughtlessly overlooked. PTL and
the Bakkers were part of a powerful drama created in and
through television. Like a real-life soap opera, the "PTL Club"
offered entertaining glimpses into the personal lives of other people. And like a compelling religious myth, the televised story of
PTL gave those lives special spiritual meaning. However, there is
little doubt the story reflected American materialism as much as
Christian faith.[15]

Televised Morality Plays

The PTL case is only one example of how American televangelism lures viewers partly through story and drama. Televangelists are performers, not just preachers or broadcasters. And some of them are actors in their own story, which has a religious plot and spiritual significance. Through television, radio, mail, and public speaking, many televangelists craft tales about their ministries that depict a world of good and bad characters centered around God's role in building the media organization. In this kind of religious public relations, TV preachers and their supporters enter their own morality play. As in many secular television dramas, the plot and characters clearly delineate good from evil.

American commercial television is largely in the business of entertaining people with stories about the ultimate triumph of good over evil. Tragedy has never been particularly popular in the United States, where most people view the tube to be confirmed in their beliefs about the world. Americans are optimistic, and so is their television. Night after night, prime-time television feeds the nation's hungry appetite for uplifting tales where the good guys get the bad guys and where all things seem to work together for good. This has been true of the vast majority of situation comedies, westerns, detective shows, and even soap operas. Commercial television is like an enormous storyteller, delivering many secular versions of the Christian Good News. On television it is not God that saves, but good sense, luck, patience, power, or money. Once in a while, love is the savior, but rarely the love of God.[16]

Televangelism and popularized commercial television increasingly share this moralistic sense of drama. On Sunday-morning television, just as during prime time, it is almost always clear who are the good and bad guys. Televangelists increasingly specialize in creating unambiguously evil characters, groups, and movements for their viewers. If someone is evil he is heretical, immoral, liberal and so forth. Certain movements and organizations are evil because they support unacceptable ideas or practices. The specific litanies of evil change from year to year, largely with the news. As TV ministries address currently newsworthy topics, from prayer in school to abortion, homosexuality, or communism, the evils have new names. Nevertheless, there are always clear statements of who or what is evil, as well as who or what is good.

In the kinds of ongoing morality plays created by televangelists, there can be no room for distinctions or comparisons. Everything must be black and white or the drama loses its power and the televangelist no longer has as much appeal. Jimmy Swaggart used a morality play to condemn dramatically both Roman Catholicism and Calvinism; he never indicated that American Protestantism owes much to either. Jerry Falwell blasted "communists" repeatedly during the early years of his national television ministry; he was simply uninterested in the fact that there are many brands of communism and socialism, including some advocated by Christians in the face of fascistic domination and persecution. Nor was Falwell concerned with addressing the ills and abuses of capitalism and democratic governments. The point here is not to argue against the basic thrust of either Swaggart's or Falwell's message. Instead, the point is that in televangelism, as in popular secular drama, there is rarely anything more than an overly simple and highly moralistic point. One is either an evolutionist *or* a creationist, for example, and the latter position requires one to adhere to a fundamentalist interpretation of the first few chapters of Genesis.

This kind of morality play, which creates simplified and polarized answers to complex questions, has been enormously divisive in the churches of the United States. Some Christians, getting their ideas about multifaceted issues from televangelists, begin carrying a self-righteous attitude that prohibits friendly discussion. Televangelism does not normally mold or change a viewer's attitudes completely, but it can help legitimize any tendency toward an extremist position in such areas as politics, morality, and especially popular theology or Christian doctrine. In some churches the religious-television viewers are among the most dogmatic and intolerant parishioners, repeatedly causing dissension and strife within the body of Christ. Again, the point here is not to embrace tolerance or open-mindedness per se, but to warn followers of TV ministries that the drama depicted on the tube is but a glimmering of the full truth. Televangelists stand to gain when *their* story becomes the viewer's story, for televangelists are only human, and they tend to do and say those things that will further the progress of their ministries, even if not their own personal interests.

In both secular and evangelistic TV programs, evil lurks somewhere "outside." During prime-time television, evil is confined to certain bad guys, from criminals to Indians to gunslingers and other obvious villains. Rarely does evil reside in the heart of the hero. Similarly, in televangelism the devil is alive and well among *other* ministries and especially non-Christians, instead of among *all* people, including televangelists. Whether it be "secular humanists" or "liberals," evil always lurks elsewhere. Morality plays throughout history have tended to affirm what people already believed rather than to question those beliefs. Especially in the case of televangelism—one among many imperfect institutions in a fallen world—this is hardly a good idea. Christians need the power of spiritual discernment, not just knee-jerk moralism. American televangelists fling too many salvos at others while carefully hiding their own transgressions.

TV Theology

It should not be surprising, then, that the tube's dramatic lure is not theologically neutral. Popular televangelism thrives on the kinds of religious ideas and biblical interpretations that cater to the visual and emotional demands of the medium. On television the highest-rated preacher will not typically be the one who is most cherished as a local pastor or gifted theologian. Television has its own internal logic, which propels religion in particular directions while stifling other approaches. John Calvin, Martin Luther, and John Wesley would have faced entirely different communication problems in the television age. So would the many Roman Catholic pontiffs. As television has become the major storyteller and perhaps the great jester in American culture, it has shifted the balance of power and authority among religious groups and Christian traditions.

In a marvelous book, *Eloquence in the Electronic Age,* rhetorician Kathleen Hall Jamieson reveals the communicative bias of television. She writes, "The central claims of Madison Avenue, of prime-time television, and of widely viewed films have replaced those of the Bible, Shakespeare, and the great speeches of the *lingua franca* of contemporary oratory."[17] Television's visual grammar is associative, she argues, making it hard for viewers to demand evidence or even to understand how they are being affected. The medium does not normally engender thought among viewers. Its rhetoric pales in significance as television delivers images that evoke emotions and feelings. When politicians look and act authoritative on the tube, viewers assume the person is ripe for office. Similarly, if a TV commercial makes a product appealing, even romantic or sexy, viewers are eager to try out the product for themselves. The attractive images and cajoling words flow endlessly, offering little time for the audience to think about what it is seeing. Unless the commercials are taped and slowly replayed, providing an opportunity for critical thought, they have simply come and gone without mindful attention.

As a result, television favors experientially validated theologies over systematically argued ones. Pentecostals, neo-pentecostals, and charismatics find the tube an attractive and effective medium, whereas reformational Protestants do not quite know what to do with it. Lengthy sermons, delivered in a literary fashion and based on systematic theology, generally flop on the tube. Meanwhile, narrative preachers who tell exciting stories about what "God is doing" in their ministries attract significant audiences. Traditional liturgies are incredibly dull on a twenty-one-inch screen, while spontaneous and animated worship formats, especially healing services, are interesting to watch. Whatever is not cast in a dramatic and, preferably, narrative form is generally prosaic viewing.

And so it goes in the United States that the spontaneous, expressive, and dramatic churches gravitate toward televised religion, while the more staid and academic traditions look on in uncertain and sometimes even critical dismay. It is too easy for the latter groups to ignore the medium or to dismiss television as inherently evil. At the same time, it is typical for contemporary charismatics and old-fashioned Pentecostals to jump thoughtlessly into televangelism without considering the theological and even spiritual risks. Every medium has its advantages, and each one invariably offers some unavoidable pitfalls. The real issue is not whether to use television for "religious purposes," since religion relates to all of life. Instead it is time to consider both the opportunities and the related dangers of televangelism in terms of the overall goal of communicating authentic Christian faith.

First, television is not particularly useful for doing deep theological inquiry. Print is far superior for that, since it lends itself to extended argument, careful reasoning, and open refutation. Television will never be the principal medium for facilitating scholarly or academic thought about Christianity, including its theology. Indeed, the Christian traditions most dependent on elitist thinkers and academic approaches to religion have the most to lose in a society increasingly dominated by television.[18]

Second, television is excellent for establishing "popular" religion—religion grounded not in an academic or elite tradition but in commonality of thought and feeling. Cultural and religious traditions are generally maintained through the spoken and written word in families, churches, schools, and other social institutions that feature interpersonal communication. Largely because images on the tube so quickly span geographic space, and also because the expense of using the medium typically necessitates mass audiences, television tends to communicate messages that are made by no one in particular for everyone in general. The result is a popular cultural mishmash of values, beliefs, and standards of action. Televangelism, for example, generally seems to most viewers to lack any traditional religious moorings. It is merely "religion," not any particular group or denomination.

Third, television facilitates the communication of emotion over thought. It encourages audiences to experience a program rather than to reflect on it. As Jamieson has argued, this is the medium's grammar. Televangelism is generally no exception, even when it tries to be more explicitly thoughtful, critical, or scholarly.

These three generalizations about the medium are not absolutes. Some televangelists, for example, are more thoughtful than others. Presumably their viewers are more thoughtful as well. Because most televangelists have apparently not faced the negative aspects of these tendencies, they have failed to present a reasonably balanced perspective on the Christian faith. There are a few exceptions, particularly ministries such as Radio Bible Class, which uses printed study materials extensively in support of its radio and TV ministry. Overall, though, televangelism promotes a popular religion devoid of either historic tradition or a thoughtful context. In the process televangelism creates a rather unstable and inauthentic faith based on emotion and experience. As we shall see, this helps make the United States ripe for unorthodox gospels of "health and wealth," and even popular sorcery.

If faith must always contain knowledge *and* belief, thought *and* emotion, television can be a serious threat to authentic faith when it is the only medium for religious communication. Much of contemporary televangelism is little more than a potpourri of powerful images and emotional words designed to attract and hold viewers. It usually does not teach very effectively. Nor does it promote thoughtful Christian action in the world. Instead, it often makes much ado about nothing, thereby belittling the very concept of faith itself.

MTV Religion

Indeed, the trend in televangelism is to say less and entertain more. The result is that it looks and sounds increasingly like MTV—a visual and aural hodgepodge that clamors for attention, changes quickly, and offers no time to make sense. Pastor Bill Hybels' comments about the younger generation are an apt expression of the dynamics behind this trend: "This is the generation that grew up on television. You have to present religion to them in a creative and visual way."[19] Similarly, Alex Clattenberg, another megachurch pastor, says it's time for churches to present a vital, dynamic and exciting faith, since young people today are not interested in a stale, dull gospel.[20]

Because it is so strongly market-driven, televangelism, even more than the local churches, represents the cutting edge of MTV-styled religion. Until recently, however, few televangelists saw any benefit to attracting audiences with flashier and quicker programming. Now that televangelism's viewers are literally dying off, the ministries' leaders are looking for ways of luring younger followers. Upbeat messages and new-styled programs are important parts of the solution. Bakker and Robertson had success with their more contemporary formats. Robertson, for example, selected Sheila Walsh, a former British rock star, as co-host on his "700 Club." The program also relied on relatively short segments to keep the flow lively and interesting.

But the comparison with MTV does not stop there. As a hyper-example of the direction of modern television, MTV illustrates how public things become private, while private things become public. Television in general, and rock videos in particular, publicly broadcast all kinds of naturally private matters, expecially sexuality. Rock videos are loaded with references to and depictions of sexual relations. Meanwhile, in the age of MTV, many public activities are privatized, including worship. Just as youth may watch televised dance and music shows privately in their bedrooms, instead of dancing with a partner or listening to music with others, televangelism's congregants may derive their public religion from the privacy of their living rooms.

Karl Rahner has asked whether or not it is appropriate for Christians to broadcast on television their own personal religious observances. He questions whether or not it is proper for holy words and actions to be made available to anyone who tunes in to a program, regardless of what they believe or think about what they see and hear.[21] The fact is that some Protestant preachers refuse to pray on camera, and for a long while the Roman Catholic church prohibited televising Holy Communion. Consider the equivalent situation of televising real (not acted) sexual relations between intimate adults. Obviously there is a difference. Nevertheless, the unwillingness of Christians to address the issue of public appropriateness suggests that, like MTV, modern televangelism is more interested in attracting audiences than in communicating effectively and ethically.

When virtually all church-related activities are aired openly to millions of people without any concern for how they might be interpreted, the activities are often perceived as little more than entertainment. Moreover, they can become outlandish spectacles for unbelievers. Does healing really belong on television? What about deep and personal prayer? And what shall we make of public prophecies directed at the church, or of "words of knowledge"? All these are regularly carried on television. Some people tune in not to be edified, but to ridicule or criticize or both. Others tune in for curiosity. Although preaching to unbelievers would certainly be acceptable, beyond that it is not clear what kinds of "Christian programming" should really be on the public airways. As we shall see in a later chapter, televangelism and its audiences are not to be equated with "the church."

It is the responsibility of that church, however, to monitor the appropriateness of its members' activities. And it is the right of critics within the church to watch for excessive uses of hyperbole, drama, and story to attract audiences for so-called religious programs. The movement toward a rapid-pace, sensationalistic, quasi-personal style of televangelism needs serious discussion by believers of all denominations. There is a growing sense that televangelism is on a dramatic treadmill, moving ever more quickly into slickly produced programming that imitates secular styles and techniques, including MTV and commercials.

Conclusion

In 1950 evangelical theologian Edward J. Carnell had already addressed the dramatic lure of television. Recognizing the medium's impact on religious communication in the United States, he sought to uphold the dramatic qualities of the gospel message while cautioning against entertainment-driven religion. He wrote in *Television: Servant or Master?* that "good preaching ought to be good entertainment . . . The gospel is good news! . . . skill and love—not challenge, bitterness, haughtiness—must characterize the ways of those dedicated to the work of announcement to men that Christ died for their sins. . . . Religious telecasting will either be good entertainment or it will die a natural death."[22] By "entertainment," Carnell really meant programming that agreeably got people's attention, that neither offended nor imitated nor upset.

Carnell's book addressed the major issue that would eventually face all televangelism: how to use the medium effectively without turning the gospel into mere entertainment. He was correct that religious communication, whether from pulpit or camera, should not be so dramatically dull that no one cares to listen or watch. Indeed, the gospel message is inherently exciting, dramatic, dynamic, and even entertaining. The problem, however, is that televangelism in the United States tends to mimic the dramatic styles and rhetorical strategies of secular communication. As Virginia Stem Owens has argued, this belittles the gospel message, turning Christ into another consumer product.[23] When Christianity is peddled like any other product, it loses its distinctiveness and especially its authenticity. The gospel must be communicated differently precisely *because* those who believe it are to be godly people, not worldly hucksters. How the gospel is dramatized on television will not just make or break the business of televangelism; it will also establish the public's notion of what it means to be a Christian. Every televangelist contributes to the world's perceptions of the Christian life and the gospel message.

Furthermore, artistry and finesse should certainly characterize televangelism. Sloppy, ill-crafted, obnoxious, or simply inferior messages have no place in the church's public presentation of itself. On the other hand, simplicity remains a virtue in human communication, which too often is clouded by fancy histrionics that detract from the message. Unfortunately, American television is like that, forsaking the simple power of an unadorned message for flashy televisual dramatics that are designed to compete head-to-head with commercial TV fare. Every year it becomes clearer that most televangelists put dramatic considerations over the veracity of their messages. They feed viewers more and more action and emotion and less and less spiritually nutritious food.

As John Shea has argued, much of the motivating symbolism of contemporary religious experience is created and distributed through popular culture. Television and the other mass media are increasingly dominant purveyors of popular religious belief and practice.[24] As televangelism has tried to garner audiences and elicit contributions, it has tended to dilute the essence of Christian faith by creating dramatic versions of it that have little or no historic or traditional moorings. For good and for bad, but mostly for the latter, televangelism turns faith into popular drama. Just as American commercial television offers cheap drama, televangelism offers a lot of emotion and action without much substance. This is not the kind of religious expression that will foster deep and abiding faith. Instead it plays with transitory feelings and shallow responses, such as calling an "800" number or sending in a contribution. There is little likelihood that most televangelism will significantly deepen the nation's faith.

Televangelism, unless carefully crafted to avoid it, has turned the preacher into an actor, the studio "congregation" into extras, and viewers into a passive audience. Along the way it has also created a story about the role of the ministry in redemptive history that is both compelling and deceptive. The goal of establishing a large, well-known ministry can become more important than the desire to truly minister to people. Dramatic techniques will attract an audience, but they will not necessarily leave that audience with anything more than an entertaining story. Televangelistic programming is too often directed toward the ministry and what it will supposedly do for the viewers, not toward God and what he has already done for a fallen world. The real goal of televangelism should be to promote the authentic gospel of God's redemption plan, from Creation to Christ's Second Coming.

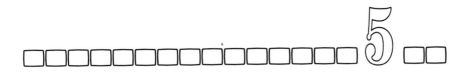

The New Sorcery

❉ ❉ ❉ ❉ ❉ ❉ ❉ ❉ ❉ ❉ ❉ ❉

D uring the summer my pre-teen son and I frequently go for long walks in the evening. We take turns selecting a route that will offer a change of scenery as well as introduce us to new neighbors and lead us to uncharted areas of town. In the late 1980s our journeys frequently took us to a transitional area marked by an unusual combination of ethnic minorities, budding young professional couples, and senior citizens. In some respects the neighborhood was a cross section of American society, primarily because the low cost of housing enabled many people to afford living there.

As we strolled regularly through this social and architectural hodgepodge we noticed that there were few people around after about eight at night. Although a few couples and individuals sat on their steps or rested peacefully in their screened porches, most residents were in their living or family rooms. The bluish glow of TV sets gave away their major evening activity. Only convenience stores displayed signs of real public life—the endless stream of automobiles to and from these 24-hour establishments that specialized in video rentals, alcoholic beverages, candy, cigarettes, and lottery tickets.

One of our treks coincided with a major case of state lottery fever. As the lottery went without a winner for weeks on end, the stakes grew into the tens of millions of dollars. The result was an incredible parade of folks at the local convenience stores. In fact, in all of our walks my son and I had never seen such a mind-boggling array of neighborhood residents as excited about anything else. We stood silently and disbelievingly before one of the stores on a muggy evening when most people would normally be sitting rather lazily at home. Instead they were lined up like fidgety chickens about to become canned soup. One man carried a rabbit's foot hopefully in his left hand, alternately grasping it firmly and opening his fist to make sure it was still there. Another had his fingers crossed. All in all, there was remarkable silence and concentration in the line as each gambler made his own pact with the mysterious forces that supposedly controlled the game's fate.

Several days later, as lottery fever became part of the state news, numerous reports humorously examined the "methods" used to play the game. According to the newspapers, individuals rarely picked numbers randomly off the top of their heads. Rather, they selected lottery numbers based on some personally meaningful numbers, such as birth dates, ages, telephone numbers, anniversaries, and the like. Once in a while the winners of a lottery would seemingly confirm the benefits of such a method by testifying that they had won precisely because they stayed tenaciously with such personal numbers for months or years of play.

As anyone who has studied state lotteries knows, they are among the most regressive taxes available to legislators and governors in the United States. Generally speaking, poorer and less-educated citizens play such lotteries regularly. One evening my son and I watched an amazing demonstration of this fact. A seventy-year-old (or more) gentleman pulled up to a convenience store in a very old, rusted, filthy automobile that sounded like a semi-muffled jackhammer. With considerable difficulty the senior citizen limped to the lottery ticket window in ragged clothes and worn-out leather shoes. In a few minutes his work was over; he hobbled back to his dirt-black car and rumbled noisily home, holding the tickets against the steering wheel.

Modern televangelism, like the lottery, is a source of hope for many needy people. Sometimes that hope is well placed, as the gospel is preached. However, many times it is not. The problem is that anyone can play the games of the televangelists. All one needs is a TV set. In a land where there are indeed many spiritually, medically, and financially needy people, some TV ministries deceptively offer the possibility of achieving victory over virtually every kind of malady. Much of televangelism is like a religious version of the lottery window—a place to turn when all other sources of hope have seemingly turned sour.

Although we do not like to admit it, Americans are a superstitious people. Science and technology have not eliminated all the irrational urges to control our destinies through various kinds of cant, superstition, and magic. Sorcery is alive and well! It exists on the tube, in the churches, and on the shelves of religious bookstores. Most importantly, the new sorcery masquerades as part of the Christian gospel, when in fact it is a reflection of the superstitious underbelly of American popular culture. In this chapter we will look at the pagan-American aspects of the "health and wealth" gospel that increasingly dominates popular televangelism. This is today's religious lottery, served by the most convenient medium of all times.

From Medicine Man to Televangelist

Americans sometimes forget the important role of medical sorcery and quackery in the nation's history. The nineteenth-century medicine show, for example, was a popularized and somewhat sanitized version of the American Indians' medicine man, a ritual specialist in the diagnosing and curing of illness. Also called a shaman, the medicine man was believed to draw on the assistance of good spirits to rid the body of evil ones. Some of these tribal "priests" were true believers although they might supplement their healing rituals with herbal cures and other treatment measures, some of which have been found to have medicinal value. Others merely used various sleight-of-hand tricks and psychology to convince patients that they had indeed been cured, usually for a price.

In many respects the medicine show was the predecessor of some forms of religious healing services and eventually even contemporary televangelism. Medicine shows were a form of itinerant entertainment that flourished in rural America. As with TV, the show was free; only the nostrums, peddled in a circus atmosphere by a so-called doctor, carried a price. The secret patented formulas, often containing alcohol, promised cures for most of the common ailments of the day. Testimonials were sometimes offered by individuals who swore to the effectiveness of such potent brews.

Medicine shows generally followed the seasonal weather from north to south, gathering crowds in the outdoors during good weather and in rented lodge halls and country opera houses during the winter. Before the medicines were peddled, the crowd had to be entertained; after all, bored citizens could be attracted to shows of virtually any kind. Performances included the seeds of urban vaudeville: dog acts, blackface minstrels, pie-eating contests, and the like. Often the medicines were finally introduced by a "professor," who might emerge from a tepee wearing buckskin and long hair in the popular image of an Indian scout. Cure-alls included liniments, laxatives, bunion and corn remedies, liver pads, hair growers, electric belts, powdered herbs, and the clichéed "snake oil."

It was not merely the actual medicine that was being sold to hopeful (though skeptical) Americans from coast to coast. Rather, the medicine man offered free entertainment in exchange for an opportunity to sell hope to a nation of individually troubled people. No matter what their ethnic or religious background, members of the medicine-show audience brought to the performances common needs and shared desires. They sought to be relieved of all their problems through medical solutions. The medicine man, in turn, hoped to rid these people of their troubles by convincing them that his magical potions and formulas would fix the body and thereby change their lives for the better. He sought to convince people that they must have faith in him and his products. Where there was such faith there was hope.

These "doctors" were experts in popular psychology. They frequently dressed like country preachers, or "men of science," with frock coat, silk hat, and Vandyke beard. They also peppered their language with religious words, such as "thee" and "thou." And they used all of the proven rhetorical devices of persuasion: testimonials, demonstrations, sympathy, fear, and so on. After all, their success depended on their ability to establish a belief in the effectiveness of the product, not on the actual merits of the product itself. They had to generate "faith" among skeptical audiences. Only such faith would produce sales. Entertainment alone was not enough.

In the early years of the twentieth century the medicine men largely disappeared. As the population became more educated, and rural areas were increasingly linked via transportation and communications media to urban centers, the market for such nostrums and potions declined steadily. Some cities hastened their disappearance by saddling medicine men with restrictive fees and civic regulations that limited or refused entry of such emotional, fast-talking, high-pressure salesmen.[1] Almost a century later, in the 1980s, the "superstition trade" was again booming in the United States, legitimately selling herbs and totems to hopeful retail customers across the country.[2] In Florida, one entrepreneur makes a bundle at his own bingo parlor, where customers purchase packets costing from $79 to $289 in hopes of winning cash, travel awards, or a beach-front condominium. Called "Big Cypress," the parlor is designed, according to the owner, to "make [patrons] happy while they're losing."[3]

Religious Ignorance

The case of the nineteenth-century medicine man shows how superstition thrives in the midst of ignorance. Uneducated rural folk, lacking even rudimentary knowledge of medicine, were relatively easy victims of these fast-talking "experts." It also documents an important American legacy that has influenced popular religious belief. Even in the nation's early colonies, people were often surprisingly ignorant of elemental Christian beliefs, let alone the nature of science and the practice of medicine. Historian Jon Butler has described how magic and astrology were important aspects of Early America's religious heritage. From the nation's beginning, there has always been a significant stream of occult or magical practices borrowed, like Christianity itself, from Europe.[4]

The point is that popular Christianity in America is not the same as the faith and practice described by its mainstream churches or examined by academically trained theologians. The nation's Christianity has typically been a combination of orthodox Christian belief and various kinds of superstition, cant, and even magic. Just as the medicine man was able to convict individuals of the effectiveness of his cure-alls, often through purely deceptive means, the popular preacher could gather a flock around a host of aberrant beliefs and practices. The "truth," as defined by mainstream Protestantism, was not always the most appealing message, especially if delivered by a rather untalented performer. People often wanted to "feel" the message, not just to know it or understand it. This democratic impulse to deliver the gospel message in a popular style seized the Christian church in America during the first two hundred years of its existence.[5] It was not about to disappear in the twentieth century, when religious ignorance was still alive and well.

In 1989 a humanities professor tested new students enrolled in college classes of religion on their "religious literacy." The results may not have been any better than they would have been two centuries earlier. Only about one-fifth of them could place the Protestant Reformation in the correct century. About the same number (probably mostly Roman Catholics) knew that Peter is believed by Catholics to be the first pope. None of them could identify the "social gospel." Most amazing of all, less than one-third could even paraphrase the first of the Ten Commandments.[6] Clearly the educational system hardly teaches students about Christian history and doctrine, let alone to believe it.

Church education classes hardly fare any better. A survey conducted in 1989 of U.S. Protestants found that only a third of them had an "integrated faith" that embraced both basic beliefs and their practical implications in life. Sponsored by six mainline Protestant denominations, the distressing study determined "that faith is not particularly well-developed" in many church members and that church education programs are "less than effective." The study concluded that many Christians hold a private faith that is largely unrelated to their practical actions in the real world. That kind of faith is merely belief or doctrine, not behavior. Moreover, many Christians feel that religious faith should not be expressed publicly or discussed with others. Finally, the study found that *adult* religious education is crucial for building mature faith. Ironically, most churches emphasize religious education for the young far more than for adults.[7]

Such flawed religious education takes place in a country where millions of people consider themselves to be religious. In *The People's Religion: American Faith in the 90's,* George Gallup, Jr., and Jim Castelli examined revealing surveys of Americans' religious faith and practice from 1930 to 1988. They found that Americans seem to be a very religious people—nine in ten say they have never doubted the existence of God; 88 percent believe that God loves them; 80 percent believe they will face God on judgment day; 70 percent believe in life after death. In fact, Gallup and Castelli determined that more Americans now say they have made a personal commitment to Jesus Christ than any time in the last twenty years. Yet, even though Americans claim religiosity, they display in such surveys an appalling ignorance of the Bible; only about one-third of Americans read it weekly. Moreover, only about 40 percent know that Jesus gave the Sermon on the Mount, fewer than half can name the four Gospels, and many are unaware that Jesus was born in Bethlehem or that he had twelve disciples.[8]

The portrait of American Christianity that emerges from these and many other studies is hardly complimentary. In a nation dotted with churches, loaded with Bibles, and with one of the highest church attendance rates in the world, there is enormous religious ignorance. Religious faith is frequently merely a popular phenomenon tied to various faddish practices or beliefs, whether they be uttering a double "Amen" after prayer, raising hands during worship, or using biblical "prooftexts" to end discussions about appropriate Christian lifestyles. Like the surrounding culture, the church and its people, Protestant and Catholic alike, are deeply and often unwittingly influenced by the world around them. As a result, faith is frequently a generalized feeling or attitude, not a firm belief in Christ, a commitment to the historic doctrine of the church, or even a recognition of the biblical basis for religious practices. In fact, because American Christians typically have no knowledge of the history of the Christian faith beyond a popular interpretation of selected sections of Scripture, their faith easily becomes an expression of popular, extra-ecclesiastical religion that cannot be linked to any particular church or denomination. Such popular religion emanates from and belongs to "the people" rather than to religious elites trained in seminaries and organizationally controlled by denominational or local church prelates. It is highly fragmented and diffuse, held together more by prevailing cultural myths than by official organizations and carefully articulated creeds and confessions. Popular religion is based on what the people actually do and believe, not what ecclesiastical specialists say they do and believe.[9]

Faith and the American Dream

In the United States, then, one can expect the Christian gospel to reflect some of the popular values and beliefs of its people, not just the historic faith and practices of the universal church. And so it does, especially among the televangelists, who are ultimately dependent on their audiences, particularly their financial supporters, for their own future. They cannot simply preach what people ought to hear, but must preach what people desire to hear. Superstitious and largely ignorant of the faith, millions of Americans are easily persuaded to believe many things that they want to believe and to hope for things that are obviously "American."

As indicated earlier, the electronic church is increasingly grounded in experiential rather than doctrinal theologies and beliefs. Televangelists testify to the veracity of their own experiences as much as to the biblical truthfulness of their beliefs. They rarely call on either the historic witness of the church, as expressed in creeds and confessions, or the collective witness of the contemporary church. Instead the televangelists offer their own personalized expressions of the gospel as adapted from and directed to American culture. To put it more strongly, the faith of some televangelists is more American than Christian, more popular than historic, more personal than collective, and more experiential than biblical. As a result, the faith they preach is highly affluent, selfish, and individualistic.

First, the new American faith reflects the nation's affluence. In the years before their fall from public grace, Jim and Tammy Bakker of the "PTL Club" were the epitome of this trend. Although they sometimes claimed to be greatly concerned about America's poor and even supported some programs to aid poverty-stricken citizens, the Bakkers' popularity grew from their middle-class vision of the "good life." Their wardrobes, automobiles, homes, and lifestyles reflected the affluence many Americans dream about and even pray for. Jim's very slogan, "You can make it," spoke of these aspirations. Faith was envisioned as a means to personal gain—more money, better clothing, a bigger home, and all of the rest of the trappings of American affluence. The Bakkers' success undoubtedly resulted partly from their allegiance to such explicitly material values.

Second, the new American faith is highly selfish. It is based far more on what God can give to the believer than on what the believer should give to God. Countless television programs reflect this trend, which replaces God-glorifying service to others with giving to others for the sake of one's self. In one sense this aspect of American religiosity turns Calvinism on its head, transforming the depraved sinner who deserves eternal death into a righteous believer who merits special blessings. According to many televangelists, the Christian's principal task is to watch out for "number one." After all, if the believer does not, who will?

Third, this new faith system is highly individualistic. It is a matter only of the relationship between the individual believer and God, rarely between the church and God, or even the individual and the church. In 1982, when I wrote to one hundred of the most popular radio and television evangelists, requesting information about their programs, only one of them suggested that I seek out a local church for membership. Ironically, that was the broadcaster for the denomination of which I was already a member! Televangelism in America has trivialized Christianity by reducing faith to a matter of personal belief. The Christian faith is far more, incorporating the faith of God's people throughout history. Unlike some religions, Christianity has turned personal faith outward to the life of the community of believers, called the church. In America, where individualism runs rampant, the church quite easily becomes trivialized as a collection of individuals.

These three aspects of televangelism's faith system—affluence, selfishness, and individualism—say much about how the broader culture has shaped the popular religiosity of American Christianity. They reflect the American Dream, whereby a self-motivated individual supposedly attains great affluence. They also reflect the impact of modernity on the church. As David Wells has suggested, modernity "vitiates any appeal to tradition or a transcendent order. Because we cannot look outward, backward, or upward, we look inward. . . . The self becomes both the object of our concern and source of values. Truth is replaced by feelings and relationships; the goal is not so much to be righteous as to be whole and happy."[10] By using his own brains and brawn, along with a few good breaks, the health-and-wealth believer supposedly can accomplish more than would normally be possible for a mere mortal. As Robert Schuller has put it, such faith can turn "your scars into stars." His "possibility thinking," like Norman Vincent Peale's "positive mental attitude," are distinctly Americanized versions of the modernized Christian gospel.

The Health-and-Wealth Gospel

Probably no version of televangelism is more clearly American than the name-it-and-claim-it, health-and-wealth, or "faith" gospel. During the last twenty years this version of Christianity has blossomed on national television, representing over half of the highest-rated religious programs. It began on TV with Rex Humbard's and Oral Roberts's programming of the 1950s and 1960s, and today includes Roberts's former pilot, Kenneth Copeland, as

well as Robert Tilton, Kenneth Hagin, Fred Price, Jan and Paul
Crouch (of the Trinity Broadcasting Network), former televange-
list Jim Bakker, and numerous others. Robert Schuller and
Jimmy Swaggart have also been influenced by the health-and-
wealth gospel, although they sometimes preach against it. Even
Jerry Falwell, an independent Baptist who once wore the "funda-
mentalist" badge proudly, and former presidential candidate M. G.
"Pat" Robertson have borrowed some of its elements.

The essential thrust of the health-and-wealth gospel is that God
intends for all faithful believers to live healthy and wealthy lives
in this world. Only the lack of personal faith keeps a Christian
from overcoming any emotional, physical, or financial problem.
Once the true believer "claims" these promises of God by faithfully
uttering them, he or she will surely live a healthy and prosperous
life. As James Goff puts it, the faith movement teaches that
"divine health and prosperity are the rights of every Christian
who will appropriate enough faith to receive them. The secret of
appropriating such faith is in making a 'positive confession'—that
is, stating in faith what one desires or is requesting from God and
believing that God will honor it."[11]

Although the specific rules that one must follow to claim the
promises of God vary among the televangelists, the basic premise
is typically the same: Believers can overcome earthly setbacks to
achieve worldly success. Eternal life is not enough. Nor is heaven.
The gospel is meant, such televangelists tell their viewers and
contributors, to free believers from the tyranny of the devil in the
here and now. Along with such freedom supposedly come the
fruits of American culture, including health and wealth. As
William Hendricks described "the theology of the electronic
church," it offers the hope that "God is unambiguously on the side
of the believer who keeps the rules or claims the promise."[12]

Although other critics have narrowly assessed the theological
character of the health-and-wealth gospel, focusing on how it
diverges from both historic Protestantism and even basic Christian doctrines such as the Trinity, they have generally overlooked
how characteristically American such heretical notions really
are.[13] Obviously the name-it-and-claim-it gospel is outright heresy.
Walter Martin has argued that some of its adherents on TV even
proclaim that human beings can become gods in this life.[14] Only
the most offbeat readings of Scripture and loose interpretations of
Christian tradition would conclude that humankind can manipu-

late God by living according to certain rules or engaging in particular ritualistic practices. As Mark Vermaire has written, "Studying wealth through the writings of . . . prosperity teachers would be like learning the proper use of pharmaceuticals from a crack dealer."[15] However, even Pat Robertson falls partly into this trap in his popular book *The Secret Kingdom,* which offers "laws" for living that will supposedly enable believers to overcome life's travails.[16] Because Americans are so optimistic and pragmatic, they believe that such a God-winning system must exist. Some televangelists take advantage of the situation by telling and selling the hopeful throngs the rules of the game.

Contemporary American televangelism is loaded with versions of this outlandish gospel of success. In fact, the airways and religious publishing houses are so filled with it that this unorthodox message now appears normal and even orthodox to many believers. A few years ago I spoke in a church shortly after Kenneth Copeland had suggested on the air that God's goal for everyone was financial prosperity. Not a single member of that Sunday school class, composed of middle- to upper-middle-class Protestants, saw anything particularly wrong with such a sermon. It was as if God had suddenly sanctified American culture in the names of prosperity, affluence, and abundance. Evidently it had not occurred to these adults that money frequently led to more problems than happiness (witness the tragic lives of so many lottery winners, whose personal relationships often disintegrate in the face of windfall millions). Nor did they consider that the love of money is one of the fundamental sins of the Christian life—even the root of evil.

Is it reasonable to believe that God would intend for all his children to live materially prosperous lives? Are not simplicity and inner satisfaction parts of the Christian life? Is not poverty, and sometimes even bankruptcy, a blessing? I offer these observations not with a smug righteousness or with any malice toward wealthy individuals, many of whom are very faithful, God-fearing people. Instead, I simply wish to suggest that worldly prosperity is a distinctly American version of the gospel, not a particularly biblical one. God's will for our lives is far more eternal than is typically acknowledged by the advocates of the health-and-wealth gospel. As the Bible makes clear, God seeks long-term growth and abiding happiness for his children, not merely short-term financial gain or quick healing—though he may deliver both.

As it is blown by the strong winds of the national culture, tele-vangelism breaks the Christian gospel from its historic anchors and increasingly shifts it to an unorthodox prosperity message. David Hazard once wrote, "Listening to some currently-popular preachers and conference leaders, you might think you mistakenly wound up at a Mary Kay convention, where God—not Mary Kay—will reward you with a new car if you play things right."[17] In their own ways, televangelists sweeten the gospel for Americans who, under the shadow of the Fall and the weight of sin, seek to fashion God in their own materialistic image. God is then envi-sioned as the greatest medical wizard or the most successful financial planner, delivering to middle-class Americans what they so desperately want—one more medical breakthrough and the world's most incredible business deal. As Jay Cormier argued, tel-evangelism often errs by offering a faith that is too comfortable rather than comforting. God asks much more of believers than a financial contribution or a "decision for Christ." And Jesus was and is more than the kind and loving Good Shepherd. He chal-lenged the comfortable rabbis and angrily drove the money chang-ers from the Temple even as he instructed peasants and prosti-tutes to call him Teacher. Christ even challenged his own disciples, who were sometimes inclined to be ideologues or judges.[18]

The health-and-wealth gospel plays well in American culture because so many citizens want to believe that the spiritual medicine works, just as nineteenth-century rural folk hoped that the mysterious snake oils peddled by the medicine man would calm their nerves, heal their bronchitis, or eliminate prostate problems. Pat Robertson's "700 Club" broadcasts were not particu-larly popular until the show's format was organized around the healing power of God. In fact, audience research showed the pro-gram's producers that viewers wanted stories about God's mira-cles in today's world. Said Robertson in an interview, "I've just come from a meeting where I learned that our audience has increased by 30 percent this last year [1982]. When we started talking about the miracle power of God our male audience in-creased by 67 percent, our female audience went up by 37 percent and total households watching us increased by 50 percent. Now we are talking to Jewish people, to Catholic people, to non-Christians, to Protestant people, evangelicals, Pentecostals. And we are talk-ing about things they are interested in. As a result, our support base has gone up dramatically. In fact, our 1982 income was up 43 percent."[19] In other words, once Robertson's "700 Club" focused specifically on stories about individuals supposedly healed by God, ratings increased dramatically and the program began competing successfully with other cable channels for viewers.

In contrast to what popular journalism has reported, few people watch televangelists primarily for advice about political candidates.[20] One study of the most popular televangelists found that health-related issues were mentioned more than any other personal concerns, including religious or spiritual problems.[21] Televangelism's appeal is essentially material and, secondarily, spiritual.

Generally speaking, then, televangelists serve the same social function as nonreligious television programs by confirming Americans' fundamental beliefs about themselves and their culture. Just as the situation comedy tends to ratify the nation's belief in the ability of the family to overcome confusion and complication, TV preachers reaffirm the belief that the individual believer can "get ahead" and solve all personal problems by calling on the name of God. Many televangelists are modern-day trumpeters of a religious version of the Horatio Alger myth, which said that through luck and pluck any ordinary person could become successful. Now God has become part of that equation for achieving personal goals and overcoming self-oriented difficulties. Through a warped faith, literally by manipulating God, one can supposedly guarantee health and wealth.

According to some televangelists, it's all in the system. The role of the health-and-wealth preacher is to uphold the Alger myth by strutting incredible examples before a disbelieving but hopeful audience. Religion becomes a kind of game show where contestants vie for personal prizes awarded on the basis of who has more faith. Some religious broadcasts are like modern morality plays that reflect the basic values and beliefs of American culture. Television is part of what Chuck Colson has called "the promised land of imagedom."[22]

Tabloid Religious TV

The spread of the health-and-wealth gospel has led to American Protestantism's own version of tabloid TV. Secular television has Phil Donahue, Oprah Winfrey, and Geraldo Rivera. Televangelism has people like Ernest Angley, Robert Tilton, Oral Roberts, and Kenneth Copeland. These kinds of TV preachers sensationalize the prosperity gospel as vigorously as people like Donahue sensationalize virtually every conceivable social issue.

According to such religious broadcasters, God works primarily through miraculous, supernatural means, not through the common, day-to-day process of guiding and upholding the Creation. In other words, for them, God is present principally when a spectacular miracle occurs rather than simply because he is who he is. Roberts developed the slogan "Expect a Miracle" to convey this view of God's handiwork to hopeful viewers of his television program. In his early years Roberts even "specialized in casting out demons, believing he had a sensitivity in his right hand which gave him 'the power to detect the presence, names and numbers of demons' in sick people."[23] Just as Donahue-type showmen largely ignore the non-spectacular aspects of life, the health-and-wealth preachers overlook the ongoing power of God in making and sustaining the world. Humankind does not have to "expect" a miracle, precisely because the miracles of Creation and redemption are already achieved. Everywhere humankind turns is evidence of the grace of God amidst pain and suffering. A sunset may not be great television, because it occurs too often to be considered "sensational." But, in spite of what some televangelists suggest, it is just as much a reflection of the authority and majesty of God as is any seemingly "divine" healing or inexplicable financial windfall.

Popular health-and-wealth theology reflects the same values that afflict the national culture generally. Just as Americans devalue the miraculous joys of day-to-day living, seeking ever more intense experiences, televangelism gravitates toward increasingly outrageous depictions of God's healing and financial power. This trend would not be so troubling if it were limited to a few fanatical or ill-directed television preachers. The truth is that more and more televangelists are moving further and further toward implicitly tabloidized views of God's work in the world. Even a conservative Baptist such as Jerry Falwell, who is certainly not a charismatic, has increasingly embraced this Americanized gospel. He speaks of the "miracle" that God is performing in his ministry by eliciting contributions to the "Old-Time Gospel Hour" broadcast. It seems that around every turn of the televangelism dial is another example of God's sensationalistic power—examples which are nearly always good for fund-raising. After all, who wants to contribute to a ministry that cannot perform miracles?

As a result, both secular and religious tabloid TV are always stretching for greater examples of God's sensationalism to hold the attention of potentially bored viewers. Health-and-wealth gospels, because of their truncated view of God's handiwork, enslave the believer to ever deeper expressions of God's miraculous power. They require greater faith for greater personal rewards. It is never enough simply to believe in Christ and to work thankfully for a better world. One must learn more techniques for manipulating God so as to garner greater wealth or heal more physical and emotional problems. If God heals a sore foot one week, he must surely be prepared to cure asthma the following week and to eliminate a heart murmur two weeks later. Or, if God raised a million dollars one month, he must raise more the next month to prove that he is really a sovereign Lord. As early as 1970 one observer remarked that the "Christian communicator must learn to tailor his messages to the audience at least as well as does Proctor & Gamble."[24] Today perhaps Phil Donahue would be an even more appropriate comparison than Proctor & Gamble.

Tabloid religious TV is not merely a simplification of the gospel but a distortion of its basic message. All preachers, including televangelists, invariably simplify complex scriptural passages and offer idealized applications of such texts. Moreover, Christian traditions of all kinds highlight some spiritual truths while downplaying others; in godly terms, there is no perfect preacher or church. Tabloid religion, however, runs against the very theological grain of the historic Christian church as affirmed in such broadly ecumenical statements as the Apostle's Creed and the Lord's Prayer. Health-and-wealth theologies challenge the biblical injunction that we pray for God's "will" instead of merely for our own wants and desires. Surely we may (and should) petition the Lord for what we *think* is best for ourselves and all humankind. Nevertheless, there is no perfect system or technique by which our faith can manipulate God for fantastic results. This is the ill-founded gospel of tabloid religion.

TV Sorcery

Like the nineteenth-century medicine man, the televangelist captivated by the audience-generating power of tabloid TV is caught in his own brand of modern sorcery. Unlike the medicine man, however, most TV preachers believe in the effectiveness of their own godly powers. The shaman was essentially a charlatan, although some ailing people were psychosomatically healed. Today's religiously inspired artist of tabloid TV generally believes in the distorted gospel of success he disseminates. He is taken in by his own televisual sleight-of-hand as well as by the typically American values of prosperity, individualism, and selfishness. Both types of crowd pleasers must give the audience what it wants to see and hear—faith in humankind's ability to overcome apparent hardships and achieve worldly success with the help of some mysterious power or secret formula.

Whether or not the sorcerer believes in his own powers is relatively unimportant. Far more significant, especially in televangelism, is whether the very system of audience-dependent communication will necessarily distort the truth and how damaging to the audience that distortion might be. Medicine man and televangelist alike, unless they are careful, will shift from being essentially harmless entertainers to evil deceivers. All sorcerers depend on the willingness of the audience to believe in their magical powers to perform extraordinary acts. Once that willingness becomes a demand for such acts, a sorcerer is no longer merely a magician but a true shaman. As tabloid religious TV increases the sensationalism stakes, leading televangelists to "up the incredible ante," the TV preacher is seen as a pseudo-god who can seemingly manipulate the world with his own words or actions. Although the televangelist may say that "only God heals" or "only God creates prosperity," his visual and aural message suggest otherwise: "You, too, can manipulate God."

That is a profoundly tempting message in a fallen world, and a cleverly deceptive one in a culture that greatly values individual power and personal initiative. Compared with the sermons of so many local pastors, who sometimes confuse theological or literary sophistication with practicality, the new sorcery is far more appealing. Most Americans are uninterested in a sermon's intellectual flair. They don't care about historical insights or linguistic nuances when interpreting Scripture; they crave practical, useful, effective techniques for improving their lot in life. Intellectualism seems irrelevant and pretentious in comparison to a simple, straightforward message that tells an audience exactly what to believe, and especially what to do. In an American cultural context the health-and-wealth gospel is among the most appealing messages. It offers a means of achieving what most people seem to want. Moreover, it does not depend upon theological sophistication, doctrinal savvy, or even scriptural knowledge. Best of all, the new sorcery does not require hard work, but only faith, regardless of how elusive.

Tabloid TV's sorcery conveys its own simple message of worldly salvation in a culture of considerable discontent with the organized church and with seemingly irrelevant preaching. As John Garrett suggested during the first decade of commercial TV, there is a crisis in American pews partly because of the verbal techniques of Protestant scholasticism, which turned sermons into theological lectures and emphasized intellectual over emotional responses. American parishioners crave relevance, stories and images, all of which they can get on the tube if not in the local pew.[25] The health-and-wealth preachers indeed give many people what they want—a relevant message that will seemingly help them to achieve the American Dream: a long, healthy, and prosperous life. And they directly deliver the message creatively and often persuasively to the parishioner's home, bypassing local pastors, denominational authorities, and other traditional roadblocks to popular success.

Just as boredom, curiosity, and hope led rural folks to the medicine show, similar motives deliver audiences to the new sorcerers. No matter how seemingly extravagant or outlandish their claims, these preachers offer amazingly appealing "good news" to hopeful and needy viewers. The new sorcery, aided by the rise of the charismatic and neo-pentecostal movements, is clearly a telling illustration of how cultures shape the gospel message, sometimes even perverting it in the name of relevance and popularity.

Post-Office Hucksters

The unorthodox gospel of televangelism is seen most clearly in the barrage of fund-raising letters sent to viewers who respond to on-air offers of various products. Televangelists frequently offer "free" books, pamphlets, and trinkets as a means of eliciting telephone calls and letters from unknown viewers. Then the viewers' names and addresses are used to solicit contributions. Some televangelists are frequently coy on the air about what kind of gospel they preach; in the "private" letters, mailed only to those who have responded to televized appeals, their real message is both revealing and frightening.

Consider the case of Pastor David Epley (Baptist Church of the Good Shepherd in Fort Lauderdale, Florida). Although not one of the major religious broadcasters, he uses the mails effectively to generate financial support for his ministry. In many respects his techniques reflect the worst aspects of televangelism's deceptive message of prosperity. Over the course of several years I received almost monthly letters from Pastor Epley, nearly every one promising me health and wealth. His mailings even let me decide what I wanted. I merely needed to check the appropriate box and send the return envelope with my "offering." Pastor Epley promised to pray personally for my needs, whether they be for relieving headaches, depression, or anxiety, or obtaining a new house or car—whatever. In fact, if the pastor did not list my particular desire, all I had to do was write it on one of the blank spaces for "other needs." To help convince me of the reality of God's healing and prospering power, Epley often included prayer-blessed tokens: a miniature bar of soap, a shiny new penny, sand and a small wooden cross from the Holy Land, a plastic glove, and even an empty plastic vial, which he would fill with anointed oil for $20 or more.

Pastor Epley's techniques are repeated over and over again among numerous televangelists. Oral Roberts, Kenneth Copeland, and others each have their own similar versions of this kind of direct-mail hucksterism. In effect they are selling various kinds of personal gain in the names of both Jesus and the televangelist, who frequently seem to be one and the same. Health and wealth of all types are made dependent on the prayers of and the offerings to the televangelist. Letters become the psuedo-personal link between viewers and God, with the televangelist as the high priest who controls the message flow. Rex Humbard writes in one of his letters that his "private study" is a place where he feels "so close to God" that he will pray for the viewer's "urgent personal prayers." Televangelist Marilyn Hickey writes that she wants to see "God bless and prosper his people as they study and read our magazine, *Time With Him.*" That magazine informs new believers that their "dreams can come true," that God's people are "possibility thinkers and doers and achievers of this generation. For them there are no obstacles in life—only challenges."[26] Hickey even tells believers in her letters that "you HAVE all the power in Jesus!" As a result, believers can "live in supernatural health" and in "divine prosperity in your finances," "experience success" and "more victory than ever before!"

In his *Believer's Voice of Victory* magazine, mailed to viewers, Kenneth Copeland offers his own prophecies direct from God. Copeland's words and God's words become one and the same. The televangelist explains how he stopped preaching the prosperity gospel for a while because he received criticism from some of his "closest friends in the ministry." Eventually, however, the Lord gave Copeland "release to preach it once again." As he explained it to readers, the Lord had "given me the release to preach it . . . with a greater anointing and a greater zeal than ever before. And this time I am preaching prosperity *through* the persecution and the criticism. I am at liberty to do what I know best, and that is to teach the abundant life in Christ." Copeland thanked viewers for "standing with" him. "And know, from the bottom of my heart, that *I want you to prosper.*"[27] Personalized letters from Copeland strongly encouraged viewers to contribute to building a new ministry center, which would help deliver this prosperity gospel to the entire world. In a booklet sent to new believers, Copeland told them, *"You have the right to live free from sickness and disease."*[28]

These kinds of personalized mailings deliver the new sorcery to interested viewers across the country. Compared with the actual broadcasts, they are even more obviously unorthodox and deceptive perversions of the Christian gospel. Such appeals display most candidly the real values and beliefs that animate many TV ministries. On the air the televangelists may couch their real beliefs in a somewhat orthodox package; in the mail they gear their appeals quite obviously to the selfish fallenness of their viewers and contributors. Regardless of whether or not these kinds of televangelists believe their own rhetoric, the messages are doctrinally bankrupt aberrations of the historic Christian faith.

The Right Stuff

As the Americanized gospel is increasingly market-driven, confirming what people want to believe about themselves and God, it is increasingly clear that the historic Christian faith no longer has the right stuff for this nation of individualism and abundance. People do not want what Buckminster Fuller called a "second-hand God." They want their own God, created in the culture's image, manipulated for personal gain, and hawked on the tube like snake oil.

Christianity Today's Kenneth Kantzer rightly criticized the "cut-rate grace" of the health-and-wealth gospel in a two-page editorial that clearly distinguished between it and historic evangelicalism. That "unbiblical gospel," he wrote in 1985, is "perverted" and makes "false promises" that lead to "unscriptural desires for wealth and material prosperity, to false hopes for perfect physical health, and in the end to false guilt and despair." Kantzer even mentioned popular televangelist Kenneth Copeland as one who mistakenly believes that humankind can be totally saved from the effects of the Fall before "the end times," when the bodies of believers are resurrected at Christ's Second Coming. God can heal, Kantzer insisted, but "God has never promised to heal here and now."[29]

One of the great dangers of televangelism is that it is able to deliver more aberrant messages to more people in less time than any previous mode of religious communication. In so doing, it has become far more than an identifiable religious movement with its own beliefs and practices. Like television programming generally, televangelism pervades American culture, distributing its diffuse messages to millions of people and crosscutting religious traditions by appealing directly to individuals. As a result, TV ministries have been shaping religious consciousness across the nation, delivering a warped gospel to hopeful Americans who represent all groups in the country's heterogeneous religious landscape. It is increasingly evident that what churchgoers consider to be the right theological stuff has been influenced by the new sorcery. The health-and-wealth gospel pervades the popular Christian media today and increasingly shapes local congregations' expectations of their pastors' preaching.

As the right stuff, televangelism has significantly influenced the nation's notions of piety. Those notions, in turn, were fabricated out of some of the most dynamic American values and beliefs. Perhaps it is not an exaggeration to say that a name-it-and-claim-it gospel may be the most remunerative and characteristic form of American Protestantism. Certainly it captures the aspirations and hopes of the lower and middle classes. It is interesting to note that many of the health-and-wealth televangelists have carved a market niche out of the usually less-educated working class and racial groups that aspire to middle-class status. In other words, the right stuff appeals strongly to people who are hopefully trying to climb out of their underprivileged place in the social order. For them especially, the prosperity gospel symbolizes the desire to get ahead in life. James Randi, in his provocative exposé of some corrupt itinerant healers, similarly found that the attendees of healing services were typically poor as well as in ill health.[30] The right stuff is most attractive to those who do not already have it.

Liberation Gospel

The new sorcery, as practiced by TV shamans and expressed in the health-and-wealth gospel, is the right stuff primarily in the United States. Some media preachers, such as Jim Bakker, Kenneth Copeland, and Oral Roberts, have garnered audiences in other nations, but the United States was always the source of their financial bread and butter. Some Third World countries in Latin America and Africa, have picked up on the new sorcery, often integrating it with native religions, but by and large prosperity preaching has been most successful in the United States. In Latin America the "liberation gospel" has been far more potent in recent years, providing a biblical context for poor and oppressed Christians to work for political and economic reform. Now, however, it appears that the new sorcery is offering its own Americanized version of a liberation theology.

By legitimizing certain American values, especially affluence, the health-and-wealth gospel liberates believers from the cultural shackles of fundamentalist faith. According to H. Richard Niebuhr's classic formulation of "Christ against culture," fundamentalist Christianity was usually militantly opposed to modern cultural life as expressed in liberal social mores and practices.[31] Fundamentalists shunned such things as make-up, revealing or ostentatious dress, worldly amusements like popular music and movies, and alcoholic beverages. They were to live separatist lives by rejecting the ways "of the world" around them. Obviously, fundamentalists were not without their own cultural definitives, just as the Amish rejected some industrial technologies like the automobile and substituted their own hand-made forms of transportation, especially the horse and buggy.

Usually, however, fundamentalists in the United States have opposed the cultural changes accompanying increased affluence. Money has created ostentatious expressions of wealth by individuals and families to distinguish themselves socially from less fortunate people—what Thorstein Veblen once called "conspicuous consumption."[32] Both what people bought and how they spent their leisure time established vivid cultural styles that separated conservative and liberal groups. Fundamentalists became the conservatives who guarded the cultural waters against the flood of worldliness represented principally in clothing and leisure activities. Across the religious spectrum, from Roman Catholicism to mainline Protestantism and certainly evangelicalism, every group has had its fundamentalists who challenged the values and practices of "modern" groups and individuals.

The health-and-wealth gospel fuels the co-optation of Christian fundamentalism by American values. Its sorcerers are magically liberating many evangelical conservatives from their self-imposed cultural restrictions. According to this new gospel, the Good News is not principally that individuals are saved from their sins, but that poor and ailing people are launched into wealth and health. Faith is the key that removes the shackles of poverty and affliction while ushering in the "fruits" of middle-class prosperity. Jim and Tammy Bakker's "PTL Club" program was the epitome of this kind of liberation; every show flaunted lifestyles that few viewers could afford but that were so very attractive. Tammy's make-up, Jim's freshly coiffed hair, both of their wardrobes, and their celebrated house-hunting and shopping all reflected a newfound freedom. As Bakker told his followers, God intended for them to be prosperous and successful.[33]

In the United States, liberation theology has taken on a task very different from its Latin American version. Although some Latin Americans from middle-class backgrounds have adopted the health-and-wealth gospel as a justification for their own privileged place in a generally poor society, this gospel is largely a North American phenomenon that embodies the hope that anyone can "make it" in life. Strongly influenced by fundamentalist attitudes toward culture, Latin American Protestantism is not nearly so vulnerable to the new gospel of cultural liberation. Televangelists have found that the United States is the most fertile culture for planting and growing health-and-wealth theologies. After all, this gospel emerged naturally from the imagination of hopeful and practical Americans who sought a faith that would work wonders and deliver abundant miracles.

Modern-Day Prophets

Are there not some "false prophets" on the airways? Consider that whereas televangelism's sorcerers are popular prophets who gain their authority from their fallible followers, biblical prophets derive authority from the inerrant Word of God. Televangelists are "inspired" by the apparent power of their messages to generate telephone calls, elicit mail, and build audience ratings, but true prophets are thankful if *anyone* heeds their messages. A prophet of the airways often tells people what they want to hear; a godly prophet preaches what people *should* hear—what they need to hear for their own spiritual good.

American televangelism has raised up a first and second generation of popular prophets whose revelations are little more than religious-sounding reformulations of secular values and beliefs. Not everyone thinks this is all bad. Ben Armstrong, for years executive director of National Religious Broadcasters, writes: "In the electric church power does not rest with the radio or television speaker—not even with a Billy Graham or a Jerry Falwell—but with the individual who has the power to turn the dial."[34] This is precisely what is so threatening about modern televangelism! Its market-driven prophets, dependent on the audience for financial survival, have no ultimate authority beyond the will of the people. As previously noted, in the United States that will is invariably the product of a rather superstitious culture that values individualism, selfishness, and affluence. Imagine an Amos or Habakkuk or even a Paul or John on television today. Their messages might indeed comfort the sick and poor, but not with a gospel of health and wealth.

Martin Marty once wrote that the "greater threat to the Christian faith today in the . . . communication field is not from the camp of the secularist but from the religionist." He realized that in a pluralistic society such as the United States any "successful" media religion must be "inoffensive to any minority, and the clarity of Biblical religion is necessarily denied." When religious media water down the prophetic witness of the Christian faith for mass consumption, "they contribute to making it a religion, a proper opinion of use to ideologist, advertiser, and demagogue."[35] Although not everyone likes or believes the new medicine men, American televangelists have packaged persuasive messages that will appeal to millions of former fundamentalists, liberated Pentecostals, upwardly mobile charismatics, and many others.

In Central America, where fundamentalism is now strongly entrenched, the new-style televangelist has not been perceived nearly as "prophetically" as in the United States. Jim and Tammy Bakker had their followers in Guatemala, Costa Rica, and other countries of the region, but Jimmy Swaggart was clearly the king of TV preachers. Almost like a Protestant pope, Swaggart was practically revered by Guatemalans (for instance), who watched him frequently in incredibly large numbers. Apparently Swaggart's old-style Pentecostalism, which favored strict moral codes and cultural taboos, was better attuned to Central America's fundamentalist ethos. Unlike their counterparts in the United States, evangelicals in nations like Guatemala had little use for the new kind of liberation theologian. They preferred modern-day prophets who preached sin and the Second Coming over those who spoke of the seemingly unattainable fruits of a health-and-wealth gospel. Only in the urban neo-pentecostal churches of Guatemala, where middle-class Catholics aspired to professional success and personal prosperity, did North American health-and-wealth preachers find interested audiences.[36]

Televangelism's prophets are typically much better at comforting middle-class believers than they are at defying these generally complacent upholders of conventional values. Rather than challenging their congregants to live truly Christian lives, such preachers feed viewers more of the existing spiritual somnolence. They seem more interested in building their own organizations and gaining popular support than they are in questioning flawed beliefs and values. Jimmy Swaggart was long an exception in this regard. But even his voice was only mildly prophetic, for it addressed almost exclusively the sins of individuals rather than the wayward and unjust ways of nations, cultures, and organizations. His calls to repentance were so personalistic that they, too, largely reflected American individualism.

Is it possible that contemporary televangelism, which so often breeds and spreads errant gospels, is one of the evil principalities and powers of our age? Surely televangelism is not "godly" simply because it uses the name of Jesus or claims to be doing the work of God's kingdom. Nor could we justify the deceptive forms of religious sorcery merely on account of anecdotal reports about how many "decisions" are made for Christ. Conversion is always made in the context of belief. What does a viewer who accepts the heart of the health-and-wealth gospel really believe? Above all, he must believe in individualism, prosperity, and selfishness—cardinal virtues of this land of opportunity.

Regardless of how religious the nation's founding fathers really were, there is no doubt that the kind of Christianity offered by the televangelists would have boggled the spiritual imagination of most Christians two hundred years ago. Today's TV gospel is not always unorthodox, but it is generally more afield from the historic Christian faith than most believers realize. If televangelists were in the media merely for personal gain, the situation would not be nearly so tragic. Instead, they are generally true believers in an aberrant gospel that promotes personal sorcery. Day after day, viewers see and hear individuals who really believe they have a prophetic calling to spread God's word. Little do they realize how much that word is more American than Christian.

Conclusion

The popularity of the health-and-wealth gospel in the United States is merely the latest saga in the history of a superstitious people. Science did not eliminate superstition. In fact, the media's popularization of scientific findings about health and psychology actually led to what John C. Burnham calls the victory of superstition over science in the United States. Ironically, the quest in journalism for objectivity led to the popularization of scientific "facts" about health without a coherent and rational context for interpreting the limited scientific methods that produced such facts.[37] As a result, Americans knew a lot of facts but they did not necessarily think more rationally or scientifically. Nor were they able to see such facts in the context of a unified Christian worldview. Media-fostered superstition prevailed in public opinion, in spite of people's confidence in their own rationality.

Televangelism has reaped the benefits of that superstitiousness for the sake of building its own media empires. Just as state lotteries give many people hope for an imminently better life that is filled with the riches of prosperity, televangelism often feeds the nation's unquenchable thirst for practical "good news" that God is on their side in the battle for health and wealth. Most televangelists have been at least mildly influenced by a new sorcery, which appears magically able to manipulate God. Some of them, such as Roberts and Copeland, are strongly committed to a prosperity gospel. Others, including Schuller and Robertson, have taken up the health-and-wealth themes without advocating the sorcery that sometimes goes with it.

For many televangelists it is not easy to accept the necessary conclusion that the authentic gospel will always be offensive and scandalous to some people. Because the gospel is a two-edged sword, condemning some people while saving others, its message will never be broadly accepted by the mass audiences of American commercial television. Most televangelists try to make the message more palatable and deceptively attractive. Many of them have warped the gospel for the purpose of building audiences, soliciting contributions and expanding the ministry. There are exceptions, such as Billy Graham, who is not really a televangelist (according to the characteristics outlined in chapter 1), and Charles Stanley of Atlanta, who continues to broadcast sermons from actual church services. Certainly the Radio Bible Class program "Day of Discovery" is the lowest-profile exception among the top-ten weekly programs.

Christ's own communication with the disciples was frequently ineffective, falling on deaf ears that wanted and expected to hear a very different message. That probably frustrated Jesus, who needed much patience to work with his own followers, let alone with a national-TV-sized audience. It appears that market-driven televangelists will invariably be tempted to "improve" their communication by adapting the content and style of the message to the viewers' hopes and value systems. Most TV ministries have succumbed to this temptation. Once that is done, however, the gospel has been misinterpreted and diluted, if not dangerously distorted.

Ironically, the church in the United States sees the danger of market-driven messages in secular television more than in religious programming. Christians blast the networks for their sex-

and-violence shows, which have been shown repeatedly to attract more viewers in the competitive audience-ratings race. Meanwhile, the same believers overlook the ways that viewer-dependent televangelism sells its theological soul to the health-and-wealth gospel as a way of building ratings and financial support.

Many American Christians maintain that believers should not criticize other believers, especially in a public forum. That is sage advice, but it ignores the necessary role of the public prophet in the church. Christianity needs critical voices that will speak openly against the principalities and powers of every age, including those that masquerade as godly people or Christ-centered organizations while prostituting their spirituality for the sake of establishing a large constituency. After all, the church must afflict the comfortable, not just comfort the afflicted. As Martin Marty has argued, the Good News will always be an "improper opinion" in the world. The gospel, by its very nature, contradicts public opinion in a fallen, sinful world alienated from God.[38] No mass ministry that is pandering to the will of its fallen audience will be able to hold true to the gospel. Instead, it will become the most devilish kind of prophet, building people up in the image of what they would like to become, not in the image of what God would have them become as redeemed saints.

The health-and-wealth gospel is possibly the most market-driven distortion of Christianity in the contemporary United States. Like the New Age movement, which includes faith healing, it captures a more socially acceptable faith that seemingly harmonizes the historic gospel with the present cultural milieu.[39] Based on business principles, where marketing is king, it attempts to feed American sheep with a decidedly American gospel of individualism, prosperity, and selfishness. In such a setting the televangelist can easily become the latest medicine man, first attracting viewers to his show with sensationalism and then selling them the latest cure for poverty or ailments. If the cure does not work, the viewer has only himself to blame; he must not have followed the directions or been a good enough magician. The eternal paradox—the promise of God to redeem believers' souls and bodies, yet the enduring hardship of so many individuals—cannot be resolved by the health-and-wealth preacher who invests our hope in this world. God is everlastingly sovereign, and *full* redemption will come only after a believer's physical death. Unfortunately, modern televangelism often denies that biblical truth, demanding full redemption here and now. God does heal and prosper his people in this world, but only according to *his* will, not the will of the majority or the will of any one individual in this materialistic and self-centered culture.

The new sorcery is ultimately human-centered as well as market-driven. It looks at what human beings can supposedly get God to do for them, not at what God has already accomplished through the death of Christ on the cross, his resurrection, and his triumphant return. Any truly God-centered gospel would recognize that people can accomplish little in their fallen state and that individuals foul up pretty badly the very things they are trying to improve. Televangelism itself shows how desperately humankind needs the Triune God, not some aberrant, self-oriented gospel. Even if health-and-wealth sorcery worked, what good would it do a fallen humankind? What would people ask for? What would they do with what they receive? Perhaps the answers to those questions explain why God has indeed decided to be our God and call us his children.

The Greening of the Gospel

T
en years ago I wrote to about a hundred of the most popular radio and television preachers and asked for information about their ministries. In a short, direct letter I requested the following: a financial statement, a doctrinal statement, and an indication of whether donations were tax deductible. I used my home address and waited for the replies. Within two weeks the first letters arrived, cheerfully delivered by my friendly mailman.

After a month it was clear that I would receive far more—and less—than I had bargained for with my simple letter of inquiry. Although I received only a few financial statements and fewer doctrinal statements, I had become the neighborhood postal drop-off point for much more. Not only would the mail frequently not fit in my wall-mounted box, but sometimes the letter carrier had to drive his jeep up my driveway to make a special delivery of a dozen or more letters, packages, and magazines—all from religious broadcasters. My friend soon inquired about the explosion in my mail: "Are you running a business of some kind out of your home?" (Not long after that, he took early retirement, moving from Michigan to Colorado.)

Months later, as I daily sorted through the deluge of mail elicited by my original letter, it occurred to me that the mailman nearly had it right. I *was* involved in a business, but I was the customer, not the seller. The vast majority of letters I received from the radio and television evangelists were designed to raise funds by peddling membership in the ministry, hawking various kinds of religious products such as books and tapes, and directly soliciting contributions. There was little doubt that my initial inquiry had largely served to get me on the broadcasters' lists of potential donors, not to generate responses to my questions. Only the tax deductibility of the donations was clearly stated in the vast majority of letters I received. It appeared that the essential purpose of these ministries was to raise funds, not edify, educate, or convert to Christ. In fact, nearly all the materials I received from these organizations over the next nine years simply assumed that I was already a Christian and that my principal vocation in life was to give money to their ministries.

Certainly there were exceptions—the ministries of Radio Bible Class and Charles Swindoll, to name two of the more prominent ones. But the overall impression generated by the deluge of mail I received was that religious broadcasting is primarily a business, not a ministry. Appeals for funds dominated the mail, just as they sometimes do the broadcasts. During the same period, I video-taped a Sunday-morning Oral Roberts telecast for use in class the next day. Since I was involved in church activities that Sunday, I did not see the program until I viewed the taping with my students the following morning. For twenty-eight minutes we watched Roberts stand in his half-completed medical complex in Tulsa and beg for contributions. Then he delivered a thirty-second homily. That was the entire program, and the students were furious—not with Roberts, but with me. They assumed that I had selected the show particularly to make Roberts look like a huckster, rather than simply an honorable man doing the Lord's work.

In this chapter I do not intend to impugn the ultimate motives of any televangelists. Indeed, I do not believe along with many ill-informed journalists that televangelists are "in it" primarily for personal financial gain. Rather, I wish to argue that televangelism as an institution is increasingly based on the techniques of modern marketing. As a result, televangelism "greens" the gospel by associating it repeatedly with pecuniary values and financial objectives. Because big-time, nondenominational televangelism is so expensive, televangelists find themselves as much businessmen as ministers. Their goals of ministry and evangelization are so confused with their financial imperatives that televangelists in the United States become de-facto entrepreneurs, managers, and fund-raisers.

Of course there is a long history of the relationship between business and religion, not excluding Christianity. In Calvinism the acquisition of earthly treasures was significantly tied to the assumed blessing of God—and not without biblical warrant. In many parts of the world, from Europe to Latin America, the Roman Catholic church was for centuries among the richest organizations. In some of its worst excesses, the Roman prelates built the church by selling indulgences to sinful members who sought the freedom to engage in evil practices while being guaranteed absolution from their sins. Even in Old Testament times the acquisition of property, agricultural production, and the collection of precious metals were associated with religious as well as secular life. The church has not always been a business *per se,* but it has typically been enmeshed in the business practices of the day. Televangelism is the modern-American version of such financial and religious entanglements.

Although today's televangelists are not usually driven by the desire to build personal capital and line their own pockets with money, they are increasingly dependent upon the strategies of modern advertising, sales promotion, marketing, and management. Accordingly, they base their organizational decisions less and less on distinctly biblical guidelines and more and more on the pragmatic goals of building large, popular "ministries." Like contemporary entrepreneurs, they repeatedly risk their existing "capital" in the effort to expand the ministry on the airways and invest in related ventures, such as universities and Jim and Tammy Bakker's Heritage U.S.A. theme park. This type of entrepreneurial spirit led Oral Roberts into the fields of medical research and hospital care; it also nearly cost him the ministry by plunging it into enormous debt, which could not easily be met through on-the-air or direct-mail fund-raising. The same spirit made it relatively easy for Pat Robertson to move from televangelism to other religious broadcasting to secular programming. From the beginning he had used the principles of successful commercial broadcasting.

Many viewers are attracted to the electronic church because of its apparent spiritual vitality, social and personal relevance, and spontaneity. Compared with their own denominations and local churches, which often seem too orderly, bureaucratic, and spiritually lifeless, televangelism seems vibrant and engaging. What such viewers generally fail to realize, however, is that the image cultivated by televangelism is not so much the spontaneous working of the Holy Spirit as it is the carefully planned result of managerial and financial decisions. Behind a program's televisual appeal is typically a relatively pragmatic group of talented technical advisors and businesspeople who have learned what "sells" on the tube and what does not.

So, even if most televangelists are not motivated principally by greed or personal financial gain, they reflect a society that puts a lot of emphasis on the worldly fruits of success, including social status, power, and prestige. And TV ministries mirror the nation's tendency to see business as the route to such success. The result is that televangelism takes on the means and methods of American business even while claiming to be in the "business" of ministry.

The Spirit of American Business

It may seem strange to refer to the "spirit" of American business, although Max Weber, in his landmark study of the relationship between business and religion, wrote of the "spirit of capitalism."[1] Just as Christianity expects believers to live "in the spirit," contemporary business practices are animated by a "spirit" of one type or another. Some businesspeople are driven by greed, others by the love of money or even a desire to serve others or to make a quality product. Commerce can be motivated by many different "spirits," some good and others clearly evil. The point is that "business" is not merely the process of buying and selling a product or service; it is also a *way* of conducting those activities and a *motivation* for doing so.

In this regard the United States is not exactly like other nations. For one thing, the American spirit of business is highly entrepreneurial. From the early colonies to the present, commerce has been fashioned by individual risk-takers who put capital into various enterprises with the hope of making a profit. For another, American business has been promotion-oriented, certainly from the late nineteenth-century to the present. More than in most countries, businesspersons in the United States spent a lot on promoting, not just producing, their products. It is safe to say that this nation provided fertile soil for the development of modern advertising techniques. Finally, American business is highly competitive. Producers, wholesalers, and retailers have always been locked in recurring cycles of competition that abated only when monopolies formed or when the government decided to regulate commerce.

This entrepreneurial-promotional-competitive spirit was enabled and abetted by the nation's sense of individual freedom. To an amazing degree, Americans have truly been free to pursue their own business interests in their own ways. Although not all individuals or social groups had the education or capital necessary to enter the business world, except as laborers for others, the American economy was fueled by a sense that anyone was free to practice business, in the broad sense of the word. Consumers may have sometimes been sold inferior products or given poor service, but they generally had the freedom to refuse to buy those products or use those services again. In other words, business freedom sometimes helped and at other times hurt the interests of consumers, especially in the short run. To protect consumers from harmful or socially damaging products (such as environmentally unsafe ones), the government has enacted regulations. The goal in such restrictions on freedom is not to interfere with the free market *per se,* but to ensure that the broader interests of society are not trammeled by greed, insensitivity, or lack of conscience.

In the United States, then, freedom has both political and economic aspects. Consumers are taught to "beware" *(caveat emptor)* precisely because economic freedom exists and government regulation has limits. Business freedom generates a plethora of new products, even if most of them fail in the marketplace. Unlike Eastern Europe, for example, America's economic challenge has not been to produce more, but to consume more. A free marketplace creates so many sellers that they have to worry about convincing people to buy their products. Hence, promotion, especially advertising, weighs heavily in American business plans. In religion, with so many different churches and denominations, there is likewise such a variety of products that sellers typically have to hawk their wares to gain an economically effective voice in the cacophony of disparate voices.

Along with this spirit of business—entrepreneurial, promotional, competitive—has come a parallel emphasis on consumption. If Americans like to produce, especially at a profit, they surely like even more to consume at a good price. The spirit of selling has produced a seemingly unquenchable thirst to buy. Americans hardly buy only to meet needs. For most of the middle and upper classes, consumption is also a way of relieving boredom and simply having fun, such as a trip to the shopping mall or a vacation. A mail-order company in Maine sells live lobsters to people all over the country. As the head of the firm's telemarketing department observes, selling the critters is only part of his problem. He answers a steady stream of calls from customers who have received their lobsters but do not know what to do next—despite the cooking instructions that are packed in each shipment.[2] Americans will sell and buy practically anything, even if they are not sure how to use the product. Birthdays and the holiday season are often stressful times for buyers, who search madly for the right gift for friends and relatives who really have all they need. Christmas shopping today epitomizes the American spirit of business, as buyers and sellers plunge head first into the world of commerce, fulfilling their roles in the ongoing drama of production and consumption.

Part of this business spirit is the symbolic significance of products and services. Producers do not just make "things"; they offer values, from optimism to youthfulness, and from sexiness to happiness. The country's economic freedom has had decidedly cultural consequences. Everywhere one turns are products that offer far more than a simple utility. Lobsters are not just a nutritional food; they are symbols of the good life and a particular level of affluence. Lobster is not for everyone; some people truly do not like the flavor. The same goes for crab, yet stores sell artificial crab legs made from the flesh of less expensive fish.

Behind the American scene always lurk images of the evils of its business spirit. In Arthur Miller's "Death of a Salesman," Willy Loman captures the pitiful vestige of a man who could never become the great businessman he had sought to become for his family and himself. Yet the decadence that frequently follows affluence is evident throughout the country. This, after all, was the nation of parvenus and plutocrats, of people whose business success created status and power without the encumbrances of European wealth, which was typically tied historically to one's family and class. As sociologist Hugh Duncan argued, the American Midwest, especially Chicago, became the most fertile soil for the new spirit of business and the resulting culture of consumption.[3] It seemed in the imagination of Midwesterners that anyone could make it, just like Horatio Alger, with enough luck and pluck. In reality, not all could, and not all would, except in their own dreams cultivated by the advertisers. Not all businesspeople were created equal, any more than were all preachers. But the dominant message was clear: "You can make it." That slogan, used by televangelist Jim Bakker, captured the fundamental mythic unity between American business and TV's popular evangelicalism.

Over the last two centuries, as the spirit of American business infused its methods and ideals into virtually every crack and crevice of society, almost everything became a product, including religion. The spirit of entrepreneurship, promotion, and competition has influenced all aspects of American life, from politics to the media and the church.

Evangelicalism and Business

Throughout the history of the United States, business and religion have shaped each other's characteristics. In particular, evangelicalism and business have exchanged values, practices, and the same overall spirit described previously. Evangelicalism, like business, has been remarkably entrepreneurial, highly promotional, and tenaciously competitive. The spirit of entrepreneurship is best seen in the long succession of evangelical leaders—from George Whitefield to Charles Finney, Billy Sunday, and Jimmy Swaggart. The promotional spirit is most evident in the unsquelchable desire among evangelicals to communicate their faith to unbelievers by using all available media and often the latest commercial techniques.[4] And the competitive spirit is obvious in American evangelicalism's penchant for schism and variety. Even more than their mainline Protestant counterparts, evangelicals have had enormous difficulty working together and forming common organizations. They apparently find it much easier to compete than to cooperate. National Religious Broadcasters, an evangelical trade group, is a case in point. Annual conventions emphasize workshops on how individual televangelists can improve their "business," while very few meetings seriously address the need to work together.

Largely because of evangelicalism's emphasis on spreading the gospel, however, it has been a champion of communication, especially persuasion. Like business, evangelicalism is expansionary and totalistic. Its ideal is to have "total market share" before the Lord Jesus Christ returns. Evangelicalism is naturally in the practice of spreading the message, converting people, and promoting the faith among unbelievers while keeping old customers coming back for more—revivalism. This affinity explains why James F. Engel, one of the most respected scholars of consumer behavior

and author of a major text on the subject, would also be an evangelical who used contemporary behavioral theories and research
to help people spread the gospel of Christ.[5] The goals of business
and evangelicalism are remarkably similar in the United States:
to establish a solid market for a product. Although it is ridiculous
to speak of Christ as a mere "product," the affinities in style and
technique between televangelism and contemporary advertising
are clear and cogent.

One of the most telling examples is the 1970s' campaign of
Campus Crusade for Christ: "Here's Life, America." Across North
America the organization enlisted local support for the campaign,
which was heralded as one of the greatest evangelistic efforts of
all time. Billboards ran the simple teaser ads, "I found it!" and
other media played supporting roles. As if it were designed to
unfold a new product, the campaign never told the public up front
what exactly the product was—salvation through Christ. Instead
the ads got curious individuals to call a local telephone number
staffed by volunteers who presented the gospel via the "four spiritual laws." Under the anonymity of a phoned sales pitch, callers
could supposedly decide whether or not to accept Christ as their
Lord and Savior. This kind of evangelistic effort clearly reflected
the techniques and strategies of American mass marketing.[6]

At least from the nineteenth-century urban revivalists to the
present, American evangelicalism has strongly reflected this type
of business-oriented approach.[7] Indeed, evangelism was increasingly defined as a problem of marketing and mass communication,
not principally as a spiritual or theological challenge. Pragmatic
American evangelicals in the twentieth century have been largely
disinterested in pursuing spiritually authentic lives and greatly
preoccupied with converting people to Christ. In fact, in many
evangelical circles the conversion experience, the moment of
accepting Christ as one's personal Savior, is the essence of the
faith. As church services repeat the formulaic altar calls and
"recommitments" over and over again, faith becomes, like a consumer product, something that can be lost and found from one
minute to the next. As with the purchase of new clothes, which for
a short time create a sense of personal newness and identity, the
cheaper versions of popular evangelicalism transform faith into
little more than a transient feeling or momentary decision. Televangelists piggyback on this phenomenon, repeatedly informing
their contributors how many "decisions" were made by people

watching their shows. It is never clear if these are old or new decisions, or, more importantly, exactly what the decision meant to an individual. In the consumer world, knowledge about a product is rarely as important as the feeling it creates for the buyer. So is it often in televangelism.

Historian Perry Miller persuasively argued that in America missionary activity and industrial development were perceived as two sides of the same work of God.[8] As we saw in chapter 2, this partly reflected the nation's technological optimism. It also was evidence of how Americans have identified evangelism with business. After all, American business exhibited the same kind of promotional hype, competitive edge, and entrepreneurial flavor that characterized much of evangelical missionary work. Methodist circuit riders paid their own way partly by selling books and pamphlets, much as today's televangelists offer premiums to keep the contributions flowing. As emotional persuaders, popular evangelists reflected the rising tide of the mass propaganda eventually called advertising. In fact a number of the legendary "founding fathers" of modern advertising were destined for careers in the ministry. Among them was Claude Hopkins, who pioneered various kinds of product copywriting in the 1920s and 1930s.[9]

Today the close affinity between American evangelicalism and contemporary business is especially clear in so-called multi-level marketing, where individual distributors recruit new distributors to sell their products for a commission. For many strong "believers" in this type of business, their work is a way of life that expresses faith in the system, not just a job or a means of making money. As pastor Steve Schlissel has noted, multi-level marketing "literature is often liturgical in form. It contains *praises* for the company and/or its leaders, *thanksgiving* for its products, *testimonies* to the greatness of both, *confessions* of doubts, and even songs of adoration." He adds that for multi-level marketers "'church' can meet in small groups (devotionals?) or large auditoriums. In the latter the atmosphere is truly reminiscent of tent revivals in both program and intensity."[10] Not surprisingly, the styles and techniques of multi-level marketing are mirrored in large segments of popular evangelicalism.

The church-growth movement also reflects the business-evangelism affinity. Like many contemporary evangelistic strategies, the movement is heavily dependent on contemporary marketing. Jeff Whan, marketing director for Church Growth International, puts it this way: "Those within Church Growth are realizing that to compete with television and movies, we had to reevaluate some of the traditional methods of church growth." He believes that tele-marketing is one of the effective methods emerging in the movement. For an average cost of only $4,000, plus many hours of volunteer time, a local telemarketing campaign can be launched. According to Whan, it is purely a matter of resources; if enough people are called, the campaign will work. One church logged 14,000 calls in one month by calling for four hours, six days a week.[11] Of course many secular businesses, from lawn care to cemeteries, use the same technique.

While churches and televangelists have adopted many business techniques, business in turn has borrowed the evangelistic rhetoric of salvation. Consumer advertising promises to save the distraught public from bad breath, inferiority, boredom, loneliness, unhappiness, unpopularity, sexual unfulfillment, and all of the other "sins" of American life. One Japanese automobile manufacturer, touting its low-cost automobiles, claims that "Datsun saves." Christ is *the* answer for the church, but only when the church gets to pose the question: "Saved from what?" In the United States there are many competing saviors from many different things, and not just sin. Everywhere one turns there are advertising and publicity campaigns hawking one type of salvation or another. They all use a hyperbolic rhetoric of salvation to create awareness and thus sell their products and services—to peddle their solutions to what *they* define as humankind's problems. Here, too, televangelists are among them, imitating the strategies of contemporary marketing that work for consumer products.

Preacher as Salesman

It should not be surprising, then, that to the casual viewer many televangelists seem to be hucksters hawking their wares. In American culture there is often a fine line between a business salesman and a preacher. Successful advertising executive Bruce Barton captured this relationship in 1924 in his bestselling novel *The Man Nobody Knows.*[12] Barton depicted Jesus as an early advertising genius and his disciples as a group of marketing executives. Jesus became the greatest entrepreneur ever—a super salesman with a dynamite product. Reflecting deep American sentiment, the hardcover edition sold over half a million copies, and the paperback remained in print into the 1990s. As historian

Patrick Allitt has argued, Barton's view of Jesus was a telling depiction of an *American* Christ who saved by selling the greatest product ever.[13]

Both on the air and through the mail, televangelists have to persuade potential contributors of the value of their ministry to the kingdom of God. They cannot just preach the Word of God; they have to persuade viewers that the ministry's work merits their financial support. Since without such support they will simply disappear from the airways, televangelists have their own appeals or selling strategies that have proved to be effective over and over again. Their persuasive tactics include promises of blessings upon those who contribute; threats that the ministry will go off the air if funds are not raised immediately; claims that contributions are synonymous with the will of God; charges that impediments to the growth of the ministry are the work of the devil; exaggerations of the ministry's impact (puffery); claims that the televangelist has a privileged relationship to God. These are the standard pitches used by these televisual hucksters—religious salesmen who use the airways to spread their own brands of popular religion.

Because such appeals are not always enough, televangelists sometimes have to offer "free" premiums as an incentive for people to contribute. To overcome sales resistance they provide a tangible product in return for a contribution to the ministry. Carl Wallace, director of administration for Robert Schuller's "Hour of Power" program, put it this way: "You can't just preach the gospel and wait for the money to come in. . . . It doesn't happen that way. You've got to offer some incentive for people to communicate with you. The minute we stop offering gifts, our revenues go down dramatically."[14]

Most televangelists, dependent on their audiences for financial support, become salesmen of far more than the gospel. Jimmy Swaggart is probably one of the top-selling gospel recording artists of all time, although his album sales were never certified by the Recording Industry Association of America because he sold them direct to consumers via television and his monthly magazine, not through record stores. Robert Schuller has sold millions of knickknacks, primarily jewelry with religious significance. In recent years Jerry Falwell has concentrated on selling enrollments in the Liberty University School of Lifelong Learning (LUSLL), an accredited home-study program leading to a bachelor's degree.

During the spring and summer of 1989, about 16,000 television viewers responded positively to Falwell's special tuition and scholarship offers.[15] From special Bibles to lapel pins and magazine subscriptions, televangelists sell products to generate a "profit" that will be used to pay media expenses and frequently to expand the ministry by purchasing land, erecting buildings, and buying the latest communications equipment.

Because of the ongoing costs of their ministries, from media bills to salaries and building overhead, these TV salesmen have to return again and again to the viewers for support. Like full-commission salespeople, they cannot rest on their persuasive laurels, hoping for a benefactor to appear or for a rich uncle to leave them a healthy bequest in his will. As a result, many televangelism programs look and sound like the home-shopping channels on cable television. One study found that if the average female viewer watched only two hours of televangelism weekly, she would be solicited for an average of nearly $20,000 in the course of a year. If the same viewer watched only preaching or revival programs (not, for example, talk shows), the figure would climb to over $33,000 annually.[16] Of course, few individuals give that much, but televangelists do elicit a considerable amount from viewers. One study of viewers in West Michigan found that the average gift was $339 per year, compared with the average gift of $420 to local churches.[17]

The selling does not stop with the audience and the supporting constituency, however. A televangelist, like any business executive, has to sell the ministry to his own staff, not just to potential "buyers." Just as some advertising agencies and manufacturers expect their employees to use their client's or their company's products, some televangelists expect their employees to attend their own churches and even to tithe. Generally speaking, televangelists are rather autocratic leaders who anticipate organizational loyalty and sometimes demand it. Not all employees are so enthusiastic about everything a ministry does, however, so they have to be repeatedly sold on the purpose and vision of their leader. Since evangelism is usually the guiding purpose that holds these organizations together, not many employees (if they are truly evangelicals) will dispute that objective. As a result, the selling job is rather easy; staff members want to believe that the ministry is a significant force for national and international evangelization, even if the day-to-day reality suggests that such an idealistic objective is inflated to mythic proportions.

Some of the most popular televangelists are notable for their personal charisma and persuasive charm. They are natural salesmen who can convince audiences to contribute while also persuading employees to work long and hard for the good of the ministry. Men such as Jerry Falwell, Oral Roberts, and Pat Robertson fit this mold perfectly. They effortlessly convey enthusiasm and excitement to those around them. Among other things, this has helped them sell potential employees on the ministry, luring them from other positions that often paid more and carried more social status in secular society.

The common evangelical goal of bringing people to Christ essentially depends on persuasive appeal. In televangelism it enables even some of the most autocratic leaders to maintain *esprit de corps* in their organizations and keep the contributions flowing into the ministry's coffers. Internal conflict can usually be dissipated when a ministry waves the evangelistic banner. Moreover, viewers who may not agree with a televangelist's politics or with his view on a particular moral issue are not likely to ignore the same banner. The ultimate product that televangelists sell—hope in the power of the media to evangelize the world—does not die easily. After the PTL scandal and even though Jim Bakker was sent to federal prison, many die-hard followers continued to support Jim and Tammy because of what they represented as media evangelists. Sexual and financial misdeeds paled in comparison to the necessity of winning people to Christ. Evangelism is an easy sell, even for autocratic leaders, who sometimes frustrate their own management with half-baked fund-raising schemes and unchallenged "visions" for the ministry.

In recent years some of the most popular televangelists have enhanced their entrepreneurial credibility by donning the clothes and adopting the language of corporate executives. Today's TV preachers look and sound less like old-style evangelists or revivalists and more like successful business leaders. During his 1988 presidential campaign, Pat Robertson understandably denounced reporters who continued to refer to him as a televangelist. Robertson wished to be known as "a successful broadcaster," or at least "a religious broadcaster," terms that conveyed far more civic responsibility and corporate success than "televangelist." He was not simply trying to distance himself from the scandal-ridden world of televangelism, as some journalists incorrectly assumed. Robertson was really at the forefront of a new breed of religious broadcasters who wished to be known more for their managerial, corporate, and professional abilities than for their narrower abilities as proclaimers of the gospel. The same kind of change took place in the public presentations of Jerry Falwell, who was increasingly depicted as a corporate leader flying around the country in his private jet, buying property for his expanding organization, establishing a respected university, and advising various political leaders. Even Jimmy Swaggart's television solicitations, compared with his preaching segments, reflected a growing sense of managerial prowess and organizational skill rather than raw evangelistic talent.

However one looks at it, televangelism reflects contemporary American business. Televangelists are preacher-salesmen who pitch their own ministries while broadly trying to sell the gospel. Their task is complicated by the need to please both employees and contributors, but it is made possible by the common goal of evangelism. No matter how godly an image they are able to cultivate, televangelists *must* be good salesmen, for without that talent they could neither evangelize nor keep their organizations intact.

Mail-Order Religion

Televangelism's popularity stems from its commanding presence on the tube, but its financial success depends to a large extent on well-calculated use of the postal service. The programs pursue personalized audience contact via the mail or telephone, which becomes the basis for follow-up appeals and solicitations. Through regular mailings to viewers and especially to known contributors, televangelists are able to (1) create a stronger sense that a viewer-contributor "owns" the ministry; (2) establish a seemingly authentic personal relationship between the televangelist and the individual viewer; and (3) enlist the audience in a national or international movement that seems to have significant power and influence. As the regular mailings elicit increased contributions, the financial aims become part of these three objectives. If viewers believe that they are part of the ministry, that they have an authentic bonding with the televangelist, and that the ministry has broad influence in at least the United States, they are more likely to become contributors. Communication through the mail thus becomes a crucial part of the business of televangelism.

During the 1970s and 1980s most of the major televangelists adopted the same direct-mail techniques that had proven successful with other nonprofit groups and some for-profit organizations, from international-aid agencies, to political fund-raisers. Televangelists hired outside consultants to fine-tune their on-air appeals, build large mailing lists, and compose effective direct-mail "packages" (which normally include a carefully crafted letter with an eye-catching design, a return card, and an envelope). A packaged concept could cost as much as $20,000 if purchased from a firm specializing in such solicitations. These kinds of mailings would frequently be used by a number of different ministries, proving that certain standard techniques were almost universally successful. Normally, however, the larger televangelism organizations would eventually go "in house" with their fund-raising after initial help from well-paid consultants. The more sophisticated in-house operations are able to target particular kinds of supporters for specific appeals. In any case, the letters are generally personalized by inserting the name of the contributor repeatedly in the letter and are written as if to a special friend, not to a stranger on a list of thousands of distant supporters.

The development of sophisticated direct-mail techniques can be seen clearly in the ministry of D. James Kennedy in the 1980s. The Fort Lauderdale pastor was best known for his "Evangelism Explosion" program, which was used by thousands of churches in the country to evangelize their neighborhoods. A gifted preacher with a direct, sophisticated style of delivery, Kennedy was a far cry from the histrionics of the Bakkers or the sheer dramatic engagement of Swaggart. Kennedy's original television program was little more than exegetical, expository preaching from his own Sunday services. More and more, however, Kennedy preached on currently hot political and moral issues. At the same time, his direct-mail appeals reflected the careful work of professional writers and designers.

Kennedy's letters are meant to engage recipients in the work of the ministry by tying the ministry to the latest public issue that is likely to motivate evangelicals. Most mailings immediately gain a recipient's attention with startling phrases on the envelope: "ACLU takes Christ out of Christmas!"; "Stop the Bloodbath: Petition Enclosed"; "How *Your* Tax Dollars Are Funding Pornographic

Art." The letter proceeds to indicate how Kennedy's Coral Ridge Ministries is going to "fight against" particular evils in society—of course with the financial support of viewers and other contributors. Kennedy's major technique has been the "petition" or "survey," in which he solicits viewers' opinions on issues that currently outrage many Americans and are widely reported in the news media. In this way the respondent comes to "own" the ministry by feeling that his or her views are being represented in public by someone with authority and media status. Kennedy becomes a viewer's personal representative in the national battles against evil.

Without using the survey technique, televangelist Dwight Thompson achieves the same personalized effect with his regular letters. This up-and-coming televangelist presents to recipients one cause after another: saving souls before Christ returns; saving youth from the ravages of despair and even suicide; helping the individual supporter to "make it to the top" in life; teaching the church how to pray effectively; helping Christians to "conquer Satan." Compared with Kennedy's letters they are far less issue-oriented and politicized. Instead they focus largely on evangelism and personal faith development. Nevertheless, the overall strategy to engage supporters in the work of the ministry remains the same. Once they join Dwight Thompson World Outreach Ministries, the letters suggest, they will be part of a major force for Jesus Christ in the world. All contributions and premiums become part of God's plan via the televangelist.

Jerry Falwell has even found that direct-mail appeals can effectively entice viewers to enroll in his Liberty University School of Lifelong Learning. Television spots on Falwell's "Old-Time Gospel Hour" generate the prospects, who respond by mail or telephone and are then sent persuasive appeals designed to move them to sign up for LUSLL courses. One mailing, an oversized card with large black and red lettering that looks like a sale announcement from a local furniture store or franchised chicken-dinner operation, announces: "For A Limited Time Only . . . We'll Cut Your Tuition By 50%." A follow-up "Compugram," designed to look like a personal telegram, reminds recipients of the tuition incentive. Later letters, mailed by the "LUSLL Scholarship Committee," announce an "outright grant" of $4,000 for new students. Finally, a card from LUSLL's Director of Admissions indicates that one of the "very last" scholarships has been reserved for the recipient.

The boom in direct-mail campaigns by televangelists underscores the general observation that few are simply in the business of saving souls. They are increasingly involved in being in *business*, which means creating causes and developing spin-off ministries that will look attractive to potential donors. By and large, contemporary televangelism survives because of its carefully cultivated business practices, including "selling" mail-order religious knickknacks, books, recordings, jewelry, and even education. Jerry Falwell's ministry is an excellent example. By 1990 it was clear that he was as much in the "business" of education as he was in the "business" of soulwinning.

Direct-mail campaigns tell the story of a ministry from its own perspective. Like secular public-relations efforts, the campaigns emphasize some parts of the story while ignoring others. They are fictionalized accounts of what the ministry really is, designed to create a sense of what the ministry *could* become if donors will help write a happy ending by opening their wallets and checkbooks and credit-card accounts. A company called "Response Unlimited" rents out the mailing lists of certain TV ministries. One list of over 200,000 "donors and responders to a full-gospel television ministry" is called "enthusiastic Christians" in the company's catalog. There are also lists of "Cream-of-the-Crop PTL Donors" (70,000), "Rex Humbard Donors" (92,000), "Jim and Tammy Bakker Donor File" (350,000), "$1,000+ Members of a Large Christian TV Ministry" (42,000 U.S., 17,000 Canada), and a list of almost 314,000 people who contributed to Jimmy Swaggart Ministries in 1986–87. Each of these mailing lists represents the response of individuals to the personalized story of a television ministry as created through the tube and the mail.

In spite of what many viewers and other supporters believe, for most televangelists direct-mail fund-raising is much more business than ministry. In 1981 one researcher documented this by writing to five of the highest-rated televangelists that he had "given his life to Christ" and asking how he could "follow him." Over the next nine months he received fifty-four mailings from those five televangelists. Forty-five were letters. The rest were books and magazines. Three of the five televangelists replied to the researcher's initial question about his conversion, but only three of all the mailings provided specific information about how to live as a Christian. Most amazing of all, only four mailings made any reference to the new convert's involvement in a local church—as if living the Christian life does not significantly involve participation in a local body of believers. At the same time, all but one of the mailings included requests for financial support.[18] Again, it appears that some of the most popular televangelists are more in the business of raising funds than encouraging church participation or religiously educating viewers.

Interestingly enough, the success of direct-mail appeals by independent evangelical organizations, especially the televangelists, has led some denominations to follow suit. Feeling the competition for funds, certain church groups have decided to experiment with the mailing techniques developed by televangelism. Although monies are raised by such strategies, there is also a tremendous amount of irritation and dissension generated among recipients. Without the self-selection process that takes place with television viewers (most of whom do not respond initially to on-air appeals), denominations run the risk of alienating their members if they employ hard-sell, emotional, direct-mail appeals. Indeed, if some viewers saw the letter sent out to targeted donors in the name of their favorite televangelist, they might never become supporters. Instead, they might join the chorus of critics who insist that Christianity should be more than a "mail-order religion."

Creating Crisis

Like any other business, televangelism must maintain its cash flow or it will be in serious financial condition. Based on the premise that their TV ministries can continue to expand, yet faced with rising media costs, televangelists usually exist on the financial edge. If revenues dip significantly over even a few months, most ministries will be faced with layoffs and may have to drop some of the stations that carry their broadcasts. Generally speaking, televangelism is a precarious and unpredictable business. (Prior to the scandal, Jimmy Swaggart Ministries was a notable exception, eliciting far more contributions than the television ministry needed to survive and expand. After the scandals of the late 1980s, he, too, was faced with serious financial shortfalls.) Some fund-raising strategies work extremely well—like Jim Bakker's Heritage U.S.A. memberships, guaranteeing annual lodgings— while others fail quietly, if not miserably. And the reasons for success or failure are not always clear, even to the people who create the televised or direct-mail campaigns.

Over the years, televangelists have learned that crisis appeals are generally the most effective ways to get new contributors or increase support among existing ones. Like the local municipality, which often can pass school millage increases only after convincing citizens that a financial crunch is endangering education, the televangelist faces the depressing fact that most people will not contribute financially to his ministry unless "proof" is given of a pressing need. After all, in the United States most television, like most religion, is free. But someone has to pay the piper! And in televangelism the piper almost always has to ask for money before anyone will pay. If threatened with the disappearance of one of their favorite programs, viewers are more inclined to lend their financial support.

So, like the local school board, televangelists face the reality of always having sooner or later to return to the trough for more funding. Driven by their own rhetoric of constant expansion, they have locked themselves into a dark closet of financial deficits with no guaranteed escape. Televangelists today essentially have two possible options. First, they can honestly and openly keep viewers informed of the precise financial state of the ministry. Few ministries do this (e.g., Billy Graham), because it will not normally generate new supporters. Or, second, they can create fund-raising campaigns based on imminent crises or on opportunities that suddenly face the ministry. Nearly all televangelists choose the latter course.

Consequently, televangelism appears on the tube and in its direct-mail appeals to be ever in need of more money, regardless of the real state of affairs. If there is no crisis, one has to be created to legitimize the heavy-handed appeals that will bring in the cash. This practice is so widespread among televangelists that it hardly deserves serious attention, except that many viewers are amazingly naive about the ways they are manipulated by Sunday-morning hucksters. Again, the motivation is not personal greed; most televangelists are not trying to fatten their own wallets. The underlying problem is the ethics of what can be called "holy deception"—duping people in the name of some admittedly noble religious undertaking. Televangelists say they wish "to save the world," which is certainly a worthwhile task that deserves Christian support. But does that goal *ever* justify deceptive fund-raising tactics? Former Assemblies of God minister Austin Miles recalls how the Bakkers pleaded tearfully for funds on the "PTL Club" while the needed money had already been raised.[19] Surely such blatant lying is not typical, but nearly all of the major televangelists stretch the truth (like advertisers) to make the situation appear worse—or better—than it really is.

Since televangelists have learned as well as other salespeople that human beings are basically lazy and selfish, they attempt to overcome the inertia regarding financial support with the kinds of crisis appeals that have already worked. Televangelists are pragmatic people and will generally do what must be done, especially if it is in the uncontestable name of evangelism.

In televangelism, then, crisis is good business, even repeated crisis, since crisis always presents an opportunity for donor participation. Sometimes the fine line between crisis and opportunity is obscure. In 1988, while Jerry Falwell faced the financial fallout of scandals in other ministries, he launched a fund-raising campaign around the "need" for a new Liberty University building. On the surface, such tactics seemed absurd. Why try to expand when donations are off and business is generally poor? The answer, of course, was that Falwell not only needed a new building; he needed another cause, another reason to raise funds, even another potential crisis. While other televangelists were desperately pleading for funds and cutting their staffs, Falwell smartly plunged ahead with a new campaign. He needed the new building, he said, to reduce a space shortage at the university that was reaching crisis proportions.

By taking risks like some of the most successful secular entrepreneurs, televangelists are assuming that expansion will bring more viewers and contributors, more "customers." Even though financial disaster hangs over them like a Damoclean sword, televangelists, who are often asset-rich and cash-poor, push on toward bolder risks and more bizarre fund-raising tactics. Oral Roberts even holed up in his university's prayer tower to make the point that unless supporters would contribute $8 million, the Lord would take him home.

When Falwell took over the financially strapped PTL after the Bakkers' departure, he immediately inherited a host of major fiscal and public-relations problems. The impact of that situation on Falwell's own on-air financial strategies was amazing. The mild-mannered, business-suited Falwell was suddenly transformed by the moment into a rather charismatic fund-raiser. In addition to pleading for funds to keep PTL solvent, he danced, clapped, and sang on the "PTL Club" program. Finally, in a publicity stunt apparently of his own design, he agreed to sail down Heritage U.S.A.'s giant water slide if a specified amount of money was raised by a given date. The viewers and PTL won the "bet," and Falwell (hardly the loser) braced himself for the wild ride on live television. Business suit and all, looking enormously uncomfortable, Jerry bore the results of his own clever scheme by taking the long plunge. Ironically, the crisis was over only temporarily since the need for even more funds would become increasingly obvious. Unaccustomed to PTL's intense crisis appeals and wildly erratic fiscal mismanagement, Falwell had met his own match in the Crisis Derby.

In all likelihood, however, it would not be possible for *any* televangelist to bail out another one, for the financial pie is only so big, and endorsing a competing ministry can bring new crises at the home office. Although Falwell's attempted rescue of PTL made him look like a hero to many evangelicals, it was also a rather fruitless exercise in terms of the growth of his own ministry. On returning full-time to his own organization, Falwell took up the cause of Liberty University more rigorously than ever. Perhaps he finally realized that there is little long-term future for a ministry based primarily on televangelism, with all its real and heightened crises. Higher education looked much more sensible and secure.

Televangelism cannot easily cope with the possibility of status quo. It is a business of expansion-related crisis—both real and imagined. Supporters want to hear about new, bigger, and better things, not about the same old programs. They expect more souls to be saved, new buildings to be erected, and the latest technologies to be mastered. Such expectations fuel televangelists' own desires to succeed at seemingly impossible tasks, such as building the Crystal Cathedral of Robert Schuller or establishing a world-class medical facility at Oral Roberts' Tulsa campus. Televangelism is a business of dreams and hopes. In that, too, it is an especially American phenomenon. Horatio Alger is a far more appealing, though certainly less realistic, role model than Willy Loman.

Compliant Competition

While televangelists depend on crisis appeals to keep them financially afloat, they are also inevitably drawn into a situation of religiously related competition. Like American business in general, televangelism has never been marked by significant cooperation, except to keep the airways open to its programs, which is why the National Religious Broadcasters was formed by evangelicals in the first place. Televangelists compete for relatively limited air time and especially for the rather inelastic evangelical dollar. There are only so many viewers and contributions to go around. As former executive director of NRB, Ben Armstrong, put it, televangelism is part of the "competitive system of private enterprise."[20]

On the one hand, competitiveness is good for televangelism. It encourages remarkable creativity in programming, especially compared historically with the rather dull shows produced by mainline church groups and sometimes aired for free. Televangelists are not without interesting formats and visually stimulating fare. Given their limited production budgets compared with commercial television, American televangelists do not do too badly at making technically good programs. They are better, in fact, than much of the prime-time fare produced both here and abroad. Televangelists have searched for successful programming ideas across the spectrum of secular shows, borrowing strategies from talk shows, variety shows, dramas, situation comedies, soap operas, and even the news and commercials. Given their explicitly religious flavor, televangelistic programs do fairly well at entertaining audiences in a society used to watching multimillion-dollar productions. Surely competition has encouraged such creativity and variety.

On the other hand, televangelism's competitiveness has undoubtedly caused enormous public confusion about the nature of Christianity. At least it has amplified existing disharmony and disunity in the churches of the nation. It seems that televangelism's business-oriented approach thrives on product differentiation—on highlighting the differences among products when in fact there may be more similarities than differences. There are so many brands of faith healers, positive thinkers, pornography blasters, patriotism pushers, and prophecy proclaimers that the essential "product," the gospel, is often lost in the shuffle to air a program with an identifiably different message. A few TV preachers, most notably Jimmy Swaggart, have vigorously attacked other televangelists on the air, if not by name certainly by message and program style. Swaggart does not like the kinds of Christianity represented by charismatics like Jim Bakker or possibility thinkers like Robert Schuller, and he made no bones about it on the air. Most televangelists, however, are like most advertisers; they rarely mention the competition in their ads.

Competitiveness tends to tune televangelists even more finely to the whims of the evangelical marketplace. As mentioned previously, if D. James Kennedy were ever to become one of the top three televangelists, he could not have stayed with the old preaching format set in a Sunday service at his Presbyterian church in Florida. He had to venture out to more risky fare and more issue-oriented fund-raising and programming. If he were a faith healer there would have been other options, but as a rather subdued television performer with a Calvinist heritage, he had limited possibilities for product differentiation. For a time—about six years—Jerry Falwell's product was a highly politicized message, but after that his organization decided to emphasize gospel preaching and Christian higher education. Falwell eventually folded the Moral Majority and once again cast his televisual lot with the preachers and teachers. Oral Roberts has shifted his basic television product so many times that it is now difficult to figure out exactly what his show is all about; indeed, that loss of specific product image may have accounted for his audience decline in the late 1980s.

As the free market of televangelism brings business values to roost in the nests of Sunday-morning religious programming, the resulting competition gives independent organizations a district advantage in the marketplace. In 1971 independent evangelical programming accounted for 67 percent of all syndicated religious fare. By 1981, as "free" time for nonindependents was largely eliminated, independent evangelicals produced 92 percent of all such programming.[21] Market competition has been good for evangelicals, who appear to be far more entrepreneurial in the use of TV and other media than their mainline Protestant or Roman Catholic counterparts.

One fund-raising expert has concluded that competition for charitable contributions in the United States is greater than ever. George A. Brakeley, Jr., has argued that charitable institutions must "work harder than ever to join a greater share" of the available contributions. He suggests that they must be aggressive and imaginative.[22] It appears that televangelism faces the same competitive dilemma, since it will take more and more programming savvy and fund-raising expertise to produce more contributions to fund its predicted growth. At the same time, supporters will expect to see and hear about tangible progress toward certain predicted accomplishments, especially world evangelization. Sheer competitiveness gave evangelicals the edge over other religious groups in the 1970s and 1980s, but now it will likely give some evangelicals the edge over others, creating a whole different kind of contest.

Proponents of a free market historically took it for granted that the best ideas and products would thereby survive while inferior ones would be eliminated. Through this kind of "invisible hand," as Adam Smith called it, excellence and superiority would be rewarded over mediocrity and inferiority. But what does that mean for televangelism? What is really the "best" program or the "superior" televisual product? The one that would attract the most viewers? Elicit the greatest contributions? Save the most souls? These are important questions that the marketplace of televangelism does not explicitly address. Competition certainly creates winners and losers, but who is to say the losers, those who can't afford to stay on the air, offer inferior products? Without some kind of objective standard for evaluating programs, the free market, as represented by a whimsical public, plays its own magical games of enhancing some programs' marketability while detracting from others.

In the United States, where so many denominations and independent groups exist, it seems that only the public at large is left to decide who has truth and who has bunkum. All televangelists are not created equal, but it is up to the so-called free marketplace, not the church or official prelates, to decide which programs fall into which category. The questionable assumption in all this is that pure competition necessarily produces better televangelism, better religion, or better anything. But, if it does work for consumer products, will it not work for spiritual communication? In some cases, probably so. There are some remarkably good preachers and teachers on the airways. But competition also penalizes the Christian church by promoting some programs that only appear to be superior because of their audience size (after all, viewers are sinners, too), and by squandering limited resources on many competitive practices. Perhaps the idea is too idealistic, but one cannot help but wonder what types of high-quality evangelical programs might result if evangelical broadcasters worked together harmoniously rather than competing quietly but determinedly in the current free marketplace of contemporary televangelism.

Consulting the Wizards

As discussed earlier, televangelists have frequently called on the services of outside marketing consultants and direct-mail writers. In some cases the consultants are evangelicals themselves. In other cases they are simply non-religious professionals who provide services for any interested clients. Some of the major televangelists and their management teams have learned much from consultants, using the advice to make changes in both programming and fund-raising.

These consultants have been the most direct and persistent source of marketing techniques for the major televangelists. They are the wizards of televangelism, the special people who supposedly know how to give one ministry the competitive edge over another. However, since almost all ministries use their advice, there is really little competitive edge left. Over the last fifteen years most televangelists have learned the same tricks of the trade—how to give their on-air fund-raising appeals a sense of immediacy; how to make contributors feel like they "own" the ministry by providing them with informational magazines rather than just financial solicitations; how to use premiums effectively; how to maximize large donations through matching gifts; and many more techniques.

The wizards of consulting have accentuated the tendency for televangelism to be more a business venture and less a ministry. Their focus is not how best to minister to people, but how to build a large, financially solvent organization. Although they know how to help televangelists raise more funds and attract more viewers, they care little about the ultimate value of the ministry itself. These professional wizards are usually neutral about the theological or spiritual values of the ministries they advise. Like hired guns in the Old West, they get paid to do a specific job, not to figure out whether the job has merit.

Some televangelists have thrived in the hands of the wizards. Most of the major TV ministries made it to the top-ten weekly ratings with their assistance. But without the freedom to evaluate the theological foundations of their clients' ministries, consultants have been able to do little more than help televangelism become more successful as a business. The ultimate responsibility for this rests with the televangelists, who naively believe that all business practices are neutral by definition. However, marketing is never neutral; it always introduces values into the process of producing, distributing, and selling products. Marketing can indeed shape the message of a televangelist, framing the very contours of the gospel preached—or not preached. As discussed earlier, the health-and-wealth gospel has been "good business." It opens up many avenues for which savvy marketing experts can design attractive appeals. But it is also a theologically bankrupt gospel that distorts the truth for a fallen humankind. That, in fact, is the inherent danger of using marketing wizards, who are good primarily at helping clients create what people want, not what they should have. A few of the better wizards are not so coldly financial, but many are.

Marketing has much to offer the religious community, but it must be marketing with a spiritual conscience and a sense of mature discernment. The secular trend, which leads wizards to give anyone the tools to get a message across, is simply unacceptable to the Christian community. Televangelists need wizards who will say "no" when a strategy might be in the immediate interests of the ministry but is clearly in conflict with the word and will of God.

Conclusion

In a cogent critique of the electronic church, Donald Oberdorfer concludes that televangelism is more in the business of marketing than the task of ministry.[23] Oberdorfer has rightly identified perhaps the most disturbing trend in televangelism—the trend toward advanced marketing techniques at the cost of meaningful ministry. Televangelists are largely caught in an escalating spiral of higher costs and stiffer competition. Their only way out seems to be to forsake ministry *per se* and charge willy-nilly into ever more businesslike ways of conducting their work. In the process they become managers rather than ministers, performers rather than preachers. Again, there are a few exceptions, even among the top-ten weekly syndicated broadcasters. Nevertheless, the overall trend is too clear and significant to be ignored. Televangelism needs to be propelled by more than business values, though it may discerningly call on modern marketing experts for assistance in figuring out how best to *minister* to people.

Almost always big-time televangelism, like the secular media, is a self-interested business. Decisions are made largely on the basis of how well they will help the organization grow. In the name of "evangelism," the *size* of a TV ministry (measured by the number of stations, audience ratings, and the like) is equated with the *quality* of its ministry to real people. Just as the commercial networks claim to be serving the public by garnering large audiences, televangelists claim to be ministering to people by building large donor lists, erecting impressive buildings, and generally increasing the size and scope of the broadcasting operation. All this is folly unless real ministry is taking place. As we shall see next, this is not the case, regardless of isolated anecdotal evidence to the contrary.

Of course this problem is not idiosyncratic to modern televangelism. Oswald Chambers writes in *He Shall Glorify Me,* "Every denomination or missionary enterprise departs from its true spiritual power when it becomes a successful organization, because the advocates of the denomination or the missionary enterprise after a while have to see first of all to the establishment and success of their organization, while the thing which made them what they are has gone like a corn of wheat into the ground and died."[24] Those are strong and provocative words, but I believe they aptly apply to contemporary televangelism, which has indeed become more concerned with its own success than its "true spiritual power." As entrepreneurial, promotional, competitive organizations, television ministries have largely replaced their spiritual drive with business savvy and marketing prowess. The result has been large organizations that look, sound, and act like corporations motivated by self-interest alone.

Generally speaking, televangelism has succumbed to what French social critic Jacques Ellul has called *"la technique."* Concerned principally with manipulating their audiences for maximum organizational gain, televangelists have put the values of efficiency and control ahead of all others. This is one of the most damaging trends of modern societies, whether they be democratic or authoritarian. People are treated as mere means to particular ends defined selfishly by organizations, from the media to government.[25] While claiming to be evangelizing the world, televangelism is actually being evangelized by the secular media and the modern spirit of pragmatic business. Malcolm Boyd cogently observes that televangelists are "ironically and demonically enmeshed in tactics" that are little more than religious versions of secular business techniques. "The gospel which we are commanded by our Lord to communicate," continues Boyd, "stands in judgment upon the means we employ to communicate it."[26] And Boyd wrote that in 1956, long before televangelism became truly big business.

Billy Graham's refusal to launch a weekly television program was probably one of the smartest decisions of his ministry. In the name of evangelism, he could have easily joined the crowd of financially strapped televangelists who are forced to become money managers and fund-raisers more than ministers. There will always be a few places in televangelism for someone such as Charles Stanley, whose ministry thrives on unsolicited small donations from many grateful viewers, or Radio Bible Class, whose literature ministry largely supports its radio and TV broadcasts. For most televangelists, however, the weekly and monthly costs of operation, to say nothing of the drive for expansion, lead almost invariably to a greening of the gospel. Business considerations overcome spiritual values, and marketing strategy dictates the thrust of a ministry. As a survey showed as early as 1984, religious TV producers themselves believe that the "emphasis on money and fund raising" is the greatest weakness in such programming.[27]

Perhaps the whole trend toward business professionalism in televangelism is badly misguided. If professionalism is defined by the world, not the church, it may be an enormously deceptive ploy to subvert the work of spreading the gospel. As long as professionalism means "holy deception" and *la technique,* this will surely be the case. As Pastor Jack Hayford once put it, such "creeping professionalism" may "erode the integrity of the Christian communicator."[28] Fund-raising alone is not the problem, as too many secular critics are too quick to suggest. The real dilemma is how televangelists can maintain their Christian integrity while being shaped by the day-to-day business needs of their organizations, both on and off the air. The issue is not just *what* televangelists do, but *why* they do it, *how* they do it, and *for whom* they do it. Put to such a spiritual test, most big-time televangelists fail to earn even a passing grade, no matter how "professional" their organizations.

The greening of televangelism reflects the American preoccupation with money, status, and power. Through the ages the churches of Jesus Christ have often been shaped by these things, but in American televangelism they have reached their zenith of influence. Most non-Americans are repulsed by the televangelism that flows from the United States. They see in it the worst of commercialization of religion and call for someone to chase the money changers from the temple. Using William Stringfellow's terminology, televangelism is "demonic" because it is clearly governed by values and practices antithetical to the gospel. Televangelism exists in a "state of alienation from God, cut off from the life originating in his life, separated from its own true life and, thus, being in a state of death."[29] Whether in business, televangelism, or the church, when the life-giving values of an organization are ungodly, it is not merely benign, but evil. So it can become in the greening of the televisual gospel when growth, fund-raising, and organizational status become more important than spiritual edification and authentic communication.

The Evangelistic Myth

❋ ❋ ❋ ❋ ❋ ❋ ❋ ❋ ❋ ❋ ❋ ❋ ❋ ❋ ❋ ❋ ❋ ❋

A s part of its own promotional campaign in favor of film evangelism, an organization called World Film Crusade offered a stinging criticism of televangelism's boasting about its audience size. "In the 'Christian' world," it wrote, "there often appears a *tenth* gift of the Holy Spirit, as it is so often observed. This is the *Gift of Exaggeration*. Church attendance, campaign contribution totals, Bible course enrollees, souls saved, and of course, television audiences, can be exaggerated in the name of the Lord."[1] In the case of televangelism, this is a particularly pronounced gift evidenced on the air and in direct-mail appeals, speeches, and media interviews. Televangelists know how to exaggerate effectively, especially when it comes to fund-raising.

In this respect, too, televangelism mirrors the broader culture. Americans love to speak of how great they are, even compared with each other—who lives in the biggest state, the most beautiful one, or the most prosperous. Television advertising, perhaps America's most popular art form, reflects the nation's hyperbolic sensibility; everything is new, better, or at least different. Products, supposedly like the people who use them, are touted as the most glamorous, gorgeous, and gifted. It is almost as if products have a life of their own. (Actually, some do: Charlie Tuna never gets selected for processing because he cannot meet the manufacturer's standards. As they say, only the "best tuna" are selected. Fishermen must use truly American nets to catch those special fish!) Day in and day out, from college football to automobiles, Americans exaggerate for fun and profit.

As World Film Crusade suggests, however, Christians are specially gifted in this land of hyperbole. Exaggeration does appear to
be a notable talent among evangelicals, particularly when they
are boasting about the growth of evangelicalism, the most soul-
saving brand of Christianity. Evangelicals like to tell themselves
and others that they are bringing many people to Christ, when in
fact there may be very little evidence to support such a conclusion.
To put it starkly, evangelicals typically exercise the gift of self-
promotional exaggeration, thus seemingly confirming what they
wish to believe about the world and especially about their own
efforts at winning people to Christ.

Televangelists are among the champions of hyperbole, and for
good reason. Their financial support generally depends upon convincing viewers and especially contributors that they are successful evangelists. Even Pat Robertson, who publicly denied that he
was an evangelist, has appealed for funds to viewers of his "700
Club" partly on the basis of how many people were being saved
via the show. Because televangelism is largely a product of American culture, and because American evangelicalism emphasizes
personal spiritual conversion, TV preachers exaggerate their
evangelistic victories more than anything else. When they speak
boldly of the number of stations that air their broadcast or of the
potential audience for their cable programs, it is always with an
explicitly evangelistic rhetoric. And anyone who challenges their
exaggerations is typically branded as "unchristian," since offering
such criticism seems to question the value of evangelism itself.

Popular support for televangelism in the United States rests on
two shaky foundations: (1) the power of the mass media to change
people's basic values, attitudes, and beliefs (the "faith in technology" discussed earlier), and (2) the ability of televangelists to use
the media to bring people to Christ. Instead of realistically evaluating these two fundamental concepts, evangelicals have assumed
them to be axiomatic. The fact is that television has not proven
itself to be so powerful and televangelists are not nearly as effective as they claim. This chapter will review only some of the more
compelling evidence in support of these conclusions.

It appears that most televangelism reaches few non-Christians
(even few nonevangelicals). Televangelists' exaggerated rhetoric
typically suggests they are saving many souls, while studies show
that neither the medium of television nor the method of televangelism is particularly effective for evangelization. Although Ameri-

can evangelicals may believe that "bigger is better," actual experience shows that the more "mass" the medium, the less powerful it is for bringing people to Christ. Instead of presenting the gospel "to the world," televangelism is communicating overwhelmingly with a relatively small segment of the evangelical community. Televangelism rarely sows the seed of Christian faith among the masses of unsaved souls.

Prime-Time Religion

Media commentators have frequently referred to televangelism as "prime-time religion," but televangelists are rarely able to afford prime time. Instead they buy time during fringe viewing periods, such as early morning, late at night, or Sunday mornings. In fact, except for Bishop Fulton J. Sheen's advertising-supported prime-time program during the 1950s, and Oral Roberts's few prime-time variety shows a decade later, religious broadcasts have rarely been aired during the high-rated evening time periods. Billy Graham's crusade broadcasts usually appear in early prime time, but not on one of the major networks. The Graham organization purchases time on individual stations across the country. There is no doubt, however, that Graham could not afford to buy such time every week. He is able to subsidize only a few televised crusades every year, partly because he does not solicit funds on the air.

"Prime-time religion," then, is really not so prime after all. Basically limited to fringe periods, televangelists reach essentially a rather small group of their own devotees. As the Annenberg-Gallup study found in 1984, religious broadcasters rarely speak to audiences outside their natural constituency. Religious programs are viewed overwhelmingly by churched people who are already quite religious.[2] In 1978, when televangelism was already well established, a survey showed that less than 5% of the 61 million unchurched Americans recalled ever having watched a televangelist other than Oral Roberts (12%) or Billy Graham (11%).[3] Interestingly enough, Graham and Roberts were the only televangelists who had had real prime-time programs. A *Christianity Today/ Gallup* poll in 1980 found that 85% of those who listen to or watch religious broadcasts profess to be converted. And some national ratings show that less than 4% of the total radio and television audience is reached by religious shows.[4]

Obviously the rise of prime-time religion has not been as dramatic as the televangelists would have their supporters believe. In the 1940s, when radio evangelist Charles E. Fuller purchased evening time for his "Old-Fashioned Revival Hour," his audience was certainly larger than the Sunday-morning audiences of today's televangelists. With few exceptions (such as Roberts, Sheen, and Graham), religious broadcasters have consolidated their audiences far more than they have expanded them. They have learned how to reach likely supporters, not how to reach enormous audiences with the gospel. Sunday morning is the most sought-after program period not because it is effective for reaching nonbelievers, but exactly because it is one of the best times for getting at the checkbooks and credit cards of believers. The same holds true for the religious cable-television networks that offer "prime" time to televangelists. Because these networks, especially TBN, provide religious audiences for religious broadcasters, they are a relatively cheap way of generating supporters for ministries hoping to expand. In marketing terms, they are an efficient media buy, since televangelists would not be reaching many who are not potential donors. It should not be surprising, then, that televangelists air their programs more frequently in areas of the country with high church attendance—those are the places where the market is already primed for fund-raising.[5] Similarly, this helps to explain why so many televangelists use religious language that would only be understandable to evangelicals.

The real audience for TV ministries is not the unchurched, who would not support the broadcasts, but the evangelical subculture that supplies the finances to keep the broadcasts on the air. The "Back to the Bible" radio ministry realized this and decided to do what few televangelists have ever attempted. It started a separate evangelistic broadcast called "Pause for Good News," knowing that the program would never elicit adequate contributions from viewers to become truly self-supporting. "The potential for the response of faith is great," said the organization's David Breese, "but the mail response is minimal. The secular listeners will rarely write and almost never make a contribution."[6] The same could be said of televangelism. Prime-time religion is really prime-time fund-raising. Televangelists almost always select the best channels, times, and days to raise funds, not the best ones for reaching nonbelievers.

The Limits of TV Evangelism

In spite of what televangelists say, and what evangelicals often wish to believe, television has never proven itself to be an effective evangelistic medium. Both because of the inherent limits of the medium and the fund-raising strategies of televangelists, there is a strong corpus of evidence that television is a poor evangelistic tool. This reality typically falls on deaf ears in the United States, where it is assumed that the number of people reached by a medium determines its power. But only a fool would argue against the historic fact that television has simply not made a major contribution to worldwide or even national evangelization. In spite of the billions of dollars spent annually on televangelism, that goal has remained little more than a dream.

Communication research long ago proved that mass media have largely been a confirmatory influence. Audiences first select programs that are generally in tune with their existing attitudes and beliefs, and then interpret those programs according to their preconceptions. This is why for many viewers the bigoted Archie Bunker of "All in the Family" was a hero, while for others he was a red-neck villain. In addition, audiences generally do not take mass-mediated messages as seriously as they do personal communication from friends, co-workers, relatives, teachers, neighbors, and the like. The media *can* influence people, but the influence is rarely as simple, direct, and one-sided as some assume. Television viewers, in particular, are quite skeptical about what they see, if it is not in harmony with what they and their close friends already believe. Although the audience is not entirely sovereign, it does carry a lot of communicative clout. The best propaganda, as Jacques Ellul explained, tells people what they already want to believe.[7]

The very concept of mass-media evangelism, then, has to be seriously questioned. And the data support such skepticism. A survey by the Institute for American Church Growth of 40,000 church-related Christians found that only .01% of them said they attend a church as a result of mass evangelism, including religious radio and television. By contrast, more than 85% said they came to Christ and the church primarily because of a friend, relative, or associate.[8] A survey of Christian Jews found that the influence of radio/TV/movies was instrumental in the conversion of less than 2%.[9] Another study of lay Christians found that evangelistic campaigns accounted for only 5% of conversions, while friends and relatives accounted for between 75 and 90% of them.[10] Research repeatedly shows that over 80% of people who have recently joined a church came as a result of the word of a friend or relative, while less than 1% came specifically as a result of electronic evangelism.[11] Sociologist Tony Campolo concludes that "it is difficult to warrant the expenditure of hundreds of millions of dollars annually to sponsor Christian television on the assumption that it is a primary instrument of evangelism."[12]

This is not to say that televised religion has absolutely no role to play in evangelism and church growth. Actually, five of the eleven largest churches in North America have significant television ministries. However, only one of them, Jerry Falwell's Thomas Road Baptist Church, sponsors primarily a national television program, "The Old-Time Gospel Hour." The other four (First Baptist Church of Houston, First Baptist Church of Jacksonville, North Phoenix Baptist Church, and Bellevue Baptist Church of Memphis) use television primarily as a local outreach ministry.[13] For many large churches, including Falwell's, local television broadcasts of worship services give the church and its pastor some visibility in the community. These shows also create the feeling among the congregation that the church is a significant factor in local religious life, a place that amounts to something important. As a result, parishioners are proud of their membership, more willing to talk about their faith, and thus more likely to be evangelistic. Moreover, the broadcasts attract new members who may transfer from other churches because of the relevance and style of preaching.

Predominately, however, televised religion has been a dismal failure at evangelizing nonbelievers, at least partly because televangelists become more interested in building an organization than in saving souls. As mentioned, these ministries often exaggerate their evangelistic data to maintain a facade of evangelistic outreach. Ministry workers know better, but they pretend that the emperor *is* wearing clothes. Sometimes their compliance stems from the fear of being fired, since few televangelists will tolerate negative publicity from the staff. More often, employees, like the ministry's supporters, simply continue to believe in the evangelistic power of their leader, regardless of information to the contrary. The evangelistic desire is so strong that individuals who know better continue to be true believers anyway.

Over the years I have learned that televangelists and their avid supporters nearly always object to data that show TV evangelism to be largely unsuccessful. They like to point to anecdotal evidence that is impossible to refute, since some people are indeed saved through these broadcasts. But the numbers remain small in proportion to the enormous expense of national television programming. Not one major study has found statistical support for the power of televangelism. On the contrary, dozens of studies have shown that televangelists preach to the faithful, not the faithless.

It appears that without local church support, televangelism is clearly not worth the money it costs. True evangelization is essentially local and interpersonal. It happens in the course of genuine relationships between believers and nonbelievers, not in the unrealistic drama experienced vicariously by the isolated television viewer. People will most likely be attracted to Christianity when they experience the emotional healing, human warmth, and personal support of local fellowship, not when they view the fabricated intimacy of the television preacher and read the self-serving personalization of religious junk mail.

In his revealing study of "700 Club" viewers and supporters, Stewart Hoover verified this in lengthy interviews. Most members of the Club were already evangelicals before they started viewing. Moreover, their conversions were emotional experiences that significantly involved personal relationships more than mass-media programming. Hoover concluded that televangelism is not converting many, even if it is seen as an evangelistic tool by its supporters.[14] Although there has been much debate on the matter, the best estimates are that there are only about 15 million regular viewers of religious television and that the vast majority are already evangelicals.[15] In other words, televangelism reaches largely a small subset within the country's evangelical community.

As Martin Marty has put it, the "media are essentially confirming and reinforcing agencies—even though they have been sold to the churches as the latter. . . . "[16] This contrasts sharply with the rhetoric of Ben Armstrong, former Executive Director of National Religious Broadcasters, who says, "Penny for penny, per capita studies indicate there is no better way to reach the largest number of people with the life-changing news of Jesus Christ than through radio and television."[17] Yet Armstrong cites not a single study.

The fact is that the mass media contribute significantly to evangelism only when they are tied to the community. Billy Graham's organization figured this out long ago, using television to publicize the ministry and help generate local church involvement in citywide evangelistic campaigns. The John Guest Evangelistic Team took essentially the same direction in the 1980s but without national television. Neither Graham's nor Guest's ministries depends primarily on television for evangelization. In fact, religious organizations that put most of their emphasis on television are less successful evangelistically.

Religious Playtime

One of the reasons that television has been a rather ineffective evangelistic medium is that few Americans view for educational purposes. Indeed, some networks and channels are called "educational" as a way of distinguishing them from most broadcasts. Most viewers do not approach the TV set with the desire to be challenged intellectually, religiously, or morally. Americans expect and want television principally to entertain them. And by "entertainment" they mean leisure-time fun or diversion; more than anything else they want to be relieved from the boredom of free time and diverted from the stress of the real world.

William Stephenson appropriately locates television viewing in the realm of human play.[18] His point is that viewers turn on the tube with playful expectations. This is considerably different from the way an individual might worship, read Scripture or participate in Bible studies.

Since most TV viewing is simply a way to spend leisure time, televangelists who try to use the tube to evangelize find that their audiences expect to be playfully entertained. A few viewers do tune in for serious worship or instruction, but most will not. The way Americans have integrated television viewing into their daily lives conflicts with a TV ministry's evangelistic intentions. To maintain an audience and attract potential supporters, televangelists normally find that they have to entertain more than teach and preach, unless of course they can educate or sermonize in an engaging way. A friend of mine, best described as a nominal Christian, thoroughly enjoys viewing late-night televangelism from his motel rooms while on business trips. He concedes that while he disagrees with the televangelists' theology, their programming is simply more entertaining than most late-night fare.

As discussed at length in chapter 5, one way to hang on to viewers is to tell them what they want to hear, namely a health-and-wealth gospel. At the same time, however, televangelists have to be concerned with *how* they communicate their message. Usually, a playfully presented program that does not take itself or its message too seriously will attract more attention than one that requires the viewer to be more than entertained. The irony is clear—televangelists have to be entertainers more than evangelists.

Television evangelism too often becomes an entertaining drama designed to elicit viewer response through telephone calls and letters. Like public television, which turns fund-raising into entertaining auctions and other phone-in campaigns, some televangelists initiate their own telethons that count converts and tabulate contributions. This type of live programming is truly engaging fare—far more so than most preaching or Bible teaching. But it cheapens religious faith by immersing it in a highly commercialized context. No matter how seriously televangelists expect viewers to take these on-air campaigns, they communicate a playful and trivialized version of religion. Authentic Christianity cannot be measured by conversion numbers or financial tabulations. Televangelists are truly playing around with the faith life of their viewers.

The medium of television steers the Christian faith toward silliness and even profanity. In Dietrich Bonhoeffer's phrasing, the tube offers "cheap grace," a perverted gospel that equates religious belief with rather meaningless responses to an entertaining message. "Cheap grace means grace sold on the market like cheapjacks' wares," says Bonhoeffer. "The sacraments, the forgiveness of sin, and the consolations of religion are thrown away at cut prices."[19] Because contemporary evangelicalism has adopted this type of popular religious expression, "cheap grace" plays well on the tube. A televangelist can shout praises to God for the money that rolled in, and no one complains that the money-changers may have entered the temple. Or he can announce exuberantly how many viewers have called to "accept Christ as their personal Lord and Savior," but no one asks if those viewers had any idea what conversion really means and what Christ actually requires of them. It is all too often like a game show or a situation comedy. Should anyone really take this kind of programming seriously?

Win Arn appropriately asks how effective televangelism is at cultivating true disciples of Christ. It may lure a few viewers, and it may raise funds, but is it helping to produce committed followers of Jesus Christ who know *whom* they are to follow and how to do so? Arn persuasively argues that "evangelism is more than proclamation. It is persuading people to become Christ's disciples and to be responsible members of the church. In this, TV evangelism is a great failure."[20] It is not enough, then, for televangelists to preach a simplistic gospel, even though it be a popularized and dramatized version. Since the authentic gospel requires not only a "yes" but also a knowledgeable commitment, television can interfere with the development of the church in America. Faith without works is dead; but so is faith without the knowledge of *what* good works are required of those who "accept Christ" and *why* they are required.

In this respect, no amount of TV "conversions" will greatly advance the cause of Christ unless the so-called converts are taught to be spiritually discerning and biblically oriented. It is outrageous for televangelists to lay the burden of this responsibility on the local church while simultaneously claiming to be evangelizing the world. A parallel situation is television news, where reporters are more involved in communicating attention-grabbing tidbits than in presenting the total picture that will help viewers understand the significance of the news. Television news plays the same deceptive game as religious television, where more televangelists say less of importance than ever before.

In this regard, the level of biblical knowledge of televangelism's viewers makes for a depressing situation. A study conducted in 1978 by the Gallup Organization for *Christianity Today* apparently proved the point. The data suggested that knowledge of the Bible is more strongly correlated with the traditional avenues of religious education, such as church attendance and Bible reading, than with listening to religious radio or watching religious TV. In fact, an examination of the data revealed that "exposure to religious television and radio are negatively associated . . . with knowledge of the ten commandments. . . . " This was true for the total population surveyed as well as for Roman Catholics and Protestants individually.[21] The unmistakable conclusion is that televangelism fosters a kind of popular religion that has little biblical content. Like newscast viewers who may think they are well informed, religious-program viewers may greatly overestimate their biblical knowledge and thus their capacity for being disciples of Christ.

Evidence suggests, then, that televangelism alone may not be as positive a spiritual force as so many supporters believe. Are televangelists truly serving their viewers? Attracting viewers is not the same as serving them. People can be attracted to things that are not good for them, especially when those things are gilded in glamour or the rhetorics of "faith." Fortunately some TV ministries are really appendages to other ministries that can actually educate viewers about the elements of the Christian faith. Radio Bible Class's massive literature ministry is an excellent example. So is Charles Swindoll's radio and publishing ministry; his show leads many listeners to his books, which offer deeper spiritual instruction in a more effective educational medium. Most televangelists, however, present little more than a superficial smattering of biblical instruction. What you see is what you get. Religiously speaking, that is not much, because the medium and its financial constraints lead televangelists to play around with the Christian faith rather than communicate it cogently and comprehensively. In televangelism, the church is using entertainment to talk to itself.

The Evangelical Big Time

In the United States the mass media connote power and authority, and being on television makes one a celebrity. I experienced this when I appeared regularly on a program carried by satellite to cable television systems across the country. Friends would occasionally call me long distance or write to say they had seen me on television. Even local acquaintances and relatives would stop me on the street to report that they had run across my televised image while scanning across their cable channels. At first I was simply surprised that anyone would find it worth a comment; after all, lots of people are on the tube every day. What was the big deal? On further reflection, I began to recognize the incredible status-making effect of television in American life. Although people do not normally take their viewing seriously (many people cannot even remember what they watched the previous evening),

they are nonetheless impressed by the very appearance of someone on the tube.

Partly because American culture is so nontraditional and show-
business oriented, television symbolizes power. To be on the tube
is to have special clout, or so people believe. The television personality is someone who is special and who matters—a person who is
different from the average citizen. Similarly, the organization
whose spokesperson appears on the tube is suddenly legitimatized
as a group that deserves attention if not respect. On the other
hand, an organization that cannot get the attention of the cameras may easily die in media obscurity. The evangelical church in
the United States has wrestled seriously with this problem since
at least the 1920s, when it was often portrayed by the media of
the day (newspapers, magazines, and then radio) as a backward
group of unsophisticated and misguided religious zealots. News
coverage of the Scopes trial, in particular, cast fundamentalists as
a rather uneducated group of ignorant folk. From that time on,
evangelicals have seized the latest media partly to regain public
respect in a culture that seemingly relegated them to the
marginal role of outsiders.[22]

The sheer power of the tube has helped modern televangelism
gain supporters in the face of unequivocal evidence that it is not
very effective at evangelism. Contributors are fairly content just to
have their favorite show on the air. And supporters are often
highly critical of anyone who judges televangelism's methods,
because they take it as a blast against the legitimacy of evangelicalism in general. Ironically, then, televangelism need not be so
concerned with doing evangelism—because its own backers, no
matter how committed to the Great Commission, are often happy
simply to have a real evangelical broadcast on the air. To them
such programs represent the ascendancy of evangelicalism on a
social ladder that was formerly controlled by either religious liberals or secular humanists.

In their own ways, each of the major evangelical television programs contributed to this quest for cultural status. Billy Graham,
though not really a televangelist as defined in this book, was an
important legitimizing presence for the rise of neo-evangelicalism
after World War II.[23] Oral Roberts gave a considerable boost to the
self-perceptions of old-style Pentecostals. Jim Bakker did the
same, but in a very different way, as discussed previously. In the
1980s, however, clearly the most important evangelical media

figure was Pat Robertson, whose CBN organization and especially his "700 Club" broadcast represented a new style of highly professional evangelical programming. Both as a presidential contender (which gave him secular media coverage) and as a sophisticated religious broadcaster, Robertson symbolized the entry of evangelicals into the corridors of national power. From the perspective of his and evangelicalism's critics, of course, Robertson was a threat. But to his followers this new status was luxuriously appealing in a media world seemingly governed by forces hostile to evangelical values and beliefs. Stewart Hoover found that "700 Club" supporters believe that a kind of "power, status and credibility goes along with being on national television."[24] For that reason, some of the program's donors were not viewers; they simply wanted to contribute to the evangelical media presence.

No doubt part of this kind of support for televangelism is a reflection of the place of evangelicals in American society. Until recent years evangelicals have represented primarily the lower social classes, but the contemporary situation has changed significantly. Falwell's Liberty University, for example, is made up primarily of first-generation college students. There are far more evangelicals today who attend college, enter professional careers, and then pursue middle- and upper-middle-class lifestyles. This alone has given evangelicals far more visibility in America. However, media presence remains an important legitimizing force for even the newly enfranchised upper-middle-class evangelicals. Robert Schuller's possibility thinking has appealed considerably to this group, which seeks official public sanctions for its privileged standing in the social order.

In other words, it is not enough for evangelicals, whatever their social standing, to have their own churches. Like other groups in society, they want to have social status and public respect regardless of how secular today's American culture seems to be. Television visibility, more than small in-house media or even other mass media, affords evangelicals the opportunity to authenticate their existence in the minds of the rest of society. Some evangelicals may dismiss this as one reason for the existence of televangelism, citing the foremost call of evangelicals to save souls. But the fact is that TV preachers are *not* saving a lot of souls. And not many of the unconverted are even watching the televangelists. Besides, there is no reason to believe that evangelicals are free from the status anxiety that characterizes American culture. Wherever one looks there are groups trying to get their names, agendas, and leaders into the media limelight. Like evangelicals, they want to make it to the big time.

Because national television is the cutting edge of image-making in the United States today, evangelicals, not unlike politicians and movie stars, hope to project their image on cable and regular broadcast channels. Even if they cannot convince the general public of evangelicalism's merits, they can at least convince themselves of their power to influence. Ironically, their message reaches few nonbelievers. Even more ironically, some of the most popular televangelists have fallen in recent years, probably lowering the perceived authenticity of evangelists and evangelicals in general.

The greatest danger of making it to the big time, as discussed in chapter 3, is in the personality cults that celebrity status may foster. Ted Baehr says that "vanity video" is always a potential pitfall.[25] Television is a two-edged sword, sharpening a group's social standing while giving it the power to cut off its own head in front of all to see. The big time can become a bad time if social status becomes a more important goal than saving souls. Evangelicals may tell themselves that everything is rosy in TV land, but mass-mediated reality can paint a different picture, especially in the hands of cynical journalists. *Everything* that evangelicals do is potential fodder for the news media.

Big-time television offers considerable potential for giving evangelicals a voice in society, but not when the church talks merely to its own members. Then it is only small-time image-making. Even the televangelists with the greatest media charisma have not been able to significantly elevate the social status of evangelicals. The job is simply too important to be carried out merely on the television screen, especially when the general public is not watching. Television gives evangelicals a self-deceiving sense of power, which they really do not have, either as evangelists or shapers of public opinion.

The Threat of Professionalism

American evangelicalism has historically been marked by what Nathan Hatch calls "democratization." In an effort to spread the gospel, evangelicals popularized their messages by translating them into the musical and rhetorical styles of the day.[26] The result was a dynamic though often oversimplified or perverted gospel that resonated principally with the masses of common folk, not with the elite. Religious orators became known for their ability to move an audience emotionally rather than for their skill at composing theologically sound or doctrinally correct messages. This type of democratization, or "popularization," was the communicative spark behind many of the revivalistic precursors of televangelism. Now, after forty years of television in the United States, the medium has become a vehicle for a new group of professional popularizers. And they have come along just as evangelicals have reached comfortable middle-class status.

In their position of increased affluence, evangelicals in America are not so strongly committed to personal evangelism. Instead they seek the comfortable "good life" admired by the broader society. Their faith still calls for saving souls, since personal conversion remains at the heart of their Christian beliefs. But one-on-one evangelism is often viewed as a rather messy business that can interfere with business and interrupt cordial relations with friends and relatives. Moreover, personal evangelism takes time away from the pursuit of affluence. If the choice is between neighborhood evangelism calling and a leisurely weekend at the cottage, there is little doubt which one the vast majority of evangelicals would prefer. After all, they reason, no one wishes to be pegged by friends and neighbors as a religious zealot.

In this social context the job of evangelism increasingly becomes the task of paid professionals. Affluent evangelicals can participate indirectly in spreading the gospel by contributing to their own churches and to independent evangelists who are in the specialized business of saving souls. Televangelists are one such professional group, and they indeed have the latest media technologies at their disposal. Since those technologies are attractive to supporters in a media-dominated society, televangelists have entered the professional landscape as the new specialists in winning people to Christ. Many evangelicals are likely to support them, if for no other reason than to assuage their guilt about their own lack of commitment to personal evangelism.

In this respect, too, the rise of televangelism reflects broader cultural currents. Clearly the trend in America is toward the professionalization of just about every occupation in which someone can claim to hold special knowledge or skills. Indeed, the term *profession* now means little more than career or job—what one does for a living. Along with such specialization is the average person's growing dependency on professionals to help him or her through life. We now have not only the traditional professionals, such as doctors and attorneys, but lawn-care specialists, child-care providers, and nearly every conceivable kind of "expert." Today's televangelists represent the mass-mediated professionalization of evangelism in a specialist-oriented society.

Unfortunately, professionalization of this kind has not helped the goal of worldwide evangelization. Although, biblically speaking, there is warrant for the special "gifts" of the evangelists, the goal of evangelization is far bigger than the limited purview of the professional soulwinner. Every evangelical is a witness, for good or bad, to the gospel. And every action of an evangelical speaks of his or her faith. Even the least-gifted lay evangelical carries the burden of the Great Commission, and not just indirectly through supporting the work of professional evangelists. In their families, workplaces, schools, communities, and churches, evangelicals are necessarily witnesses to the gospel of Jesus Christ. *Personal* evangelism is far and away the most effective form. When evangelicals shift this responsibility to professionals in the name of increased specialization, they do serious injury to the task of saving souls and building up the church of Jesus Christ.

Televangelism has become the most visible form of such professionalization in the evangelical church. Evangelicals generally know who the televangelists are, at least by name and image. And they can be moved by the polished rhetoric of a televangelist who claims to have special knowledge and techniques for winning people to Christ. As the laity relaxes into comfortable lifestyles, professional evangelists are expected to take up the slack by turning people to Christ more effectively and efficiently. The laity willingly gives up its own evangelistic role in favor of these specialists, much like drivers who depend entirely on professional mechanics to keep their cars going. It is wrongly assumed that televangelists will keep the church going and growing! As James A. Taylor has written, ". . . if Jesus had had TV, if Paul had had the printing press, Christianity might never have survived. The early Christians would have been tempted to leave the job of evangelism to the communications experts."[27]

As should be abundantly clear by now, the rise of the new professional evangelists is not necessarily a boon to the growth of evangelical churches in the United States. Some local congregations, especially charismatic ones, have indeed gained new members as a result of televangelism. But in most cases this has been due to the evangelistic thrust of the local membership, not merely because of religious broadcasts. Churches that are focused on evangelism will generally grow, whether or not they have their own broadcasts. When a pastor and a congregation evangelize naturally, the church becomes an open fellowship that gladly and gratefully accepts new members. In the most aggressive of such congregations—where soulwinning is the principal thrust of evangelical life and most of the members agree to witness to their friends—membership will usually skyrocket. The large churches mentioned earlier use television to maintain their visibility in the community as well as to help convince their own members to be lay evangelists.

To the extent that professionalization of the clergy takes such evangelistic responsibilities away from the laity, it is a stumbling block to church growth. Televangelism is a significant threat in this regard since it creates the illusion that a few major media professionals are harvesting the world for Christ. In fact such harvests are few and far between; televangelists talk mainly to the church rather than to unbelievers. And, with few exceptions, televangelists help some churches at the expense of others, by shifting denominational loyalties of viewers rather than converting unbelievers. Televangelism is not the answer to worldwide evangelization. In the United States, where evangelicalism has become increasingly middle class, it is the problem. Nevertheless, professionalization is appealing as a seemingly easy way of supporting evangelism while making sure that someone else is responsible for doing it.

Conclusion

Ironies can turn to tragedies, and that may be the case with American televangelists. Historically, evangelicals took to the airways, as they did to other mass media, principally to spread the gospel of Jesus Christ. Television represented the largest risk ever because of its enormous cost. To subsidize their work, the religious broadcasters turned to the audience for support. As a result, televangelism was necessarily yoked to its evangelical contributors. Of course, not all—not even most—evangelicals would become financial supporters. Nor would all supporters watch the programs. But televangelism was so dependent on its viewers for its financial lifeblood that it could not really evangelize. As televangelists were forced to buy TV time and create programs that appealed to people who were already converted, evangelism became mere rhetoric rather than reality. Nothing has proved that more than the barrage of Sunday-morning programs aimed at the churchgoing crowd.

Finances are not the only problem, however. Televangelism has not been able to seriously evangelize because the mass medium it depends on for spreading the word focuses on an anonymous audience. Television cannot easily change people's attitudes and beliefs, which are shaped largely by interpersonal relationships and local groups, such as the family, peer group, and church. The tube is a highly influential medium, but it is rarely crucial in determining an individual's basic allegiances. This is why personal contact is far more important as an evangelistic medium. When the gospel is communicated in the context of a warm and caring relationship, it is much more powerful than when offered through the fabricated intimacy of the television screen. The Holy Spirit can and sometimes does work through television, but the gospel exists more personally and compellingly when communicated and exemplified among people who are literally gathered in the name of Christ. Ultimately, then, evangelism remains the task primarily of the local church and the individual believer, not the professional televangelist.

Christians today face the sobering realization that the vast majority of big-time evangelism campaigns have been dismal failures, producing far more commotion than worthwhile communication. Missions researcher David Barrett has identified hundreds of plans to evangelize the world, but few that got anywhere. Most "collapsed or fizzled out within five, ten or fifteen years." The major reasons: ". . . administrative fiascos, personality clashes, irrelevant doctrinal disagreements, prayerlessness, apathy, shortages of funds, embezzlements, absence of workers, rise of other agendas," and so forth. The remaining ones, says Barrett, seem "barely possible of achievement" unless Christians work together in "completely new and unprecedented ways."[28] It is rather ridiculous that in such a historical context the televangelists would suddenly become the answer to the problem of world evangelism. Unfortunately, such triumphalistic rhetoric surfaces repeatedly in the programming and direct-mail appeals of TV ministries.

Indeed, as the end of the second millenium draws near there appears to be more than the usual amount of it.

James F. Engel perceptively concludes that the church's preoccupation with evangelistic strategy and methodology can actually interfere with true evangelism. When the church is "healthy and vital," he insists, "evangelistic methods will have real validity. Otherwise, Christians run the risk of turning the Great Commission into the Great Commotion."[29] Televangelism is already a lot of commotion that has gotten in the way of fulfilling its calling. Fortunately there are a few major exceptions. Still, the church has to face the fact that televangelism speaks largely to the saved while deceptively appealing for funds on the basis of its alleged evangelistic power. There may be considerable hope in new kinds of televangelism, but it is too easy to let the lights, images, and microphones lure the church from its historic mission. There comes a time when church leaders must seize hold of their collective wisdom and theology and make the hard decision about whether the billions of dollars spent on glitz and glamour would be more effectively spent on lay education and training. If the laity is not a witnessing body, no amount of televangelism, no matter how well produced, will save the world. To believe so is sheer folly. In America, though, it is a common folly.

All this is not to say that evangelicals should not be on television. It is merely to report that contemporary televangelism is largely an evangelistic flop. Perhaps evangelicals should accept the soulwinning limits of television and claim the medium for other important purposes, such as news, drama, and documentary. Not all Christian television need be explicitly evangelistic, nor should all television be evaluated solely in terms of its evangelistic power. The Book of Genesis makes clear that humankind was created by God to have dominion over all the earth, from business to the arts, not just over the ecclesiastical church and its Great Commission. As things now stand, however, many evangelicals have too narrow a view of the Christian life. Here, too, evangelicalism can be particularly restrictive, since most American evangelicals seem to equate *Christian* communication with evangelistic messages. Like the surrounding culture, which tends to turn everything into hype and salesmanship, evangelicals look pragmatically for the altar call or decision-for-Christ in practically every medium they use.

Early on, Christian television found its special niche in American culture as primarily an evangelistic vehicle. The result has been less than the wisest use of the church's resources. Instead of taking a hard look at themselves, televangelists have contributed to this unfortunate development by participating in programming in which they preach mainly to other Christians while claiming to reach unbelievers. It is time for televangelists and the rest of the church to consider a different approach—one better suited to the medium and more in tune with the role of interpersonal relationships in the conversion process. Decades ago Billy Graham adopted this idea in his televised crusades, which not only led to some conversions, but—perhaps even more importantly—mobilized, trained, and motivated local churches in the name of ecumenical evangelization. Compared to most televangelism, Graham's "old-fashioned" model is still superior as a way of helping to fulfill the Great Commission. The question remains, however, as to what other uses Christians might find for television.

The Congregation as Audience

In the 1980s televangelist Jimmy Swaggart rode the crest of his success with a proposal that shocked some observers and dumbfounded others. He offered to install free of charge a satellite receiver and dish antenna at any church that would carry his Sunday-morning worship services from Baton Rouge. Billed as a church-growth idea, the proposal would have delivered Swaggart's ministry directly to the pulpits of local churches. Congregations could use television monitors or video projectors to reproduce the televangelist's image in the sanctuary—and could then advertise Swaggart as their main attraction.

Swaggart's proposal elicited some of the worst fears of televangelism's critics, who had been saying for years that evangelical broadcasting was competing with the local church. It seemed that Swaggart was making a play to establish his own denomination by becoming a kind of mass-mediated super pastor shepherding a flock of distant congregations. From the early days of radio, many pastors worried that glib and persuasive broadcast preachers might eventually steal the sheep of local churches; members would stay at home to listen to their favorite radio celebrity instead of attending church. Through a kind of Darwinian survival of the fittest, the more talented religious broadcasters might drive many local pastors out of the ministry.

History shows that such fears are at best misguided. Although the local church has much to fear about contemporary televangelism, pastoral competition is hardly the most worrisome aspect. Religious broadcasting has not driven the local church out of existence. Studies conducted in the 1980s have proved that very few people watch religious television instead of attending a local church. Quite the contrary is the case, since religious-television viewers tend to be active in a congregation. In marketing terms, they are "heavy users" who combine local and mass-media religion in their lives. As mentioned earlier, the vast majority of televangelism's viewers are already converted. By and large, they do not use televangelism as a substitute for the local church.[1] There are many shut-ins who can worship only via the tube, but these are obvious exceptions.

Moreover, studies show that televangelism does not siphon off contributions that would otherwise go toward local church budgets. This is another misconception that fueled pastors' fears about religious broadcasting's impact on their congregations. Once again, the person who gives to the televangelist tends to be the one who gives to the local congregation. The more highly religious person, who both attends a local church and watches one or more religious shows, generally will contribute to both.[2]

What, then, is the impact of televangelism on the local church and on denominational Christianity in the United States? Swaggart's proposal never really met with success, in spite of his popularity. Indeed, in the face of many people's fears, televangelism has not eliminated the local church or traditional denominations. However, this is not to say that televangelism is benign. The older fears about its impact on church attendance and giving were misguided but not wholly without validity. Televangelism's effects are more subtle and more profoundly disturbing. It appears that televangelism does not compete as much as it subverts the local church. Its impact is not principally on local church attendance and contributions, but on parishioners' sense of the faith, styles of worship, and church life. Swaggart would not likely be able to establish his own mass media denomination, but he and other popular televangelists have significantly altered many Christians' beliefs, attitudes, and sensibilities.

In short, televangelism's popular religiosity has seriously challenged the traditional, institutional and denominational church. Because it is so market-driven, televangelism has created popular expectations that have forced many pastors and denominational prelates to change the ways their churches are organized and the ways church life is practiced. Televangelism has helped introduce to congregations such things as entertainment-oriented worship, charismatic preaching, individualistic thinking, and anonymous attendance. It has turned the local congregation increasingly into an audience, even as the televangelists have unsuccessfully tried to transform their audiences into congregations. Instead of driving people away from the church, televangelism is changing their very conception of the church and its functions.

Televised Denominations

From the beginning of religious broadcasting, some denominations have worried that media-generated Christianity would hurt their denominations. Protestant and Roman Catholic church leaders alike were concerned about this possibility. (Two Roman Catholic priests—Charles Coughlin on radio and Fulton J. Sheen on television—attracted significant followings in the 1930s and 1950s, respectively.) Because American Protestantism is so varied and dispersed, personality-specific fears have rarely surfaced in public discussion of religious broadcasting. Instead, primarily mainline Protestants have worried that televangelism would lead mainline members to the more evangelical denominations. After all, evangelicalism has been far more visible on television than mainline Protestantism.

Fears about the rise of new denominations organized around effective broadcasters have been largely misguided. History shows that the airways cannot really sustain a denomination, though broadcasting can do much to advance the visibility of specific local churches. The most successful televangelists have usually been the heads of their own independent churches (Jimmy Swaggart, Jim Bakker, Jerry Falwell, Rex Humbard). Others have been influential but not omnipotent leaders in their denominations (Robert Schuller, D. James Kennedy, Charles Stanley). Independent televangelists may have built large local congregations, but they have failed to translate that success into a denominational organization, partly because many of their viewers and supporters are themselves fiercely independent. Meanwhile, denominationally affiliated televangelists, whose broadcasts are typically not supported officially by the denomination, have not been able to gain major influence over the ecclesiastical structures of their denominations.

At best, televangelists have created quasi-denominations organized around their programming and direct-mail fund raising.

The TV screen is their primary pulpit, while the postal service passes the collection plate. Membership is expressed symbolically through the creation of a "club" or some other category of affiliation, such as a broadcast "family." In 1990 Robert Schuller boldly offered membership in his own "church" to viewers who contributed a particular amount. This designation was largely meaningless, however, since Schuller's denomination, the Reformed Church in America, would hardly consider such people to be real members. This kind of media-endorsed church membership has been little more than a rhetorical technique to give viewers a clearer sense of identity with the broadcast ministry. A few viewers, especially elderly ones, might actually feel like members of the television church, but they are never given the same kinds of privileges and responsibilities that characterize local church membership—except, of course, the monthly tithe to the televangelist, which roughly parallels the commitment that congregants make to support their local church. Even "attendance" is not required. As Stewart Hoover found, not all "700 Club" patrons are actual viewers.[3]

If televangelism is not creating broadcast-based denominations, however, it is still likely leading to the decline of old-style denominations. Televangelism is surely one factor in what sociologist Robert Wuthnow calls "the restructuring of American Christianity." According to Wuthnow, denominational loyalty based on family, ethnicity, tradition, and the like is giving way to new distinctions within Protestantism that are based largely on ideology. Even within a specific denomination, such as the turbulent Southern Baptist Convention, there can be rather pronounced divisions between liberals and conservatives over social and hermeneutical issues. Televangelists fuel these debates by offering clear positions based on their own biblical interpretations. As we saw earlier, such polarized messages help raise funds as well by creating a sense of social or spiritual crisis. If Wuthnow is correct, as I believe he is, televangelism will not create its own denominations as much as foster conflict and dissent within existing ones. At the same time, televangelism will encourage the American religious community to be passionate about the implications of its faith for public life.[4]

Televangelism will not need to create its own denominations so long as there are plenty of local churches that offer worship experiences and ideology similar to these found on popular broadcasts.

The Assemblies of God denomination, for example, has been especially blessed with the broadcast-related fallout from mainline
denominations. The "700 Club" and "PTL Club," along with Swaggart's program, appealed to many viewers who sought membership in Assemblies congregations. In some areas of the country
the Assemblies churches took offerings for designated televangelists, voluntarily staffed local crisis-centered or prayer telephone
lines promoted on their programs, and cooperated in distributing
food and clothing to locally needy families from funds raised on
the air or through direct-mail appeals. This type of cooperation
between local congregations and some TV ministries has been
greatly overlooked by critics who mistakenly think that all televangelism robs the local church of significance. Pat Robertson's
"Operation Blessing" alone raised millions of dollars annually for
local projects. In effect, it used CBN as a clearinghouse and fund-
raising organization for the benefit of local communities. Of course
it also benefited Robertson's ministry by integrating it successfully
with local church activities. Jim Bakker's "People That Love" centers, commended by President Ronald Reagan, functioned similarly, though not on the scale of "Operation Blessing."

Moreover, televangelism is necessarily too dynamic to become
the center of a denomination. Forced to follow the winds of the
market, most televangelism is too busy trying to survive. Denominations require a fairly high degree of formal organization to
make them function ecclesiastically. Televangelists, on the other
hand, normally have to be able to create and eliminate building
projects and other fund-raising plans practically overnight, so they
need to place power in the hands of one or a few people, not in
large committees, delegations, synods, conventions, and the like.
Televangelism thrives partly because it is not bound by the kinds
of decision making and accountability characteristic of most North
American denominations.

Finally, televangelism is unable to establish the kinds of disci-
pling that are necessary for organizations to perpetuate themselves. Television cannot create long-term disciples, only temporary supporters or followers. As James A. Taylor put it, "The
media have too many built-in handicaps—from trying to talk to
someone who isn't there, to being unable to discern until it's too
late."[5] So far no televangelists have founded media organizations
that would definitely survive their own deaths. Robertson,
Roberts, and Falwell have all started universities as a means of

perpetuating their ministries, apparently believing that televangelists will come and go but educational institutions have a chance to survive. No doubt this is partly because educational institutions create disciples who are as much committed to the goals of the university as to the idiosyncratic vision of any particular educational leader, no matter how charismatic he might be.

The Invisible Church

If televangelism is any type of religious institution, it is part of what Thomas Luckmann has called "the invisible church."[6] It is a congregation without a real church—just a collection of believers tied together loosely by their allegiance to a television ministry or its leader. They do not necessarily even believe exactly the same thing, though they share a liking of the same televangelist and a taste for the same programming. And they certainly are not part of the same church organization.

In this invisible church the enjoyment of the show substitutes for the enjoyment of interpersonal relationships that exist in a real congregation. Because the tube cannot provide dialogue and touch, it cannot sustain fellowship and genuine trust among viewers. Its congregants never meet one another, so they share only a viewing experience, not a relational one. Any interaction is mediated through the show. The televangelist decides what viewers will know about each other—who watches, why, how frequently, when, and with what contributions. He controls the flow of messages from one invisible viewer to another, except for serendipitous meetings between fellow members of the audience. The direction is not purely "one way," from preacher to audience, since viewers are encouraged to write letters or telephone a prayer line. But televangelism's communication is essentially a series of monologues designed to create the impression of membership, relationship, and even accountability.

Yet, the lack of dialogue in the invisible church is an attraction for some viewers. Televangelism always accepts individual viewers as they are, not as the church would like them to become. Unlike a real personal relationship in a local congregation, where relationships demand some degree of openness and authenticity, televangelism requires neither. Because the viewers are unseen, they need not reveal anything about themselves, let alone shake a hand or exchange pleasantries. Attending the invisible church is a private matter that takes place in the nonthreatening space of one's own residence. And no TV minister will challenge or reject a viewer by name. Individual human personality, which becomes the currency of congregational relationships, is completely absent among the television audience. For people threatened by social vulnerability, that is probably a matter of great comfort.

Televangelists are, in a very different way, similarly anonymous in the electronic church. They appear to be highly visible, as their images and electronically reproduced voices are repeatedly projected on the tube, both in live programming and through videotaping. But individual viewers cannot have dialogue with their favorite televangelist. They do not know much, if anything, about that televangelist's real life—except the carefully selected facts doled out on the air, in mailings, and promotional autobiographies. In this context the televangelist, too, is not a real person but merely an audiovisual showman managed by sound technicians, camera operators, editors, directors, and producers.

The local pastor, by contrast, exists as a fallible human being with the same basic needs as his congregation. Parishioners know where he lives, how his children behave, what he wears during the week, and all of the other day-to-day practices that tell people a lot about others. Because he cannot hide behind promotional hype, this shepherd must meet his flock in the flesh. His personality cannot be controlled like a broadcast image, but invariably enters the pulpit colored for better or worse by the relationships he has with congregants.

In some of its most celebrated and popular programming, American televangelism implicitly denies the centrality of the church in the life of the believer. Like the Docetics of early Christianity, who denied the reality of a historical Jesus, the new televisual heretics deny the reality of the body of Christ except as an imaginary group of isolated individuals—an invisible church.[7] Without its interpersonal relationships and minus the oral culture that existed both in Jewish tradition and the early church, the body of believers cannot activate the unique personalities that God gave each individual. Believers express their God-intended qualities *in* and *through* their relationships with other members of the body of Christ. To put it even more powerfully, Christ's personality, as communicated via the Holy Spirit, takes up residence not just in the heart of the individual believer, but in the collective life of the congregation. Without the fellowship of other believers, the individual Christian is but an undeveloped personality awaiting a community in which to become what God has intended. Through prayer, preaching, and Scripture, Christians find their godly personalities and experience the fruit of the spirit. But it is through Christian community that they learn to exercise those personalities for the good of others and the glory of God.

American Christians often forget that Christianity is the collective faith of a people, not merely the personalized beliefs of individuals. The Scriptures present the gospel essentially as the story of an ancient people, the life of a contemporary people, and the hope of a future people. In each case the Good News belongs to a community, not just to isolated individuals. And its promise is to be embraced *in* that community, in the flesh and in real time and place. This sounds odd to some Americans, who are nurtured on individualism, but it is clearly a biblical theme that runs through the Scriptures. When televangelism promotes an individualistic gospel, it interferes with the establishment of rich communities of belief in the United States. The reality of this problem is reflected in the incredible mobility of individuals from one church to another, and in the lack of communal commitment in so many congregations. Many churches have become mere collections of individual believers who happen to be in the same place for worship. Few congregations reflect the kind of unified faith life that fosters deep relationships and encourages individuals to find collective expression as the people of God.

To the extent that televangelism establishes the model for American Christendom, it contributes to the problem of alienation in the church and in society as a whole. Televangelism does not and cannot restore dialogic, face-to-face communication; nor can a congregation that approaches church life as if it were building a televangelistic ministry. The loneliness, fear, anxiety, and sheer isolation that so many modern people feel all beg for real relationships. The congregations of Jesus Christ can meet some of those needs—certainly better than televangelism. But a congregation that looks to televangelism and individualistic gospels for a model of church life will likely make matters worse rather than better.

Today's American churches probably bear stronger witness to the individualism of the surrounding culture than to the body of Christ. Just as viewers gather silently and anonymously to watch their favorite TV programs, Christians drive across town on Sunday to sit passively next to people they hardly know and to observe the preacher. The alienation characterizing postindustrial American society is reflected in the weakness of bonds among members of local congregations. Televangelism does little to strengthen those bonds and, unfortunately, the church increasingly resembles the society and the television programming that surrounds it. Rex Humbard used to have an annual televised Communion service, "inviting all believers who are watching at home to gather around their television sets."[8] One wonders what the Lord thinks of that contemporary version of the Last Supper.

There is no doubt that televangelism has succeeded partly because it seemingly offers hope to people whose own churches have not met their spiritual and emotional needs. William Fore of the National Council of Churches argues that this was a factor in the growth of televangelism during the 1970s and 1980s. "To their everlasting shame," writes Fore, "the mainline churches have simply failed to understand and meet the needs of a significant number of people in their communities, people who are searching for a satisfying religious experience, but who have not found it in the mainline churches. These people, many of them alienated, unfulfilled, forgotten or ignored, but also many dynamic, independent and searching, are going to find what solace they can from the superficial and ultimately harmful ministrations of the electronic church."[9] Fore may have overstated how "harmful" televangelism is, but he certainly has identified the reasons for its allure in modern society.

TV-Styled Worship

While televangelism alters Americans' concept of the church, it also transforms their notion of worship. As the congregation becomes an audience, the worship service is presented as entertainment. Across the Protestant and Roman Catholic spectrum, local congregational worship seems more and more like a Hollywood production. Although the televisual influence is not the only one, show-business elements are unmistakable in contemporary worship. The key words used by advocates are "relaxed," "informal," "interesting," and "relevant"—but the inevitable result is TV-styled services. Televangelism has helped submerge worship into popular culture, and the effects have been mostly negative. For the sake of maintaining or building congregations, local pastors and churches have imitated the styles of entertainment popular with the generation nurtured on TV. Says television critic Neil Postman, ". . . on television, religion, like everything else, is presented, quite simply and without apology, as an entertainment . . . [T]he television screen itself has a strong bias toward a psychology of secularism."[10]

The popularity of televangelism among the churched has led many people to assess the state of local worship. When viewers find something they like on the tube, whether it be the histrionics of Jimmy Swaggart or the faith healing of Oral Roberts, their new taste in programming alters their expectations for their own church. As a result, pastors compete (whether or not they want to) with the likes of D. James Kennedy, Charles Stanley, and Kenneth Copeland. Like schoolteachers, preachers suddenly realize that the tube shapes their pupils' feelings about learning. Congregations accustomed to being part of a TV audience are more easily bored by routine, less likely to follow a lengthy or complicated sermon, and visually tuned to the performer at the pulpit. Either the pastor improves his act or members of the congregation will switch channels or complain to each other about the uninteresting services.

This kind of televisual competition is not all bad if it encourages pastors and their congregations to discuss the elements of worship in the hope of making the service more spiritually meaningful. Tradition—the living faith of the dead—can easily turn into traditionalism—the dead faith of the living. When that happens, worship can become a boring and rather meaningless ritual. Every generation has to reassess the adequacy of its patterns of worship. Sometimes the problem is simple; the congregation may simply need to be reeducated about the meaning of the different parts of a liturgy. On other occasions an assessment indicates that the styles and forms of worship have at least partly outworn their usefulness. As culture has changed, worship has remained relatively static; it is time for changes designed to introduce the age-old truths of the gospel in new liturgical packages.

Such a quest for meaningfully relevant worship, however, is too easily victimized by popular fad and fashion. Worship can be so tuned to the surrounding culture that it is little more than a celebration of secular values. Ben Armstrong is right, I think, when he declares that religious radio and television have "broken through the walls of tradition we have built up around the church . . ." He is wrong, however, when he adds that we are therefore left with "conditions remarkably similar to the early church."[11] The early church had inherited some of its own traditions from the Jews and adapted them for the Greek mind, so it was not really a tradition-free church that simply "did its own thing," to use modern vernacular. Televangelism is an odd combination of tradition and market-driven, popularly styled, entertainment-oriented faith and practice. It steals from the Holiness tradition, from the Reformational traditions, and even from Roman Catholicism. Each show does it differently, but they all blend the old and the new—with more and more emphasis on the latter. Armstrong's view of religious broadcasting is naively romantic, as if modern communications technologies will magically revert the modern church to its tribal origins, just as Marshall McLuhan thought they would usher in a global village. In reality televangelism introduces a lot of entertainment where there once was worship.

Baby-Boom Religion

The rise of entertainment-oriented worship cannot be separated from the growth of television and the flowering of the baby-boom generation. Indeed, baby-boomers, the roughly 76 million adults born between 1946 and 1964, are the first generation raised on the tube. Most of them could not imagine life without television, and except for cable reruns some of them would not even recall TV without color. Baby-boomers represent roughly one-half of the adult population in the United States and are *the* major market for a vast array of consumer products. As church-growth expert Elmer Towns has said, their personalities have been shaped as much by the Beatles, BMWs and the Bomb as by the Bible.[12]

Baby-boomers have had a significant impact on the contemporary church, especially evangelicalism, which has generally been more open to adapting its strategies and worship styles for the television generation. Towns believes that baby-boomers have formed 2,000 to 3,000 of their own churches, which are largely nondenominational and which do not stress doctrine. According to sociologists Wade Clark Roof and David A. Rozen, this generation is more religiously and spiritually fluid than any recent one. Boomers are governed by what Roof and Rozen call "calculated choice," which is based less on tradition or deep religious commitment than on the types of personal preferences that influence consumers at the shopping mall. As a result, boomers join a church "not on the basis of doctrine or denominational loyalty, but because of a first-rate child care program, congenial music or preaching lively enough to compete with television."[13]

Although primarily older people watch the televangelists, baby-boomers have established the churches that have the greatest televisual appeal. Willow Creek Community Church in suburban Chicago, for example, became the second-largest congregation in the United States by luring baby-boomers to nontraditional Sunday worship services. Designed for what the pastor calls "seekers," the services are "much more attractive, less boring, more visual and less audio," says Lyle Schaller. "They are more the agenda of the people than that of the minister . . . especially . . . the music, preaching, skits and attention grabbers."[14] Willow Creek has learned how to attract boomers by appealing to their cultural sensibilities. Elmer Towns says of this generation, "Boomers who go to church must worship God as intently as they 'worship' the Beatles."[15]

Across the spectrum of Christian churches, the television generation is having a significant impact. Wherever a church or religious broadcaster is trying to grow, principally by attracting a younger audience, the market drives worship toward the styles of contemporary entertainment. This is reflected in the popular music used in church services, in the applause used to thank performers, in the variety-show format of some church services, in the integration of drama with worship, in the upbeat styles of worship, in the shorter sermons loaded with stories, in the theater-styled "worship centers," and even in the smorgasbord approach to church education programs. Not all of these trends are entirely bad, but they clearly mirror changes in society resulting from the ascendancy of the TV generation. Like the MTV cable channel, worship is faster-paced, more visually tuned and musically based. As a church telemarketing campaign in Aurora, Colorado, determined, visitors want "unconventional praise instruments and practical services" for a "relaxed, casual atmosphere."[16] More and more, it sounds like churchgoers want church to be like a popular music concert or a TV variety show with a sermonette.

In the 1980s some innovative televangelists discovered the same phenomenon. While the more traditional preaching programs attracted older audiences, the newer talk/variety shows began luring younger viewers, including many baby-boomers. Jim

Bakker's "PTL Club" was moderately successful at enticing the new crowd. Pat Robertson's "700 Club" was even more successful, eventually adding former British rock music star Sheila Walsh as a regular co-host of the show. In some ways the entire charismatic movement of the 1970s and 1980s reflected the trend toward popularized worship as entertainment. More openly emotional, musically oriented, and physically dramatic, the charismatic movement made for good television as well as exciting worship. It was not surprising that Bakker and Robertson, hosts of the two most popular daily Christian talk/variety programs, were both tied to that movement.

For good and for bad, televangelism accentuated the rising influence of the baby-boom generation on the American church. Some traditionalism was overturned, yet along the way some essential traditions were probably abandoned as well. On the tube and in the new boomer-styled churches, there was often less concern about historic Christian doctrine than there was about feelings and emotions. All in all, the changes suggested that Christians were increasingly acting like audiences, whether at home while viewing the tube or at church during worship. Some supporters believed that the change signaled a welcome trend toward more participative worship and a more vital faith. Although that might be partly true, it is also likely that the new entertainment-oriented faith was at least somewhat the product of directors and producers as much as pastors and priests. Even the most seemingly spontaneous worship services and religious television shows were often carefully planned entertainment.

Viewers as Consumers

While worship has moved toward entertainment, the local church has found it increasingly difficult to get its members involved in church activities and programs. Like the television viewers, many church members do not expect to have to work for a place in the pews. Church membership has tended to mean little more than joining the Sunday audience. Like the character Chance in Jerzy Kosinski's novel, *Being There,* the parishioner becomes a rather passive member of the television generation. Participation means viewing the screen or, better yet, watching a live performance, but rarely giving of one's talents and gifts. Television viewing becomes the metaphor for attending-and-not participating in the life of the congregation. Robert Schuller captured this in his "Crystal Cathedral Church of the Air"; a membership required only that a viewer (1) pledge at least $25 per month for the next 12 months, and (2) sign a "Statement of Commitment" that eschewed historic Christian doctrine in favor of letting one's mind, heart, eyes, hands, and feet help other people. Schuller's electronic church reflected the direction of many real churches in American culture.

In the United States, TV viewers and church attendees alike are consumers. They have little direct participation in producing the program on the tube or in sustaining the church. A congregation-as-audience exists to "buy" the products, whether they are videotapes, religious jewelry, church pews, or the services of a pastor. Money is the medium of exchange, and "giving" (really "buying") is the type of exchange that links religious producers and consumers. Although the local church is not nearly as commercial as televangelism, the metaphor is increasingly the same: religious consumers buy their entertainment. They trade money for spiritual feelings and a legitimate place in the audience. Fortunately, most congregations refuse to be totally co-opted by this commercial impulse.

Interpersonal relationships tend to focus the work of the local congregation on real human needs and palpable religious faith. On the tube, however, consumerism runs rampant; practically every sermon is tied to an appeal for funds and a report on the status of the ministry. Faith and consumption are nearly one and the same: "He who believes, gives. He who doesn't give, must not believe." This kind of giving is not essentially the result of gratitude before God, but the carefully planned consequence of professional fund-raising appeals. The religious television audience thereby becomes an assured market of faithful buyers.

John Lankford writes that especially since World War II, Americans have ceased putting a premium on work and have become enthusiastic consumers.[17] The result for the church is a generation of congregants who view their relationship to the church very differently from their predecessors. Television and televangelism are not the only culprits. The fruits of economic growth, upward mobility, and increased leisure time have profoundly shaped American society. As television became a symbol of the new affluence and the primary form of domestic entertainment, the local church was forced to adapt to the new consumer culture.

Many Americans found the local church to be boring, irrelevant, time consuming, and even "expensive," since it did not seem to deliver as much value as various forms of sports and other popular entertainment. People still flocked to church on Sundays, but more as a matter of duty or tradition than faith and inspiration. Sunday-afternoon sports on television rivaled church attendance figures, while the Super Bowl ratings surpassed even Christmas church attendance. Although football was exciting enough to keep viewers tuned in for several hours on Sunday, most one-hour church services stretched the attention span beyond what some congregants could muster. Only in charismatic church circles, where exciting services easily lasted two hours, could religion challenge football's televisual clout.

Particularly since the 1960s, Americans have changed churches almost as easily as they switch television channels. Gary Leazer of the Southern Baptist Home Missions Board predicts that Americans will increasingly act like "religious consumers." He says that if "one denomination does not offer a particular item, people will go to another faith to find it."[18] The church in America increasingly resembles the product marketplace, with believers seen as consumers of religious fads. Again, some change is necessary to make the gospel and worship relevant, but much of the change is little more than savvy marketing to the TV generation, which is easily bored and rather self-seeking. Nationally speaking, the church looks more and more like a mass consumer group being carved up by market-driven research. In the name of church growth and relevance, local congregational life has been pushed in the same entertainment-oriented direction as televangelism.

Televangelism represents the forefront of the consumerization of the American church. On-the-tube, religious participation is little more than watching and giving, though most viewers do not do even the latter. Membership is expressed symbolically through the act of contributing and the resulting "gifts," such as "Jesus First" lapel pins and "special edition" Bibles. In this church of the airways, the gospel is a "product" that calls for little more than a telephone call or a donation. There is no need for commitment and sacrifice, which come with relationship, not mass-media consumption. One great hymn says "Trust and Obey." According to much televangelism, all one need do is "watch and consume." Unfortunately, that is also the theme of many local churches bent on competing in the marketplace.

The Useful Audience

Today's view of the congregation as an audience is poor ecclesiology, but great for marketing. Once the body of Christ is transformed into a passive group of consumers, it can most easily be used by televangelists for their own purposes, which usually include ministry growth. When an audience is primarily a congregation, it must be allowed to shape the guiding vision of the ministry. And it must be served as well. If an audience is *only* an audience, whether in commercial broadcasting or televangelism, it exists largely for the benefit of the broadcaster. These are harsh words, but they are proved true by televangelism's dismal record. As Lutheran broadcaster Donald N. Oberdorfer put it, "We continue to think of ourselves as being transmitters of the Gospel rather than being in a ministry of communication."[19]

How could this happen? The answer is simple but disturbing: Virtually every televangelist must seek an audience of contributors who will help build the ministry. Whether or not there is any real ministry taking place is relatively inconsequential. On commercial television the networks do not care whether their audiences are being served by the broadcasts. All they wish to do is maximize the ratings and enhance the company's profitability. They wrongly assume that high ratings mean the public is being served. (Actually, Americans watch more television than ever but say in surveys that it is worse than ever.) Similarly, the televangelists believe that if their audiences and/or contributions increase they must be serving their viewers. In fact, bigger audiences and larger contributions mean little more than bigger audiences and larger contributions. Such yardsticks say absolutely nothing about the quality or effectiveness of a ministry. Neither do conversion statistics unless a televangelist knows what those decisions-for-Christ mean in the lives of the converts. As noted earlier, except for anecdotal evidence, there is no reason to believe that televangelism really ministers to most people any more than commercial broadcasting really serves "the public interest" (as is supposedly required by law).

Once the body of believers becomes a mere audience, it can be manipulated for the self-perpetuation of so-called television ministries. The audience is a mere means to an end—organizational expansion. Audiences are not personalized, but quantified and abstracted. Every viewer is a number on the marketing charts, a mere blip on the computer or a dot on a graph. Although each of those viewers has a personal life history, their stories are collapsed into the abstracted audience. Even when the televangelist announces a telephone number for "personal prayer," he is not the one to answer the calls. Every call becomes part of the statistics of the ministry. The best television ministries refer all calls or letters to local churches, but most do not. They are content to use the audience for their own purposes.

Hasidic Jewish scholar Martin Buber once distinguished between two kinds of relationships. The "I-thou" relationship is characterized by special regard for each other. In this relationship individuals treat each other as humans created in the image of God. They seek to empathize and to serve each other. The "I-it" relationship, on the other hand, is based largely on the selfish desire of individuals to use others for their own benefit. People are viewed as mere means toward self-seeking ends.[20] Unfortunately, most broadcasting, including televangelism, is based on "I-it" relationships between broadcasters and their audiences. Because the relationships are impersonal, and because broadcasters of all kinds are part of larger organizations with their own goals, it is nearly impossible for these mass communicators to be authentic in what they project.

Even in televangelism it is difficult for the viewer to know the agenda and purposes behind the scenes of a program. It is usually unclear whether or not the televangelist is acting on a real desire to serve or merely the need to raise funds. Some televangelists are remarkably authentic individuals who say what they mean and mean what they say. But the temptation to say what will attract an audience and thereby elicit contributions is always strong in televangelism, whose very existence depends on the financial gifts of supporters to pay the monthly bills. Many televangelists therefore distort the truth or even lie to keep the ministry going. The rhetoric of exaggeration is a major part of this type of manipulation. Televangelists have claimed audiences ten times larger than they really are. They have exaggerated the number of conversions resulting from the ministry's programming. They have misled viewers and contributors about the impact of their ministries on public policy. And they have done all these things with a view of the audience as a useful means to the ministry's growth.

Megachurch Mania

The closest thing to televangelism incarnate in the local church is the so-called megachurch. Researcher Lyle E. Schaller believes that there are over 1,000 megachurches in the United States, including one of every 300 Lutheran parishes, one in every 200 Southern Baptist churches, one in every 600 United Methodist churches, and one in every 300 churches that carries the word *Presbyterian* in its name.[21] The independent megachurches are the most like televangelism in style and substance. However, even the denominationally affiliated ones are not dependent on the denomination for their survival. To the contrary, their denominations are often dependent on them as the cash cows. These large churches are not all the same, but they tend to rise in response to the "erosion of institutional authority," says Schaller.[22]

No longer satisfied with traditional worship, yet seeking some kind of spiritual experience, many Americans have found at least temporary answers in megachurches. Some of these large churches appeal specifically to baby-boomers. Not surprisingly, they have adopted some of the entertainment-oriented techniques that appeal to that generation. Overall, however, the mega-churches reflect far more than the boomer sensibility. In at least five ways the megachurch movement reflects trends in American culture generally and televangelism specifically.

First, megachurches typically are organized around the charismatic power of one or more pastors. They are mini-personality cults that invest an enormous amount of authority in particular people. Some of the denominationally affiliated churches are less like this than the independent ones, but personality is clearly a drawing card for most.

Second, megachurches frequently use TV-styled worship as a means of attracting new members from more traditional churches and from the secular culture. Worship tends to be dramatic and entertaining. It relies on popular music, including live performances using musical instruments not traditionally associated with worship. Generally speaking, worship is patterned on a variety-show format.

Third, the megachurch's size creates a congregational anonymity that mirrors mass society as well as the television audience. Many people who would not otherwise step foot in church are attracted to such a large, impersonal group. For at least a while, they find comfort in numbers and the feel of the congregation as an audience rather than a closely knit body of believers. Of course, many megachurches eventually require members to join small groups within the congregation.

Fourth, megachurches offer a smorgasbord approach to ministry that mimics the abundance of contemporary entertainment for the individual consumer. Such churches seek to present something for every taste and desire rather than one or two programs for the entire congregation. They are more like a well-stocked video store than a single television channel. Megachurches use target marketing to keep together a rather heterogeneous congregation.

Fifth, megachurches are willing to change rapidly with the shifting whims of the marketplace. They will quickly add or eliminate programs according to congregational needs and desires and will easily alter the order or form of worship to make it more meaningful or more attractive to visitors. Megachurches will introduce new architectural models and novel decorative schemes to set a particular mood for a given style of worship. In short, megachurches are remarkably dynamic organisms that refuse to let tradition dictate contemporary practice.

These characteristics suggest that megachurches are at the cutting edge of the American church growth movement. By incorporating aspects of popular culture and marketing into church planning, they have bridged the gap between the television generation and more traditional Protestantism. Whether or not they have gone too far is not a matter to take up in depth in this book. The fact that they are popular and apparently growing, however, indicates that they have found the pulse of American culture. Part of that pulse is quickened by television, including televangelism.

Conclusion

In a remarkable way, televangelism has established the model for much congregational life in the United States. Even people who dislike televangelism, especially the baby boomers, often find that they enjoy the kind of anonymous, entertainment-oriented worship of large and growing churches. The most difficult thing to find in these changes is a balance between change and continuity. If the gospel is truly to be popular, it must be presented in a contemporary fashion. But if achieving popularity requires the gospel to be distorted, there is no use in spreading it through contemporary means.

This chapter has suggested that the trend toward viewing the congregation as a passive audience is at least somewhat bad for both the church in general and the individual believer. Televangelism, along with other forms of popular programming, has changed how many Christians respond to worship, what they expect from a church, how they think of congregational participation, and even how they define authentic faith. For good and bad, megachurches are at the cutting edge of implementing the television model in the church of Jesus Christ. They have attracted many members who might otherwise have left the church or never come in the first place. Indeed, megachurches have been far more effective evangelistically than televangelists. However, the appeal of megachurches, like the popularity of TV-styled worship in general, is not itself an indicator of how spiritually sound and ecclesiastically proper these churches really are.

In his own assessment of the megachurch phenomenon, Lyle Schaller suggests that there is at least a likelihood that "the children of today's megachurch members will want something new and different: small, intimate congregations."[23] Schaller's observation indicates that the megachurches may not be meeting all the needs of even the baby-boomers. To put it broadly, in a television society people still desire close-knit relationships and interpersonal communication. As created in the image of God, humankind wants to be more than an audience. Because it seeks the "I-thou" relationships that should characterize the body of Christ, neither televangelism nor the megachurch is the zenith of Christian community. Each is more a product of American mass society than a final solution to its problems. Interpersonal communication is the medium in and through which deep and meaningful relationships are created and maintained. Any congregation grounded deeply in such communication will likely minister to people more effectively than one that is not.

Schaller is probably correct in the sense that megachurches, like televangelism, meet particular needs while overlooking others. Many Christians want more relevant, dramatic, and entertaining worship than they have been able to get in their own traditional congregations. But religious television programs need to address more than a statistically defined audience. They must address the universal need to be affirmed personally as a distinct human being—to be more than an anonymous viewer. This need will likely surface more frequently among members of the new-styled TV and megachurch "congregations." As that happens, there will likely be even better opportunities for ministry.

Redeeming the Electronic Church

Several years before the televangelism scandals of the 1980s I wrote a cautionary article about religious broadcasting for a denominational magazine. Instead of merely criticizing televangelism, I encouraged viewers to select carefully which TV ministries they might support. Based on my own experiences writing to televangelists, I indicated that all viewers should request two documents before contributing to any religious broadcasters: a doctrinal statement and a financial statement. My reasoning was straightforward and, I thought, common sense. Why not support televangelists whose beliefs are in tune with your own and who are good financial stewards?

I could never have predicted the response to my article. A few people wrote positive letters to the magazine's editor. Others wrote critical ones, blasting me for either not saying enough good things about televangelism or, more frequently, for seemingly criticizing their favorite TV preacher. Strangely enough, critics of my article typically supported televangelists who were at theological odds with the tradition represented by the denomination that sponsored the magazine. The most nasty letters arrived at my home and office. They questioned my integrity and especially my faith. One unsigned letter even told me where to go in no uncertain terms. Most shocking of all was a letter sent to the magazine's editor by an executive of one of the major televangelism organizations. In that personal note the executive criticized the editor for publishing an article written by an uninformed and misguided professor. He encouraged the editor not to publish my articles. His goal was clear: to have me censored from the magazine of my own denomination.

As anyone who has publicly spoken or written about televangelism knows, there are many supporters who believe there is no place for criticism in the kingdom of God. Christians are supposed to criticize the secular world, not the church and its people. Even in the face of scandals, there are many true believers who naively see the work of God wherever and whenever his name is evoked and religious words are uttered. From that perspective, critics of televangelism are suspect and their faith is challenged. They are often viewed in the same way that former Vice President Spiro Agnew once described the nation's news reporters: "nattering nabobs of negativism."

While I do not wish to defend all critics of televangelism, I do want to assert the ongoing need for criticism and admonishment within the church. Televangelism, too, must continually be watched and evaluated by the Christian community. It does not stand independently before the American public like family businesses or corporations that are legally monitored by government regulators and a few watchdog groups. Televangelism is part of the universal church of all believers in Christ. The people of God therefore have a responsibility to ensure that it actually reflects the Word of God and the work of his people. Televangelism exists for the church, not the church for televangelism. Moreover, the church exists to serve God, not to further the interests of specific ministries or to elevate the celebrity status of particular religious personalities.

This final chapter offers some suggestions for bringing televangelism under the critical purview of the church. The need for this is abundantly clear. As each previous chapter has shown, televangelism, as the most publicly visible manifestation of the church, continually risks becoming more American than Christian. Based on business principles and shaped by American values, televangelism is steadily steering Christianity toward a popular, entertainment-styled faith that would barely be recognized by the historic church. This is precisely why critics of televangelism are so strongly attacked by many of its supporters, whose own faith has been shaped more by American culture than by the gospel of Jesus Christ. Although they often do not recognize it, Christians who blindly follow the televangelists are usually sailing in the winds of American popular religion. Scandals are mere storms that cause a few shipwrecks. Once the storm passes, most televangelists set sail confidently from their ports of refuge. Life goes on as usual. Scandals will not redeem televangelism. Much more is needed.

1. *Televangelists should be sponsored by either a large church, a denomination, or a board of directors composed primarily of people greatly respected in public life.*

I believe the only way to truly achieve accountability for televangelism is to put a leash on its individualistic spirit. As long as televangelism is essentially a collection of independent organizations without a church home, there cannot be meaningful accountability. In other words, televangelism needs to be anchored in the church, not in American culture. It must be shaped by the goals and values of the Christian community instead of by the spirits of business or entertainment. This cannot be achieved by any amount of government regulation or even by industry-wide self-regulation. True accountability can grow only when individuals within televangelism must answer to knowledgeable and authoritative Christians outside the ministry. As things now stand, most televangelists are only distantly accountable to their constituency, much like secular broadcasters are only commercially linked to their viewers. This kind of market-related answerability is simply unacceptable in the Christian community, which places many values above economic success and public popularity.

Some people suggest that televangelism merely needs a stronger self-regulatory group such as National Religious Broadcasters (NRB) or the Evangelical Council for Financial Accountability (ECFA). Such monitoring is certainly helpful, since it gives televangelists a chance to work with each other on matters of mutual concern and interest, including ethics. However, in televangelism, as in the business world, self-regulation has too easily slipped into public relations. Self-imposed standards are generally too loose or nonspecific to protect either the customers or the general public. After all, self-regulatory groups want to attract as many members as possible, so they generally establish weak ethical codes that create only the appearance of genuine self-regulation. If the standards are too tough, few organizations will join. If they are too loose, membership means very little. So they ride the middle road between meaningful regulation and mere public relations, steering back and forth depending on the public mood. It is a sad commentary on the NRB that it first began taking ethics seriously during the scandal-riddled 1980s.

Both NRB and ECFA remain rather ineffectual enforcers of weak standards of accountability. Although ECFA has generally taken a tougher ethical stand than NRB, it has thereby lost members to the latter. Meanwhile, NRB concentrates far more on advancing the common interests of religious broadcasters than on keeping their houses clean. By their very nature, both NRB and ECFA pretend to function as ecclesiastical authorities when in fact they cannot really deal with anything more than gross financial misconduct. They are largely unable to examine or seriously act on the most important issues of all: the personal spiritual lives of their members and the content of the televangelists' broadcasts. For example, PTL was an NRB member during its crazy, prescandal years, while rumors about unbiblical conduct flew through the religious community. Some members of NRB clearly proclaim aberrant gospels, yet nothing is done about it. Meanwhile, ECFA struggles to attract more televangelists, who too frequently believe that NRB membership is adequate for accountability purposes.

Televangelism needs direct spiritual authority, not just businesslike self-regulation. Although the local church is in the best position to provide such authority, small churches can easily be controlled by large TV ministries and charismatic personality cults. Televangelists such as Charles Stanley, D. James Kennedy, and Lloyd Ogilvie have willingly and effectively placed themselves under the authority of a local congregation. Moreover, in each case the local congregation is also part of a denomination that seriously oversees the activities of its churches. These two levels of authority provide significantly more internal criticism than is found among most televangelists.

By contrast, Jimmy Swaggart and Jim Bakker were remarkably independent. Both had their own local churches, founded as mere extensions of the television ministry—partly to ensure nonprofit status in the eyes of the Internal Revenue Service. Moreover, although both were ordained by the Assemblies of God, they were effectively permitted to operate as independent ministries. Their apparent financial success, which resulted in donations to the denomination, and their ability to attract newcomers to the denomination endeared them to assemblies officials. To its own credit, the denomination eventually defrocked both televangelists.

Nevertheless, the situations that lead to such abuses of religious authority still exist. As denominational cash cows, these types of televangelists carry a lot of weight at the home office.

Televangelists can create enormously powerful personality cults and successful fund-raising organizations that insulate them almost completely from the authority of local churches or denominations. Few local elders or denominational officials will seriously tangle with such a ministry unless gross ethical or moral violations are made public. Then these spiritual leaders feel compelled to act to protect the public image of the church or denomination. Stopgap defensive tactics, aimed more at saving face and putting out fires than at ensuring ongoing accountability, are not adequate for the the church, which must have much tougher controls than the business world or government if it wishes its voice to be heard.

Over and over again, scandals in religious broadcasting have shown that the churches in America refuse to clean up televangelism. Like ethics in government, ethics in televangelism is nearly always seen as somebody else's problem. Denominational officials are so scared of putting their own ecclesiastical standing on the line that even if they are openly critical in private conversations, they refuse to take a stand in public or in the denominational press. Similarly, local pastors avoid criticizing the TV ministries so they can maintain good relations with their congregations. Virtually every church has its own fans of televangelism, and many of them are among the most active and vocal members. As a result, weak-kneed local pastors or denominational prelates are part of the problem rather than part of the solution. Only when scandals are leaked to the public media do these church leaders say anything about the aberrant gospels, outrageous fund-raising techniques, or unacceptable personal lifestyles of the televangelists.

Unless televangelism is under the actual authority of the church, the church will be increasingly preempted by the organizational needs and interests of the televangelists. A significant part of the blame for the contemporary state of televangelism in America rests with none other than the church's refusal to exercise its authority. Most televangelists will have to be convinced to submit to the church's control, but at the same time the church must be willing to act. This task requires church leaders who will courageously risk their own standing so as to bring public scrutiny to televangelism. Critics of televangelism will be criticized in turn by enthusiastic believers in the cults of personality. Debates

between church leaders and televangelists invariably elicit vocifer-
ous complaints from the latter group's supporters. Because critics
in the church at large often remain fearfully or disinterestedly
silent, the louder voices can rule the roost and increasingly fashion the church after the image of televangelism.

The only possible solution to this ecclesiastical crisis in authority is for the church to take seriously its communal responsibility.
Denominations and their local churches must critically examine
the organizations and programming of any religious broadcasters
under their domain. Since virtually all the major televangelists
are ordained by denominations, the structure for this surveillance
is already in place. The problem is that most denominations look
carefully at only those broadcasters whom they subsidize financially. They tend to ignore denominationally ordained televangelists who are financially independent and even celebrate those
who attract members and contribute to the denomination. In both
cases, denominations are simply abrogating their responsibilities
as overseers of the ministry of the church.

Certainly there will always be independent televangelists free
of the authority of any denomination. At best, such televangelists
will have their own local congregations that theoretically sponsor
the broadcast ministry even though most of the financial support
is provided by viewers. In these situations it is absolutely crucial
that boards of directors be composed primarily of nonmembers
who are greatly respected in the religious and professional communities. Independent ministries of this type need the helpful
counsel and advice of such people. More than that, they need
Christian overseers who will be more committed to the integrity of
the ministry than to its internal success, because their own
integrity rests on the activities of the ministry. Only if a board of
directors really feels that it has something personally to lose,
namely its own standing in the Christian community, will it likely
exercise true authority over the ministry. Today most boards of
directors in televangelism are far more committed to the growth
and prosperity of the ministry than to its institutional integrity.
Instead of representing the church, and hence Christ, they represent the ministry.

Organizations such as NRB and especially ECFA should be
lauded for their attempts to pressure televangelists to replace
family-run boards with directors who reflect broader representation. But it is not nearly enough to limit the number of ministry

employees or televangelists' relatives who may serve on boards. Such restrictions are of little help when the real struggle is between American individualism and ecclesiastical authority. In most cases unleashed televangelism creatively destroys the authority of the church. It disintegrates ecclesiastical control while elevating personal feelings and personality cults to greater and greater status in the church. If televangelists do not establish boards composed of individuals willing to put their own Christian integrity on the line, viewers should turn off the sets and cease writing checks of support.

2. The Christian media should do a far better job of evaluating and assessing televangelism in America.

Other Christian media are partly responsible for the current state of televangelism in the United States. Concerned more about their own circulations or audience ratings, they have generally shied away from reporting on televangelism. Most Christian media managers know that personality cults exist in televangelism, that messages are not always faithful to the gospel, that there is financial corruption and immoral conduct, that self-regulatory attempts have largely failed, and that boards of directors are composed of impotent sycophants. Nevertheless, Christian editors and producers remain largely silent in their own media, fearing that readers and viewers will run to the competition if they come down too hard on televangelism or particular televangelists. The best policy, they reason, is to let the church take care of the situation. Apparently it never occurs to many Christian media professionals that they, too, are part of the church.

As anyone who has closely examined them knows, Christian media are among the least insightful and critical observers of American life. Like televangelists, but in different ways, they tend to tell an audience what they think it wants to hear rather than what it should be hearing. A radio journalist once appropriately remarked, "The most difficult people to interview are politicians and church people: they always say what has to be said and never what they are thinking."[1] So it is among most Christian printed media, which largely see their duty as edifying and informing readers rather than providing them with a critical perspective on contemporary culture or the church. Of course there are Christian journals of critical comment and opinion, from

Sojourners to *Christian Century* and the satirical *Wittenburg Door*. But these are relatively small-circulation publications read largely by fellow critics. Large-circulation evangelical periodicals, such as *Moody Monthly* and *Christianity Today,* take comparatively soft stands on important issues, including televangelism. Even more telling is the fact that the vast percentage of Christian publications are boring denominational conduits of ecclesiastical news or endless repetitions of the delights of personal piety. A few lack almost any critical edge and seem even to celebrate televangelism and encourage Christian personality cults. *Charisma,* for example, has virtually become the *People* of evangelicalism, profiling various televangelists as if they are the saints of today. The pages of such publications are loaded with contemporary hagiography.

In Christian broadcasting the situation is even worse. Christian radio and television personalities frequently attack various secular evils, from abortion to communism, but rarely do they turn their sights on themselves. The direction of these prophetic voices is almost entirely one way, aimed at the evils of the surrounding world instead of at the logs in their own eyes. Somewhat ironically, it was Jimmy Swaggart's irritation with the personal life and programming of fellow televangelist Jim Bakker that led partly to the latter's downfall. Swaggart's criticisms were carefully directed through limited-access media instead of being broadcast over syndicated television. Christian broadcasters will snipe behind the scenes, but rarely will they challenge each other on the air. For the sake of solidarity and mutual interest, televangelists publicly ignore problems within their own ranks. So do Christian radio and television newscasters and talk-show hosts. Too often they act like one happy family, suggesting to the public that they are all equally yoked to the church and its mission.

There is strong biblical warrant for avoiding public arguments among Christians. The church is certainly not called to turn its disagreements into dramatic media events, as happened with Falwell, Swaggart, Bakker, and others in the scandals of the late 1980s. Public criticism can easily become a mass-mediated sport observed gleefully by the rest of the American people. At the same time, however, Christians are public citizens who should care about the image of their church in the world. Christian columnists, commentators, and preachers must not remain silent on controversial religious matters. Instead, they must offer well-considered comments that transcend personality clashes and specific conflicts among contending parties, whether ecclesiastical leaders or televangelists. Like the Old Testament prophets, Christian media should relate timeless truths to contemporary problems or issues rather than allowing themselves to be lured into narrowly defined battles of the moment. The heresies of some televangelists, for example, must be recognized as age-old distortions of the gospel, not merely popular assertions of contemporary preachers.

Televangelism and the church desperately need "prophetic voices" in the public arena that will challenge and admonish. By this term I do not mean predictions or prophecy, although a prophetic voice must suggest what are the likely consequences of televangelism's heresies and the church's commercialization. Rather, in the contemporary world, a prophetic voice is biblically tuned to the principalities and powers that shape society and culture, including the church and televangelism. It reveals the follies of humankind's ways while suggesting godly answers, solutions, and directions. Unlike the audience-driven "false prophet," the authentic prophetic voice turns the gospel on society like an enormous light that discerns evil shadows from radiant spirituality, egotism from humility, and fact from fiction. And it shines the light not just on individual souls, but collectively on the organizations and groups that abuse power and authority.

The amazingly strong lure of televangelism's personality cults scares most Christian media into silence. One Roman Catholic television columnist for diocesan papers learned this the hard way. He received more response to a column cautioning readers about watching televangelists than from any other article he wrote in eleven years. Letters "poured in from around the country," accusing him of being "anti-ecumenical, pre-Vatican II, unsaved, bigoted, and blind to the dearth of Roman Catholic preachers on the tube."[2] He rightly concluded that most Catholics probably watch televangelists rather uncritically and naively, as do Protestant viewers. It is not easy for Christian publications to enhance the church's critical awareness of televangelism, for the true believers in personality cults can be highly intimidating to anyone who even suggests that there are problems on the airways or in the corridors of the ministries.

Two decades ago Martin Marty appropriately called for a "Christian interpretation of the media world."[3] Since then little has changed in this regard. The evangelical church, in particular, has wrongly assumed that Christian media are effective substitutes for this badly needed critique of the media world. It is one thing for evangelicals to be present *in* the media and an entirely different matter for them to offer the surrounding culture a critique *of* the media and American life. Indeed, it is easier to proclaim a simple, distorted gospel than to provide a prophetic voice in the media wilderness. If mainline Protestant media have too easily dismissed televangelism as an outrageous perversion of the gospel, evangelical media have far too uncritically accepted televangelism as legitimate Christian broadcasting. As I have argued throughout this book, televangelism might be far more American than Christian.

Marty's call for a Christian critique of the media world is even more relevant in the age of big-time televangelism. Most Christian journalists remain silent—although this and other books have offered at least the beginnings of such a critique.[4] Christian media find it far easier and less risky to ignore the evangelicals' own media world than to analyze, examine, and evaluate it. Only when scandals create victims and villains do religious media look critically at themselves. Most of the time they are frustrated but content to exist in a world where secular communicators dominate the culture. They prefer to float in safe waters rather than risk swimming against the tide of complacency. Happy to survive, they rarely muddy the waters by raising a prophetic voice in the contemporary world.

Where *are* the prophetic voices in today's religious media? Why are religious publications so Pollyannish? Why do the editors of evangelical periodicals turn their eyes away from the obvious abuses of religious authority launched under the name of televangelism? One answer is that these publications simply find it good business to keep their noses out of trouble and to affirm the joyful spirit of a universal church where everything is supposedly in good and decent order. The more troubling possibility is that Christian publications have followed the winds of evangelicalism's narrow view of piety. As Richard Mouw has cogently argued, the evangelical church tends to be "other worldly," when in fact it should practice a "holy worldliness."[5] Marty's concept of the Christian critique of the media world requires a holy engagement with the world rather than a retreat into the comfort of personal salvation or a submersion into the delights of an intimate relationship with Jesus Christ. Here, then, is the fundamental problem with so many Christian media in today's world: They feed on a tepid gruel of individual edification while the church desperately needs a second course of reasoned critique.

Of course any kind of prophetic media voice will be controversial. Even this book will likely stir up some dissent and conflict within the church, although I do not claim to have the final answers about televangelism. Nevertheless, we cannot let the possibility of disharmony or contentiousness silence any type of prophetic voice. Nor should we permit the difficulty of discerning the true spirits of televangelism to lead us to anti-intellectualism. I hear repeatedly from American evangelicals that I should not speak about televangelism unless I have something good to say. What nonsense! Christians are called to engage the world, to subdue it, to redeem it. Televangelism, too, begs for redemption, both as a collection of individual souls and as part of the media world.

It is time for Christian media to face the reality of life in a world where the institution of television plays an enormously important role. As I have suggested throughout this book, television largely reflects the basic values and beliefs of American culture. And this is true not just of its programming; those same values and beliefs also guide how television is used in society by Christians and non-Christians alike. In short, television is not simply the will of individuals, but also the product of social and cultural forces that influence how the medium is used. Like other social institutions, television is one of the principalities and powers of the modern world, shaping the culture and being shaped by it. It is wrong for most Christian media to ignore their responsibility to interpret and evaluate these dynamics—and evangelical periodicals are especially negligent in this regard. Christian media are called on to pull their heads from the sands of Pollyannishness and focus their attention on the culture around them. After all, that culture shapes the church as well as the secular world.

The lack of an evangelical critique of televangelism was especially obvious during the scandals of the late 1980s. For one thing, evangelical publications started reporting on the scandals only *after* the stories were broken by the secular media. Why were evangelical periodicals not the first ones to report the problems? For years the *Charlotte Observer* had been reporting on misdeeds at Bakker's Heritage U.S.A. Why did the vast majority of evangelical media ignore those reports, which eventually won the Pulitzer Prize for reporter Charles Shepard? Even after the scandals permeated the news for several months and eventually over a year, evangelical media continued to report the stories as if they were isolated events instead of symptoms of deep problems in American evangelicalism. The evangelical media portrayed the scandals as little more than the result of bad personal judgments by particular televangelists. In reality the scandals revealed significant tears in the fabric of evangelical life and the authority of the church. As a result, evangelical media and their secular counterparts generally focused on simplistic cures such as greater self-regulation and tougher ethical codes.

I believe it is fair to say that Christian printed media contributed to the scandals by failing to provide the church with an ongoing critique of the media world and television in particular. Like the general population, the average Christian is television illiterate—what novelist Jerzy Kosinski calls a "videot."[6] He or she understands little about television—its influence, institutional values, dramatic biases, personality cults, and technological specifics. Understandings of the medium are so superficial that most Christian readers had neither the intellectual power nor the spiritual discernment to make sense out of the scandals. For them, like the wider culture, the scandals were largely a humorous or ridiculous interlude on the nightly news.

It is not surprising, then, that little changed in televangelism after the scandals. For a year or so it was considerably more difficult for some televangelists to raise funds, but the content of their programming and the behind-the-scenes practices of their organizations hardly changed after the scandals. Evangelical media turned the scandals into one more morality play that would be worked out for good once the scoundrels were out of the picture. Meanwhile, it was really business-as-usual in the land of televangelism. Instead of badly needed structural change, such as stiff denominational supervision, all that really changed was the decline of one personality cult and the elimination of another one. For most Christians that was apparently enough—and the religious media expected little more of them.

3. Religious education desperately needs to address the implications of living in the television age.

It would be unfair to place too much of the blame for contemporary videocy on the religious media. The churches themselves are also to blame. Generally speaking, denominations and local churches have missed opportunities to provide their members with minds and hearts capable of discerning the spirits of contemporary American culture. Evangelicals, for instance, have focused their critique almost entirely on television's exploitation of sex, violence, and profanity, while largely ignoring the far more widespread issues of racism, materialism, sexism, nationalism, and ethnocentrism. If anything, television is dominated more by the celebration of materialism and hedonism than by the depiction of sexual scenes or violent actions. Television offers viewers an orientation to life and a constellation of values, not only offensive images or naughty words. Similarly, televangelism provides a way of defining and experiencing religion. It is far more than sermons, fund-raising, and spiritual chitchat. In other words, the media world, especially television, animates and perpetuates the spirits of modern society. Even individuals who do not watch much television must live in a world shaped by these spirits. Like the rest of the media world, televangelism deserves serious attention in religious education.

Most American adults watch fifteen to twenty hours of television every week. If they are "religious," they go to church for about an hour of worship, perhaps for another hour of Sunday school and a few minutes of informal fellowship. Members of congregations typically also meet with each other or their pastors for another hour or two every week, briefly read the Bible and a religious publication or two, and pray a little at meals. Meanwhile, the spigot of television is running profusely, shaping all Americans' way of life as well as their notions of worship, prayer, and religion generally. Until the church seriously addresses this incredible imbalance between the time allotments for television and church activity, most Christians will not be able to identify alternative values and beliefs to counter those hawked by the media world. The fact is that most local congregations and denominations seem increasingly irrelevant to many Americans. In this situation religion does not shape life. Instead, religion is shaped by the surrounding culture. Only the new megachurches, founded on televisual principles, seem to be able to compete effectively. And these churches often provide the most highly attended religious education classes.

Televangelism will not be redeemed until the educational work of the church is redeemed. Partly because of poor preaching, and partly because of weak religious education, most Christians are ill-equipped to view the media world from the vantage point of the Christian faith. From the perspective of most church education programs, the guiding philosophy about the media world seems to be *caveat emptor*—let the buyer (viewer) beware. Instead of providing an aggressive evaluation of televangelism and the rest of the media world, the church pretends that it can carry on its work effectively as it has in the past, with but a few minor adjustments. Worship styles are changed to fit the new television culture, educational videotapes are increasingly substituted for printed materials, and seemingly perfunctory criticisms are leveled from the pulpit at television's sex, violence, and profanity, but rarely are the media brought into critical focus. Like a naive used-car buyer, who knows little about automobiles and even less about how to locate a dependable one, the average Christian adult cannot separate the wheat from the chaff on the television screen. He can spot the obvious problems, like a rusted fender or a sexually explicit scene, but is nearly blind to the underlying problems. Among the televangelists he is able to discern only the most gross examples of pulpit histrionics, megalomaniacal sermons, or excessive financial appeals.

On the one hand, the church simply needs to improve Christians' doctrinal quotient. In these days of cultural illiteracy there is an awful lot of religious ignorance. The success of the health-and-wealth gospel, for example, depends on such ignorance. Contemporary congregants need to know what their faith is really all about—what is essential and what is not, which beliefs are Christian and which ones are merely American, what the historic church has taught and what the Bible actually says. Without this kind of biblical and doctrinal foundation, the beliefs of particular denominations or traditions can easily turn into a confusing collection of contradictory ideas in the minds of many people. Religious ignorance in Martin Luther's day led him to write catechisms in question-and-answer formats. The Calvinists had their versions as well. In today's media world it appears that it is time once again for creating basic catechisms that teach the essentials of the faith in a relevant and prophetic style. How else can Christians be instructed in the essentials of the faith while some televangelists hawk the latest versions of historic heresies?

On the other hand, the church needs to address directly the specific values and beliefs of American culture, including televangelism. The age-old truths of the Christian faith must be focused particularly on the television world in which the modern Christian lives. The conflicts and tensions between Christian faith and modern culture could provocatively animate both the methods and themes of contemporary religious education. It is one thing to teach biblical history and Christian doctrine in a vacuum. It is far more edifying to relate that information to the current cultural environment. The fact that so many Christians easily become staunch believers of televised personality cults should concern local pastors and Sunday school teachers, but it should also motivate them to create educational programs and craft sermons that help congregants discern the spirits of televangelism.

The local church is the most promising vehicle for this type of religious education. After all, it is the apparent irrelevance of the local church that leads some believers to televangelism's experiential gospel of success, and it is the impersonal character of many local congregations that drives some members to the artificial intimacy of the tube. A strong local body of believers, joined in fellowship and service and embracing a shared critique of the media world, would be strong competition for television of any kind. Religious education, when grounded in real community life, could effectively fend off challenges from the broader culture or even from televangelism itself. Moreover, it might lead to new ideas about how to use the media in ways that attract lost souls to the warmth of local community instead of to the pseudo-intimacy of the direct-mail solicitations and computer-generated letters used by so many televangelists. So long as religious education is relevant and relational, it will be an effective environment for building a defense of the historic Christian faith against the onslaught of the media world, especially television.

However, many churches and denominations will be tempted to mimic in their religious education programs the styles and techniques of the surrounding culture. In the past this idea has significantly affected youth education, which now uses video and computers to teach, but which may actually be more entertaining than instructing. A few years ago I was inadvertently scheduled to speak on Super Bowl Sunday to a youth group in a Southern church. Initially I expected no one to attend. Little did I realize that the problem would be solved by bringing a television set to the church! When it was time for me to speak, the tube was turned off. Once I finished, it was turned back on. Meanwhile, during my entire presentation some of the youth were glancing at the darkened screen as if the set were on. I felt like a commercial break during the real sermon: six hours of Super Bowl television. My travels have shown that a growing number of church youth groups have their own television sets and VCRs permanently installed in meeting rooms. Youth leaders tell me that educational videos are the only way to get some kids to attend their meetings. Young people will not pay attention to most youth leaders, they say. Only videos seem to work. Undoubtedly some of the videos are truly educational. But the church must ask itself whether the uncritical adoption of educational video amounts to importing the media world into the congregation without benefit of critical translation.

In recent years adult religious education has similarly shown signs of being co-opted by the television age. Various religious celebrities regularly appear in local churches via film and video. I arrived at a church one evening only to be told that I was the second speaker. The first, I was informed, was a well-known evangelical personality. Playing second fiddle to an evangelical leader did not bother me—but I *was* irked by the fact that the leader was pre-recorded through the marvels of videotaping. As several congregants whispered to me, "You've got a tough act to follow," I suddenly realized I was competing with someone I did not know and had not even made a personal appearance. I knew I would lose before I even began, because the quality of my presentation would be judged relative to someone else's carefully edited, well-rehearsed, effectively photographed video. I was truly an afterthought, and some people began leaving before I even started my presentation.

I am not arguing that the church should abandon film or video in religious education. Instead, I want only to point out that professional media tend to establish the technical standards for what people expect from the church. Some educational videos are certainly better than others—technically and pedagogically. Overall, however, religious video swerves toward entertainment and away from education. Like televangelism, it promotes religious celebrities while pandering to the audience through various dramatic principles. In other words, religious video might be projecting a particular entertainment-oriented style of instruction more than it is truly educating congregations. The content of most religious videos is quite thin, as if the producers are striving for a lowest-common-denominator approach to Christian education that will be acceptable to the widest range of churches and pastors. Some of them have virtually lost any biblical or theological moorings; instead they advance their own versions of the self-help philosophies discussed in the chapter on health-and-wealth gospels. Video can be used quite effectively in religious education, especially when it is combined with printed materials, but the tendency is for religious videos to mimic the communication styles, standards, and messages of the television world.

I hope that religious publishers produce educational tapes that will help Christians see the media world for what it is—a challenge to living the life of Christ in the modern world. I also hope that producers will address seriously the world of televangelism. Realistically speaking, this will not happen so long as churches and denominations continue to support the entertainment-oriented, personality-driven videotapes that have already been so commercially successful. Instead of anchoring believers in the historic Christian faith, educational videos have typically promoted their own versions of popular religion, many of which distort and subvert the gospel message.

4. The secular news media must take religion far more seriously than they have in recent decades.

As I suggested in the first chapter, American news media report poorly on religion. The televangelism scandals of the 1980s were the latest sensational fodder for the nation's religiously uneducated newcasters. I am not arguing that all print and broadcast reporters ought to be religious, or that every news medium should invent religious news where there is none. Rather, I think that the media's remarkably inadequate job of covering religion further lowers the nation's religious quotient and helps guarantee the spread of popular religion, including much televangelism.

During the Bakker-Swaggart scandals I was called daily by various local, regional, national, and even international media. With few exceptions, reporters did not know enough about religion to ask me reasonably articulate questions. They confused fundamentalists with all evangelicals. They typically saw little difference between charismatics and Pentecostals. They knew virtually nothing about such major Protestant traditions as Methodism, Calvinism, and Lutheranism. Even more incredible, they often confessed to never having watched a single religious broadcast. Although they were apparently not anti-religious, they were certainly igno- rant about the American religious landscape. In one case a news- magazine printed my descriptions of the theological stands of the major televangelists almost word for word. The reporters or edi- tors may have checked my descriptions with other sources, but the important point is that the people who wrote the story seemed to have no idea what they were writing about. They were completely dependent on other people to make sense of televangelism. This is not the case with American politics or economics. Why should it be the case with American religion?

In a land where religion is such an obvious and important aspect of society, it is a travesty of good journalism that so few mainstream news media take it seriously.[7] Most newspapers limit their "religious" reports to sensational stories such as the scandals or to the regular religious page, which is usually little more than a bulletin board for local church events, coupled with publicity releases about the latest local changes in ecclesiastical leadership. Simply put, religious reporting is either ghettoized or sensation- alized. In the nation's news media the real issues of life are almost all political or economic, not religious. This is why the tel- evangelists first hit the headlines in 1980; they appeared to be a right-wing threat to more liberal candidates in national and state elections.

Thanks to the news media's disinterest in religion, the Ameri- can public finds it increasingly difficult to connect religion with public life. There are almost no stories or columns on how religion has influenced American culture or on how an individual's faith has shaped his or her actions in public life. President Jimmy Carter's admission that he was "born again" was little more than a curiosity to most White House reporters and political colum- nists. Since then the term has been used regularly by journalists to refer to anything that has been restarted or turned around. We hear now about a new kind of born-again politician, such as Gary Hart during his reactivated campaign for the presidency in 1988. The pervasive net of the news media seems to secularize and politicize virtually everything in sight, leaving little room in public life for religion. Even in the case of public debates over abortion, the role of religious faith in the pro-life movement has been trans- formed into mere lifestyle politics. Again and again, modern jour- nalism separates religious faith and practice from the news, creating a media blindness that seems to deny religion's relevance for understanding the human condition.

If the religious media and Christian educators have their roles in helping to build an informed and critical church, so do the country's secular communicators. Although newspapers, news-magazines, and broadcast news programs should not be sectarian or evangelistic, they must contribute to the nation's understanding of its own religiosity. Try as they might to isolate religion from the cultural milieu, journalists will not be able to meaningfully interpret much of what is happening in the United States without examining both organized religion and personal faith. If the news excludes religion, it misses one of the most important areas of American life. More than that, journalists must see that religion is integrated with all other aspects of contemporary culture and society. News without religion is news that ignores the dynamics of faith and the actions of faithful people. It is therefore incomplete—so it is hardly real news. Indeed, the tenacity of religion in the face of modern secularization is one of the great facts of modern American life. Only the most uninformed journalists could conclude differently. Pollster George Gallup, Jr., has tried almost single-handedly to reiterate this point to the nation's news media.[8] Except for an occasional report about one of his latest polls, the fact goes unheeded by American journalists.

Most Americans, then, depend on the news media not just for the latest political, economic, and disaster stories but also for a general survey of American life. These media provide the country's primary record of public events, orienting the population in its own place and time. We pick up the daily newspaper or watch the nightly news not just to be informed, but to verify our existence, to find out who we are as a people, to participate in the ritual of public life. As Pogo said, "We have met the enemy, and he is us." For good and bad, the news is us. We can only hope that journalists will recognize that religion, good and bad, is part of the lives of individuals and their country. Instead of focusing narrowly on scandals or schisms, pariahs or personality cults, the news media should look more carefully at the streams and currents of American religious life that have shaped the character of the nation and continue to impact aspects of society. News journalists contribute to the media world as much as do the televangelists. They are the secular prophets of American public life, and they might well learn something from the church or even from a televangelist.

5. *Christians should be more careful about which religious broadcasters they will financially support.*

Televangelists are supported by people who either watch the program or at least believe in the ministry.[9] Without that support, televangelism would disappear within a few months. Only the denominationally subsidized or heavily church-supported ministries would likely stay on the air. Because the days of free broadcast time for religion are largely over, it is the donors who keep religion on the airways today. This suggests an enormous responsibility for Christians, whose financial decisions actually determine which televangelists will thrive and which will disappear. Although Christian and secular media, pastors, religious educators, and ecclesiastical officials all must do their part to redeem televangelism, in the end the actions of televangelism's supporters will be the decisive factor. Every dollar sent to one televangelist is a reward for a job well done, while every cent withheld from a different televangelist is a vote of no confidence.

Much financial support for televangelism is based on blind faith. Contributors do not send money to a TV ministry on the basis of accurate information as much as out of hope that the ministry *will* accomplish what its leader says it *can* accomplish. When the claims of the televangelist and the hopes of the patrons are the same, contributions will follow. I have yet to meet a contributor to televangelism who did not have faith in the ministry's goals. Some supporters are not very knowledgeable about a ministry, but they are true believers. They feel good about donating to the cause of world evangelization, the alleviation of poverty, or the many other appeals used widely among televangelists. Supporters are primarily moved by a spirit of generosity, not a fear of godly retribution or divine disappointment. In short, they usually give because they want to, not because they feel that they have to for their own spiritual future. Some of the health-and-wealth preachers do elicit funds based on the promise of a godly return on investment, but other televangelists are not so crass.

Moreover, I have yet to meet a supporter who really seemed incapable of making a reasonable decision about sending money to a televangelist, although I am sure such contributors exist. The problem is that too many supporters *want* to believe in the televangelist and his dreams. Such strong desires lead to a blind faith that the money will be used wisely and effectively for the kingdom of God. Contributors are largely naive and not necessarily well-informed about the ministry itself.

The best advice I can offer potential or existing supporters of televangelism is to request information that might make their faith in the ministry less blind. In my view, any ministry that will not provide a doctrinal statement and a financial balance sheet does not deserve contributions. Most do not offer to provide such documentation. When I wrote to a hundred of the most popular radio and television ministries in the early 1980s, only a handful of them sent me financial statements, and fewer sent me statements of their doctrinal beliefs. The irony was clear; ministries that claimed to be communicating the gospel would not even provide a clear affirmation of what they believed. It was as if secrecy was more important than candor and evangelization.

The vast majority of viewers never even request such information. Based only on what they see and hear on the broadcasts and what they read in the carefully crafted mailings, most supporters are content to assume that the ministry deserves their contributions. This is simply naiveté on their part. Like local churches and nonbroadcast ministries, televangelism represents a wide range of preachers and potential contributors. Some TV ministries are far more effective than others at evangelism, edification, and entertainment. More than that, televangelism varies enormously in how efficiently the money is used. Some organizations spend 20 or 30 percent of their budgets on fund-raising, while others spend only a small percentage. The impression that viewers receive of how money is spent is often very different from the behind-the-scenes reality. For all these reasons, viewers should become better informed about which televangelists they will support.

Certainly any information provided by the TV ministries should be viewed somewhat skeptically. After all, most televangelists send out material so as to promote their ministries, not to offer an objective assessment of them. Letters and magazines are part of televangelism's public-relations efforts. So are some of the doctrinal statements, which are often so general that they could apply to nearly any TV ministry. Audited financial statements are considerably more objective, but they give no indication as to what the ministry actually believes, only how it allocates its spending. All of this suggests that doctrinal and financial statements are the very minimum that contributors should expect from the televangelists they support.

Just as the church should be held accountable for the overall state of televangelism, individual viewers should be responsible for using their limited resources wisely and intelligently. Christians need input from pastors, religious educators, and the religious and secular media, but in the end they must make the decisions themselves. As televangelism has followed the cultural currents of the United States, it has become increasingly difficult for viewers to discern the spirits in the TV ministries they support. Because televangelism is so appealingly steeped in American values and beliefs, supporters carry a heavy burden. They must distinguish between truth and falsity, charisma and personality cult, historic doctrine and the new sorcery. In that task they cannot only blame others for their own lack of perception.

6. Denominations and especially ecumenical evangelical organizations should be much more involved in producing and financially supporting religious broadcasts.

It is a sad fact that the church in America has turned over religious broadcasting almost entirely to independent organizations that are only indirectly affiliated with denominations or cross-denominational groups. For one thing, this has plunged televangelism into the kind of competitiveness that simply should not characterize the church of Jesus Christ. For another, independent religious television has nearly guaranteed that the programming will become a matter of business and marketing rather than authentic religious faith. Dependent on viewer contributions, televangelism is not really free to spread the gospel or to explore other edifying programming, from drama to news or documentary. Like commercial television, televangelism gives the audience what it wants. In the process it is selling the gospel or at least distorting it.

I am not calling for a wishy-washy organization that will dole out money uncritically to a quasi-ecumenical broadcaster or will start supporting existing televangelists. Instead I am suggesting that churches, denominations, and lay leaders combine their talents to produce and fund new programming that would be devoid of the negative aspects of contemporary televangelism, from personality cults to perverted gospels. Denominational involvement would help guarantee accountability; by and large, the existing denominationally subsidized broadcasters are accountable to a qualified board and a concerned constituency.

The possibility of such an undertaking is not as remote as some skeptics might suggest. The Lutheran Layman's League provided a possible model decades ago when it launched "The Lutheran Hour" on radio and "This Is the Life" on the tube. It was helpful that some of the air time was provided free by particular stations. But more important was the fact that extensive lay involvement in both production and fund-raising enabled the projects to succeed, even within the limitations of one small denomination's resources. Today all the program time would almost certainly have to be purchased rather than partially donated by stations or networks. But with evangelical cooperation there is little doubt that even prime-time drama might be supported. The Family Channel has tried some of this on cable, but within the limited scope of CBN's own fund-raising ability.

Considering the present state of televangelism, it is truly amazing that any viewers hear the pure gospel and find reason to believe in Christ. There is such a cacophony of disparate voices that the theological noise and religious competition tend to give the impression that the church is a commercial product rather than a spiritual giant. Egos must be kept in check, and denominations can help accomplish that—even as lay leadership could greatly help in encouraging creativity.

Conclusion

Televangelism needs to be saved from its own success. As perhaps the most characteristically American form of religious communication, televangelism has indeed prospered over the last two decades. And, in spite of what the secular and some religious news media suggest, scandals will not destroy contemporary televangelism. Such thinking is the folly of modern journalism, which sees virtually every tragedy as a turning point in the lives of individuals and nations. Televangelism's scandals have always been mere setbacks in the growth of an enormously popular and successful form of religious expression. Sensational exposés will come and go, like hurricanes or tornadoes, but the people involved will always begin rebuilding once the storm passes. Some organizations will barely feel the winds, while a few—the most fortunate of all—will actually thrive on the misfortunes of their disgraced counterparts.

The basic problem is that televangelism's success has generally been formulated in distinctly American terms: individualism, bigger buildings, larger budgets, more efficient computer systems, newer technologies, increased public visibility, and so forth. These have become the icons of televangelism. While its ministerial effectiveness is nearly impossible to measure, such worldly signs of success are tangible and conspicuous. Like secular corporations or even the modern family, America's televangelists openly display their material success for all to see. Surely Jim Bakker's ostentatious lifestyle was part of the reason for his popularity. Supporters specifically and the church generally have a right to determine what is legitimate success, in terms that reflect Christian doctrine.

Televangelism's sins, then, are also the sins of American culture. Although there are certainly exceptions, televangelism reflects the spirit and direction of a land of materialism, hedonism, consumerism, and ethnocentrism. This book has admittedly de-emphasized some of the positive aspects of televangelism and American society—especially generosity, creativity, and resourcefulness. My goal has been simply to set the record straight for both critics and supporters about the roots of contemporary televangelism's problems. Televangelism and American culture are mutually supportive, each shaping the other for good and bad. Perhaps the most that we could hope is that each would be transformed by truly prophetic voices crying in the wilderness of modern life.

Notes

❊ ❊ ❊ ❊

Introduction

1. Thomas Luckmann, *The Invisible Religion* (New York: Macmillan, 1967), p. 36.
2. Richard N. Ostling, "Many Are Called," *Time,* 27 February 1989, p. 79.
3. Barbara Dolan, "Full House at Willow Creek," *Time,* 6 March 1989, p. 60.
4. Ed Golder, "It's Saturday Night," *Grand Rapids Press,* 21 January 1989, p. D1.
5. Marshall McLuhan, *Understanding Media* (New York: McGraw-Hill, 1964); Neil Postman, *Amusing Ourselves to Death: Public Discourse in the Age of Show Business* (New York: Viking, 1985).
6. Jamie Buckingham, "Interview with Pat Robertson," *Charisma,* April 1983, p. 26.

Chapter 1: *Beyond the Stereotypes*

1. Theodore Caplow, Howard M. Bahr, and Bruce A. Chadwick, *All Faithful People: Change and Continuity in Middletown's Religion* (Minneapolis: University of Minnesota Press, 1983).
2. This estimate is based on my own careful analysis of many audience studies. For a review of the variety of findings and conclusions about the size of the audience for televangelism, see the following: Paul H. Virts and David W. Clark, "Religious TV Audience Does Measure Up," *Religious Broadcasting,* September 1985, pp. 28–30; Jeffrey K. Hadden and Anson Shupe, *Televangelism: Power and Politics on God's Frontier* (New York: Henry Holt, 1988), chapter 8; Ben Armstrong, "How Big Is the Religious Radio-TV Audience?" *Religious Broadcasting,* May 1981, pp. 33–37; Stewart M. Hoover, *Mass Media Religion* (Beverly Hills, Calif.: Sage, 1988) pp. 63–69.
3. For a speculative biography, see Robert Bahr, *Least of All Saints* (Englewood Cliffs, N.J.: Prentice-Hall, 1979).
4. I cover early evangelical radio in detail in "Evangelical Radio and the Rise of the Electronic Church, 1921–1948," *Journal of Broadcasting and Electronic Media* 32 (Summer 1988): 289–306.
5. "Big Churches Learn Radio 'Savvy' to Counter Revivalist Air Racket," *Newsweek,* 22 January 1945, pp. 74–76.

6. See, for example, Dave Berkman, "Long Before Falwell: Early Radio and Religion—As Reported by the Nation's Periodical Press," *Journal of Popular Culture* 21 (Spring 1988): 1–11.

7. This was widely reported in print and electronic media. I have not been able to look at copies of the older printing of the book, so I was not able to confirm the reports.

8. Rex Humbard, *Miracles in My Life* (Old Tappan, N.J.: Fleming H. Revell, 1971), pp. 106–123; Rex Humbard, *To Tell the World* (Englewood Cliffs, N.J.: Prentice-Hall, 1975), pp. 25–28.

9. David Edwin Harrell, Jr., *Oral Roberts: An American Life* (San Francisco: Harper & Row, 1985), pp. 267–271.

Chapter 2: *Faith in Technology*

1. "New Figures Show Per-member Giving Drop," *Christianity Today,* 19 March 1990, p. 48.

2. Malcolm Muggeridge, *Christ and the Media* (Grand Rapids, Mich.: Eerdmans, 1977), p. 23.

3. Ibid, p. 41.

4. Ibid, pp. 45–46.

5. Virginia Stem Owens, *The Total Image: Or Selling Jesus in the Modern Age* (Grand Rapids, Mich.: Eerdmans, 1980), pp. 40–41.

6. Quoted in Frank A. Reel, *The Networks* (New York: Charles Scribner & Sons, 1979), p. 96.

7. David Marc, *Demographic Vistas* (Philadelphia: University of Pennsylvania Press, 1984), p. 7.

8. Harold W. Blodgett, *The Best of Whitman* (New York: The Ronald Press, 1953), p. 256.

9. Reinhold Niebuhr, "Introduction," in Wilbur Schramm, *Responsibility in Mass Communication* (New York: Harper & Brothers, 1957), p. xi.

10. Daniel Boorstin, *The Republic of Technology: Reflections on Our Future Community* (New York: Harper & Row, 1978).

11. David Paul Nord, "The Ironies of Communication Technology: Why Predictions of the Future So Often Go Wrong," *The Cresset* (alumni magazine of Valparaiso University), March 1986, p. 16.

12. Quoted in Daniel J. Czitrom, *Media and the American Mind: From Morse to McLuhan* (Chapel Hill, N.C.: University of North Carolina Press, 1982), p. 9.

13. Stanley L. Jaki, "The Three Faces of Technology: Idol, Nemesis, Marvel," *Intercollegiate Review,* Spring 1988, p. 39.

14. Tim LaHaye, *The Hidden Censors* (Old Tappan, N.J.: Fleming H. Revell, 1984).

15. Carl L. Becker, "Progress," in W. W. Wagar, ed., *The Idea of Progress Since the Renaissance* (New York: John Wiley & Sons, 1969), pp. 9–18.

16. Martin E. Marty, *Protestantism* (New York: Holt, Rinehart and Winston, 1972), p. 87.

17. Howard P. Segal, *Technological Utopianism in American Culture* (Chicago: University of Chicago Press, 1985), pp. 74–75.

18. Howard Mumford Jones, *O Strange New World* (New York: Viking, 1965).

19. V. L. Parrington, *American Dream: A Study of American Utopias,* 2nd ed. (New York: Russell & Russell, 1964).

20. See, for example, Leo Marx, *The Machine in the Garden* (New York: Vintage Books, 1950).

21. Perry Miller, *The Life of the Mind in America* (New York: Harcourt, Brace & World, 1965), p. 52.

22. David Paul Nord, "The Evangelical Origins of Mass Media in America," *Journalism Monographs* 88 (1984).

23. Quentin J. Schultze, "Evangelical Radio and the Rise of the Electronic Church, 1921–1948," *Journal of Broadcasting and Electronic Media* 32 (Summer 1988): 289–306.

24. David Edwin Harrell, Jr., *Oral Roberts: An American Life* (San Francisco: Harper & Row, 1985), pp. 268–270.

25. Rex Humbard, *Miracles in My Life* (Old Tappan, N.J.: Fleming H. Revell, 1971), p. 111.

26. Paul Crouch, "He That Hath an Ear," *Praise the Lord* 16 (August 1989): 2.

27. World Mission Teams, *Status Report on the Great Commission* (St. Petersburg, Fla.: World Mission Teams, 1987).

28. Robert S. Fortner, "Saving the World? American Evangelicals and Transnational Broadcasting," in Quentin J. Schultze, ed., *American Evangelicals and the Mass Media* (Grand Rapids, Mich.: Academie/Zondervan, 1990), pp. 307–328.

29. Eugene R. Bertermann, "The Radio for Christ," *United Evangelical Action,* 1 March 1949, p. 3.

30. Jerry Falwell and Elmer Towns, *The Church Aflame* (Nashville: Impact Books, 1971), pp. 74–75.

31. Quoted in Czitrom, *Media and the American Mind,* p. 9.

32. Ibid., p. 10.

33. Ben Armstrong, *The Electric Church* (Nashville: Thomas Nelson, 1979), pp. 8–9.

34. Ibid., pp. 172–173.

35. Paul Crouch, "Christian TV Means Souls," *Praise the Lord* 16 (April 1989): 2.

36. Paul Crouch, "Milano—On the Air," *Praise the Lord* 16 (May 1989): 2.

37. Gerard Straub, *Salvation for Sale* (Buffalo: Prometheus, 1986), pp. 160–162.

38. Armstrong, *The Electric Church,* pp. 10–11.

39. Ibid., p. 171.

40. Jerry Falwell, *Strength for the Journey* (New York: Simon & Schuster, 1987), p. 312.

41. Frederick Ferré, *Shaping the Future* (New York: Harper & Row, 1976).

42. Boorstin, *The Republic of Technology,* p. 11.

43. Tim Unsworth, "What Does the Future Hold for U.S. Catholics?" *U.S. Catholic,* April 1990, p. 8.

44. James W. Carey and John J. Quirk, "The Mythos of the Electronic Revolution," *The American Scholar* 39 (1970): 219–241, 395–424.

45. Jacques Ellul, *The Technological Society* (New York: Alfred A. Knopf, 1964).

46. P. M. Rice, "Interview with Pat Robertson," *Your Church,* May/June 1979, p. 5.

47. Niebuhr, "Introduction," p. xx.

48. Quoted in George W. Cornell, "Christian Groups Hope to Evangelize World by 2000 A.D.," *Grand Rapids Press,* 17 October 1987, p. C4.

49. Paul Crouch, "South Africa—Born in a Day," *Praise the Lord* 16 (June 1989): 2.

50. W. H. Foulkes, "Radio Evangelism," in J. M. Bader, ed., *The Message and Method of the New Evangelism* (New York: Round Table Press, 1937), p. 230.

Chapter 3: *The Cults of Personality*

1. See 1 Corinthians 1:26–29 NIV.

2. Jennet Conant, "Billionaire Bashing," *Newsweek,* 30 May 1988, p. 67.

3. S. A. Witmer, *Education with Dimension: The Bible College Story* (Manhasset, N.Y.: Channel Press, 1962), p. 36.

4. David L. Clark, "Miracles for a Dime: From Chautauqua Tent to Radio Station with Sister Aimee," *California History* 57 (1978–79): 354–363.

5. Quentin J. Schultze and William D. Romanowski, "Praising God in Opryland," *The Reformed Journal,* November 1989, pp. 10–14.

6. Nathan S. Hatch, *The Democratization of American Christianity* (New Haven, Conn.: Yale University Press, 1988). Also see Quentin J. Schultze, "Keeping the Faith: American Evangelicals and the Mass Media," in Schultze, ed., *American Evangelicals and the Mass Media* (Grand Rapids, Mich. : Academie/Zondervan, 1990), pp. 23–45.

7. Richard Quebedeaux, *By What Authority: The Rise of Personality Cults in American Christianity* (San Francisco: Harper & Row, 1982).

8. David Edwin Harrell, Jr., *Oral Roberts: An American Life* (San Francisco: Harper & Row, 1985). Also see Oral Roberts, *The Call* (New York: Avon Books, 1971).

9. Jerry Falwell, *Strength for the Journey* (New York: Simon & Schuster, 1987).

10. Dennis Voskuil, *Mountains into Goldmines: Robert Schuller and the Gospel of Success* (Grand Rapids, Mich.: Eerdmans, 1983).

11. David Edwin Harrell, Jr., *Pat Robertson: A Personal, Political and Religious Portrait* (San Francisco: Harper & Row, 1987). Also see Pat Robertson, *Shout It from the Housetops* (South Plainfield, N.J.: Bridge Publishing, 1972).

12. Charles E. Shepard, *Forgiven: The Rise and Fall of Jim Bakker and the PTL Ministry* (New York: Atlantic Monthly Press, 1989). Also see Jim Bakker, *You Can Make It!* (Charlotte, N.C.: PTL Enterprises, 1983).

13. Some media have reported that Robert Schuller is not an evangelical. Although his own teachings do not appear evangelical to some people, he is officially a pastor of the Reformed Church in America, which certainly has evangelical roots. Theologically speaking, that denomination is probably closer to evangelicalism than mainline Protestantism. Therefore, I will include him as an evangelical leader. Clearly he appeals to far more than evangelical viewers, but so do many other televangelists. Norman Vincent Peale, Schuller's mentor, was a member of the same denomination.

14. Robert C. Toll, *The Entertainment Machine: American Show Business in the Twentieth Century* (New York: Oxford University Press, 1982), pp. 54–55.

15. J. Elwin Wright, *The Old Fashioned Revival Hour* (Boston: The Fellowship Press, 1940), p. 196.

16. I discuss Fuller and other early radio evangelists at length in "Evangelical Radio and the Rise of the Electronic Church, 1921–1948," *Journal of Broadcasting and Electronic Media* 32 (Summer 1988): 289–306.

17. Malcolm Muggeridge, *Christ and the Media* (Grand Rapids, Mich.: Eerdmans, 1971). Also see Virginia Stem Owens, *The Total Image: Or Selling Jesus in the Modern Age* (Grand Rapids, Mich.: Eerdmans, 1980).

18. Malcolm Boyd, "Communicating the Gospel Through Commercial Media," *Encounter* 18 (Autumn 1957): 409.

19. J. S. Kater, Jr., *Christians on the Right* (New York: Seabury Press, 1982), p. 106.

20. I cover this somewhat in "Evangelical Radio," p. 294. Also see Stewart M. Hoover, *Mass Media Religion* (Beverly Hills, Calif.: Sage, 1988).

21. Kenneth S. Kantzer, "The Charismatics Among Us," *Christianity Today,* 22 February 1980, pp. 25–26.

22. Pierre Babin, "The Spirituality of Media People," *The Way,* Supplement 57 (August 1986), p. 47.

23. Joseph Ferullo, "Flacking in the Fields of the Lord," *Channels,* March 1987, pp. 45–48.

24. A different interpretation of the importance of the South in contemporary evangelicalism and televangelism is offered in Grant Wacker, "Uneasy in Zion: Evangelicals in Postmodern Society," in George Marsden, ed., *Evangelicalism and Modern America* (Grand Rapids, Mich.: Eerdmans, 1984), pp. 17–28.

25. Todd V. Lewis, "Charisma and Media Evangelists: An Explication and Model of Communication Influence," *Southern Communication Journal* 54 (Fall 1988): 97.

26. Joseph Bayly, "The Nouveaux Famous," *Eternity,* September 1985, p. 88.

27. Kenneth L. Woodward, "Following Dad to the Pulpit," *Newsweek,* 8 February 1988, pp. 62–63.

28. In the case of "Day of Discovery," the TV ministry of Radio Bible Class, Martin De Haan did become the principal replacement for his father, Richard. However, the Radio Bible Class ministry is so oriented toward literature as well as the electronic media that the succession to Martin was not really a test of a television ministry.

29. One possible exception to this rule is the cult that still surrounds deceased faith healer William Branham. A few people still seek out films of Branham's healing services in hopes of personal healing.

30. Harrell, *Pat Robertson,* p. 207; John B. Donovan, *Pat Robertson: The Authorized Biography* (New York: Macmillan, 1988), p. 157.

31. James R. Adair, *M. R. De Haan: The Man and His Ministry* (Grand Rapids, Mich.: Zondervan, 1969), p. 160.

32. Richard Kieckhefer, "The Cult of Saints as Popular Religion," *Explor* 7 (Fall 1984): 42.

33. See, for example, James Breig, "Catholics Should Boycott TV Preachers," *U. S. Catholic,* May 1984, pp. 12–17.

34. Charles Colson, "The Celebrity Illusion," *Christianity Today,* 11 December 1987, p. 72.

35. Neil Postman, *Amusing Ourselves to Death: Public Discourse in the Age of Show Business* (New York: Viking, 1985).

Chapter 4: *The Lure of Drama*

1. The Marx-Freud-Barnum idea is adapted from John Garrett, "Modern Methods of Evangelization," *International Review* 46 (April 1957): 190.

2. William Stringfellow, *A Simplicity of Faith* (Nashville: Abingdon, 1982), pp. 88–90.

3. David L. Clark, "Miracles for a Dime: From Chautauqua Tent to Radio Station with Sister Aimee," *California History* 57 (1978–79): 354–363.

4. For a somewhat similar argument, see Razelle Frankl, *Televangelism* (Carbondale, Ill.: Southern Illinois University Press, 1987).

5. "The Gospel Boom," *Saturday Evening Post,* April 1979, p. 36.

6. This illustration is adapted from Thomas Clancy, "Nine and a Half Theses on Religious Broadcasting," *America,* 7 April 1979, p. 272.

7. Quoted in *Saturday Review,* 12 October 1968, p. 77.

8. On average, Swaggart's show uses over a hundred audience reaction shots to enhance the program's sense of spontaneity and to deepen its dramatic thrust. See David E. Davis, "A Structural Analysis of Four Religious Programs: The Effect of Program Structure on Ethos," paper presented at the annual convention of the Speech Communication Association, Chicago, Ill., 3 November 1984.

9. William R. Rauscher, *Church in Frenzy* (New York: St. Martin's, 1980), p. 110.

10. Joshua Hammer, "A Season of Sleaze in TV News," *Newsweek,* 11 June 1990, p. 71.

11. William Martin, "Perennial Problems of Prime-Time Preachers," published lecture delivered at Baylor University, 20 October 1987.

12. Jon Nordheimer, "Bible Belt Image Galling to Charlotte," *New York Times,* 24 June 1987, p. 8.

13. "A Disneyland for the Devout," *Newsweek,* 11 August 1986, p. 47.

14. Art Harris and Michael Isikoff, "The Bakkers' Tumultuous Return," *Washington Post,* 12 June 1987, p. D3.

15. For a similar argument, see Joe Barnhouse, *Jim and Tammy: Charismatic Intrigue Inside PTL* (Buffalo: Prometheus, 1988).

16. I argued this at some length in *Television: Manna from Hollywood?* (Grand Rapids, Mich.: Zondervan, 1986).

17. Kathleen Hall Jamieson, *Eloquence in an Electronic Age* (New York: Oxford University Press, 1988), p. 29.

18. Also see my essay "The Place of Television in the Church's Communication," in Tyron Inbody, ed., *Changing Channels: The Church and the Television Revolution* (Dayton: Whaleprints, 1990), pp. 23–40.

19. Barbara Dolan, "Full House at Willow Creek," *Time*, 6 March 1989, p. 60.

20. Andrew Kuyvenhoven, "Aim at Youth," *The Banner*, 25 April 1988, p. 8.

21. Karl Rahner, *The Christian Commitment* (New York: Sheed & Ward, 1963).

22. Edward J. Carnell, *Television: Servant or Master?* (Grand Rapids, Mich.: Eerdmans, 1950), pp. 96–97.

23. Virginia Stem Owens, *The Total Image: Or Selling Jesus in the Modern Age* (Grand Rapids, Mich.: Eerdmans, 1980).

24. John Shea, *Stories of God* (Chicago: Thomas More, 1978); *Stories of Faith* (Chicago: Thomas More, 1980).

Chapter 5: *The New Sorcery*

1. See Gerard Carson, *One for a Man, Two for a Horse* (Garden City, N.Y.: Doubleday, 1961); Stewart Holbrook, *The Golden Age of Quackery* (N.Y.: Macmillan, 1959); James Harvey, *The Toadstool Millionaires* (Princeton, N.J.: Princeton University Press, 1961).

2. John Schwartz, "The Superstition Trade," *Newsweek*, 13 June, 1988, p. 52.

3. Pat Jordan, "In Florida: Filling the Hours with Bingo," *Time*, 25 April 1988, p. 13.

4. Jon Butler, "Magic, Astrology, and the Early American Religious Heritage, 1600–1760," *American Historical Review* 18 (April 1979): 317–346.

5. Nathan O. Hatch, *The Democratization of American Christianity* (New Haven. Conn.: Yale University Press, 1989).

6. "Hardly Headstrong," *Christianity Today*, 5 February 1990, p. 52.

7. George W. Cornell, "Mom Ranks Top on List of Religious Influences," *Grand Rapids Press*, 17 February 1990, p. B3.

8. George Gallup, Jr., and Jim Castelli, *The People's Religion: American Faith in the 90's* (Princeton, N.J.: Princeton Religious Research Center, 1989); The study is summarized in Galen Meyer, "Faith Without Works—or Knowledge," *The Banner*, 26 February 1990, p. 5.

9. My argument here is adapted from Peter W. Williams, *Popular Religion in America* (Englewood Cliffs, N.J.: Prentice-Hall, 1980).

10. David Wells, "Assaulted by Modernity," *Christianity Today*, 9 February 1990, p. 76.

11. James R. Goff, "The Faith that Claims," *Christianity Today*, 19 February 1990, p. 17.

12. William Hendricks, "The Theology of the Electronic Church," *Review and Expositor* 81 (Winter 1984): 64.

13. See D. R. McDonnell, *A Different Gospel* (Peabody, Mass.: Hendrickson, 1988); Bruce Barron, *The Health and Wealth Gospel* (Downers Grove, Ill.: InterVarsity Press, 1987); Michael Horton, ed., *The Agony of Deceit* (Chicago: Moody Press, 1990).

14. Walter Martin, "You Shall Be As Gods," in Horton, ed., *The Agony of Deceit*, pp. 89–105.

15. Mark Vermaire, "Living with Wealth: On the Way to an Answer," *The Banner*, 18 December 1989, p. 10.

16. Pat Robertson, *The Secret Kingdom* (Nashville: Thomas Nelson, 1982).

17. David Hazard, "Holy Hype," *Eternity*, December 1985, p. 32.

18. Jay Cormier, "Cues From the Television Evangelists: The Challenge to the 'Non-Electronic' Church," *America*, 26 March 1988, p. 326.

19. Jamie Buckingham, "Interview with Pat Robertson," *Charisma,* April 1983, p. 26.

20. G. Melton Mobley, "The Political Influence of Television Ministers," *Review of Religious Research* 25 (June 1984): 314–320; Robert Abelman and Gary Pettey, "How Political Is Religious Television?" *Journalism Quarterly* 65 (Summer 1988): 313–319, 359.

21. Robert Abelman and Kimberly Neuendorf, "How Religious Is Religious Television Programming?" *Journal of Communication* 35 (Winter 1985): 106.

22. Charles Colson, "Jane Fonda's Farm Policies," *Christianity Today,* 18 October 1985, p. 72.

23. David Edwin Harrell, Jr., "Healing in Protestant America," in Henry L. Letterman, ed., *Health and Healing: Ministry of the Church* (Chicago: Wheat Ridge Foundation, 1980), p. 66.

24. Lucien E. Coleman, Jr., "Christian Communication in the 1970s," *Review and Expositor* 67 (Winter 1970): 73.

25. John Garrett, "Modern Methods of Evangelization," *International Review* 46 (April 1957): 182–190.

26. Marilyn Hickey, "Dreams Can Come True," *Time With Him,* August 1984, p. 16.

27. Kenneth Copeland, "I've Received My Instructions. Our Calling Is Made Clear," *Believer's Voice of Victory,* January 1985, pp. 2–3.

28. Kenneth Copeland, *Welcome to the Family: A Guide to Salvation, the Baptism of the Holy Spirit, and Healing* (Fort Worth: Kenneth Copeland Ministries, 1979), p. 29.

29. Kenneth S. Kantzer, "The Cut-Rate Grace of a Health and Wealth Gospel," *Christianity Today,* 14 June 1985, pp. 14–15.

30. James Randi, *The Faith Healers* (Buffalo, N.Y.: Prometheus, 1987).

31. H. Richard Niebuhr, *Christ and Culture* (New York: Harper, 1951).

32. Thorstein Veblen, *The Theory of the Leisure Class* (New York: Funk & Wagnalls, n.d.).

33. Jim Bakker, *You Can Make It* (Charlotte, N.C.: PTL Enterprises, 1983).

34. Ben Armstrong, *The Electric Church* (Nashville: Thomas Nelson, 1979), p. 9.

35. Martin Marty, *The Improper Opinion* (Philadelphia: The Westminster Press, 1961), pp. 63–64.

36. See Dennis A. Smith, "The Gospel According to the United States: Evangelical Broadcasting in Central America," in Quentin J. Schultze, ed., *American Evangelicals and the Mass Media* (Grand Rapids, Mich.: Academie/Zondervan, 1990), pp. 289–305.

37. John C. Burnham, *How Superstition Won and Science Lost* (New Brunswick, N.J.: Rutgers University Press, 1987).

38. Martin Marty, "The Gospel and Public Opinion," *Lutheran World* 10 (January 1963): 1–9.

39. The New Age movement is discussed in Otto Friedrich, "New Age Harmonies," *Time,* 7 December 1987, p. 62.

Chapter 6: *The Greening of the Gospel*

1. Max Weber, *The Protestant Ethic and the Spirit of Capitalism* (New York: Charles Scribner's Sons, 1958).

2. "Nation-wide Lobster Delivery Puts Maine Town on the Map," *Grand Rapids Press,* 5 February 1989, p. A12.

3. Hugh Dalziel Duncan, *Culture and Democracy* (Totowa, N.J.: The Bedminster Press, 1965).

4. I take this up in depth in Quentin J. Schultze, "Keeping the Faith: American Evangelicals and the Media," in Schultze, ed., *American Evangelicals and the Mass Media* (Grand Rapids: Academie/Zondervan, 1990), pp. 23–45.

5. Engel's books include *Contemporary Christian Communication* (Nashville: Thomas Nelson, 1979); *How Can I Get Them to Listen?* (Grand Rapids, Mich.: Zondervan, 1977); *What's Gone Wrong with the Harvest?* (Grand Rapids, Mich.: Zondervan, 1975).

6. For an interesting study of the ineffectiveness of this campaign, see Win Arn, "A Church Growth Look at Here's Life America," *Church Growth: America,* January/February 1977, pp. 4–30. Bright claimed that the campaign caused a dramatic drop in crime and a leveling-off of the divorce rate in 1976 and 1977. See Russell Chandler, "Campus Crusade at 30," *Christianity Today,* 22 January 1982, p. 35. Also see Bright's own history of the project in *A Movement of Miracles* (San Bernardino, Calif.: Campus Crusade for Christ International, 1977). For another critical assessment see C. Peter Wagner, "Who Found It? Did the Here's Life America Blitz Work?" *Eternity,* September 1977, pp. 13–19.

7. Razelle Frankl, *Televangelism* (Carbondale, Ill.: Southern Illinois University Press, 1987).

8. Perry Miller, *The Life of the Mind in America* (New York: Harcourt, Brace & World, 1965), p. 52.

9. See Claude C. Hopkins, *My Life in Advertising* (New York: Harper & Brothers, 1927).

10. Steve M. Schlissel, "Multi-Level Warnings About Multi-Level Marketing," *Messiah's Mandate* vol. 2, p. 9.

11. Ed Golder, "Growing Church Puts God First," *Grand Rapids Press,* 4 November 1989, p. B1.

12. Bruce Barton, *The Man Nobody Knows: A Discovery of the Real Jesus* (Indianapolis: Bobbs-Merrill, Grosset & Dunlap, 1925).

13. Patrick Allitt, "The American Christ," *American Heritage,* November 1988, p. 139.

14. Quoted in Dennis Voskuil, *Mountains Into Goldmines: Robert Schuller and the Gospel of Success* (Grand Rapids, Mich.: Eerdmans, 1983), p. 56.

15. This and some of the other information about Falwell's ministry were obtained through interviews of people in Lynchburg, Virginia, in the fall of 1989.

16. Robert Abelman and Kimberly Neuendorf, "How Religious Is Religious Television Programming?" *Journal of Communication* 35 (Winter 1985): 110.

17. Barry R. Littman and Daniel T. David, "The Consumption of Religious Television Programming: A Multidisciplinary Analysis of Televangelism," unpublished paper.

18. Peter Horsfield, "Evangelism By Mail: Letters from the Broadcasters," *Journal of Communication* 35 (Winter 1985): 89–97.

19. Austin Miles, *Don't Call Me Brother* (Buffalo, N.Y.: Prometheus, 1989), p. 272.

20. Ben Armstrong, *The Electric Church* (Nashville: Thomas Nelson, 1979), p. 134.

21. Peter Horsfield, *Religious Television* (New York: Longman, 1984), p. 92.

22. George A. Brakely, Jr., *Tested Ways to Successful Fund Raising* (New York: AMAOM, 1982), p. xi.

23. Donald N. Oberdorfer, *Electronic Christianity: Myth or Ministry* (Taylors Falls, Minn.: John L. Brekke & Sons, 1982).

24. Quoted in James F. Engel, "Great Commission or Great Commotion?" *Christianity Today,* 20 April 1984, p. 52.

25. Jacques Ellul, *The Technological Society* (New York: Alfred A. Knopf, 1964).

26. Malcolm Boyd, "The Crisis of the Mass Media," *Christianity and Crisis* 16 (28 May 1956): 70.

27. Robert J. Schihl, "Television Program Producers: A Profile and Survey," *Religious Broadcasting,* February 1985, p. 49.

28. Jack W. Hayford, "Character Before Communication," *Religious Broadcasting,* February 1985, p. 33.

29. Stringfellow spoke vigorously on occasion against religious broadcasting. However, I applied his view of the demonic to televangelism in these quotes. Were he alive today, I believe he would have been sympathetic with this critique. See William Stringfellow, *Free in Obedience* (New York: Seabury, 1964), p. 62.

Chapter 7: *The Evangelistic Myth*

1. World Film Crusade, *Winning the World,* March 1986, update to the first edition, p. 123a.

2. George Gerbner et. al., *Religion and Television* (Philadelphia: The Annenberg School of Communication, 1984), vol. 1, p. 52.

3. William Martin, "Mass Communications," in Charles H. Lippy and Peter W. Williams, eds., *Encyclopedia of American Religious Experience* (New York: Charles Scribner's Sons, 1988), p. 1722.

4. J. Thomas Bisset, "Religious Broadcasting: Assessing the State of the Art," *Christianity Today,* 12 December 1980, p. 30.

5. Peter Horsfield, *Religious Television* (New York: Longman, 1984), p. 97.

6. Quoted in John W. Bachman, *Media: Wasteland or Wonderland?* (Minneapolis: Augsburg, 1984), pp. 115–116.

7. Jacques Ellul, *Propaganda* (New York: Alfred A. Knopf, 1965).

8. Win Arn, "Is TV Appropriate for Mass Evangelism?" *Christianity Today,* 16 October 1987, p. 50.

9. "What Makes One Turn to Jesus?" *The Banner,* 16 April 1984, p. 22.

10. Russell T. Hitt, "Diversity Marks Evangelism Methods," *Eternity,* September 1987, p. 34.

11. Martin Marty, "I Think," *The Lutheran Standard,* 2 January 1979, p. 12.

12. Tony Campolo, *20 Hot Potatoes Christians Are Afraid to Touch* (Dallas: Word, 1988), p. 72.

13. John N. Vaughan, *The World's Twenty Largest Churches* (Grand Rapids, Mich.: Baker Book House, 1986), pp. 139, 155, 164, 180. The size of the churches was determined by averaging weekly morning worship, Sunday School attendance and total adult membership.

14. Stewart M. Hoover, *Mass Media Religion* (Beverly Hills, Calif.: Sage, 1988), pp. 68, 178.

15. William Martin, "Perennial Problems of Prime-Time Preachers," lecture delivered at Baylor University, 20 October 1987. Also see Stewart M. Hoover, "The Religious Television Audience: A Matter of Significance or Size?" in Robert Abelman and Stewart M. Hoover, *Religious Television: Controversies and Conclusions* (Norwood, N.J.: Ablex, 1990), pp. 109–129, and Jeffrey K. Hadden and Anson Shupe, *Televangelism: Power and Politics on God's Frontier* (New York: Henry Holt, 1988), pp. 142–159.

16. Martin E. Marty, "Needed: A Christian Interpretation of the Media World," *Lutheran World* 19 (1972): 111.

17. Ben Armstrong, *The Electric Church* (Nashville: Thomas Nelson, 1979), p. 135.

18. William Stephenson, *The Play Theory of Mass Communication* (Chicago: University of Chicago Press, 1967).

19. Dietrich Bonhoeffer, *The Cost of Discipleship* (New York: Macmillan, 1963), p. 45.

20. Win Arn, "Is TV Appropriate for Mass Evangelism?" p. 50.

21. Gary D. Gaddy and David Pritchard, "Is Religious Knowledge Gained from Broadcasts?" *Journalism Quarterly* 63 (Winter 1987): 840–844.

22. R. L. Moore, *Religious Outsiders and the Making of Americans* (New York: Oxford University Press, 1986).

23. This is discussed in George M. Marsden, *Reforming Fundamentalism* (Grand Rapids, Mich.: Eerdmans, 1987).

24. Hoover, *Mass Media Religion,* p. 185.

25. Ted Baehr, "Tangled Christian Telecommunications," *Christianity Today,* 20 November 1981, pp. 34–35.

26. Nathan Hatch, *The Democratization of American Christianity* (New Haven, Conn.: Yale University Press, 1989).

27. James A. Taylor, "No Miracles from the Media," *Christian Century,* 30 May 1979, p. 614.

28. Quoted in "Most Evangelism Schemes Fail, Researcher Says," *Washington Post,* 25 July 1987, p. B15. Also see David Barrett and James Reapsome, *Seven Hundred Plans to Evangelize the World* (New Hope, Penn.: New Hope Publishers, 1988).

29. James F. Engel, "Great Commission or Great Commotion?" *Christianity Today,* 20 April 1984, p. 52.

Chapter 8: *The Congregation as Audience*

1. George Gerbner et al., *Religion and Television* (Philadelphia: The Annenberg School of Communication, 1984).

2. Ibid.

3. Stewart M. Hoover, *Mass Media Religion* (Beverly Hills Calif.: Sage, 1988), p. 80.

4. Robert Wuthnow, *The Restructuring of American Christianity* (Princeton, N.J.: Princeton University Press, 1988).

5. James A. Taylor, "No Miracles from the Media," *Christian Century,* 30 May 1979, p. 614.

6. Thomas Luckmann, *The Invisible Church* (New York: Macmillan, 1967).

7. Mark R. Sills, "The Docetic Church," *Christian Century,* 21 January 1981, pp. 37–38.

8. Quoted in Peter G. Horsfield, *Religious Television* (New York: Longman, 1984), p. 56.

9. William F. Fore, *Television and Religion* (Minneapolis: Augsburg, 1987), p. 101.

10. Neil Postman, *Amusing Ourselves to Death: Public Discourse in the Age of Show Business* (New York: Viking, 1985), pp. 116, 119.

11. Ben Armstrong, *The Electric Church* (Nashville: Thomas Nelson, 1979), p. 9.

12. Ed Golder, "The Baby Boom Bulge," *Grand Rapids Press,* 7 April 1990, p. B1.

13. Ibid., p. B2.

14. Quoted in Russell Chandler, "Marketing Poll Shapes a Very Successful Church in Chicago Area," *Grand Rapids Press,* 30 December 1989, p. B2.

15. Golder, "The Baby Boom Bulge," p. B2.

16. Barbara Meyer, "Reach-Out-and-Touch Program Doubles Church Attendance," *The Banner,* 19 February 1990, pp. 22–23.

17. John Lankford, "Religion and Post-Industrial Society in America: Some Implications," *Historical Magazine of the Protestant Episcopal Church* 47 (1984): 415.

18. Quoted in George W. Cornell, "Baptist Futurist Sees Fluid Atmosphere Ahead," *Grand Rapids Press,* 5 May 1990, p. B4.

19. Donald N. Oberdorfer, *Electronic Christianity: Myth or Ministry* (Taylors Falls Minn.: John L. Brekke & Sons, 1982), p. 15.

20. Martin Buber, *I and Thou* (New York: Scribner & Sons, 1958).

21. Lyle E. Schaller, "Megachurch!" *Christianity Today,* 5 March 1990, p. 20.

22. Ibid., p. 22.

23. Ibid., p. 24.

Chapter 9: *Redeeming the Electronic Church*

1. Quoted in Pierre Babin, "The Spirituality of Media People," *The Way,* Supplement 57 (Autumn 1986), p. 50.

2. James Breig, "Catholics Should Boycott TV Preachers," *U.S. Catholic,* May 1984, p. 12.

3. Martin Marty, "Needed: A Christian Interpretation of the Media World," *Lutheran World* 19 (1972): 105–114.

4. See especially Donald N. Oberdorfer, *Electronic Christianity: Myth or Ministry* (Taylors Falls, Minn.: John L. Brekke & Sons, 1982); Virginia Stem Owens, *The Total Image: Or Selling Jesus in the Modern Age* (Grand Rapids, Mich.: Eerdmans, 1980); Malcolm Muggeridge, *Christ and the Media* (Grand Rapids, Mich.: Eerdmans, 1977).

5. Richard J. Mouw, *Called to Holy Worldiness* (Philadelphia: Fortress Press, 1980).

6. "A Nation of Videots," in Horace Newcomb, ed., *Television: The Critical View,* 3rd ed., (New York: Oxford University Press, 1979), pp. 351–366.

7. I take this issue up at length in "The Media and a Public Faith," *University of Detroit Law Review* 65 (Summer 1988): 619–642.

8. See, for example, *The Gallup Report,* April 1987.

9. Stewart M. Hoover, *Mass Media Religion* (Beverly Hills, Calif.: Sage Publications, 1988), p. 80.

Index

✣ ✣ ✣ ✣ ✣